Black Manhood in James Baldwin,
Ernest J. Gaines, and August Wilson

Black Manhood
in James Baldwin,
Ernest J. Gaines,
and August Wilson

KEITH CLARK

University of Illinois Press

URBANA AND CHICAGO

© 2002 by the Board of Trustees
of the University of Illinois
All rights reserved
Manufactured in the United States of America
C 5 4 3 2 1

∞ This book is printed on acid-free paper.

Library of Congress Cataloging-in-Publication Data
Clark, Keith, 1963–
Black manhood in James Baldwin, Ernest J. Gaines, and
August Wilson / Keith Clark.
p. cm.
Includes bibliographical references and index.
ISBN 0-252-02727-2 (acid-free paper)
1. American literature—African American authors—History
and criticism. 2. American literature—Male authors—History and
criticism. 3. American literature—20th century—History and
criticism. 4. Gaines, Ernest J., 1933– —Characters—Men.
5. Baldwin, James, 1924– —Characters—Men. 6. Wilson, August—
Characters—Men. 7. African American men in literature.
8. Masculinity in literature. 9. Men in literature. I. Title.
PS153.N5C49   2002
810.9'896073—dc21   2001004431

For my mother, Millicent Lowery Clark

Contents

Acknowledgments

I AM INDEBTED to many—far too many to name in this limited space. I must begin by expressing my heartfelt appreciation to my professors and mentors at the University of North Carolina at Chapel Hill: J. Lee Greene, my dissertation advisor whose towering and prodigious intellect always enlightened and humbled; Trudier Harris, an indefatigable scholar and thinker and unwavering mentor whose magnanimity has buoyed me personally and professionally; and James W. Coleman, whose stoic brilliance has remained a guiding light.

I also wish to recognize Joanne M. Braxton, Carroll Hardy, Ross Posnock, and Robert Hemenway, professors whom I encountered as an undergraduate and master's student at the College of William and Mary and the University of Kentucky, respectively. Each proposed academia as a viable and legitimate career option for a fledgling near–business major and encouraged me graciously.

I express my gratitude to a host of scholar-friends who've either read manuscripts for me or engaged me in conference-hall chats about my work: Herman Beavers, Ken Brown, Warren Carson, Hazel Ervin, Karla F. C. Holloway, E. Patrick Johnson, Sandra Shannon, Claudia Tate, Linda Wagner-Martin, and Helena Woodard.

I am fortunate to have supportive colleagues at George Mason University: Marilyn Mobley McKenzie, a dear sister-friend whose words of encouragement and guidance have enabled me to press on when feeling most pressed; Lorraine Brown, whose quiet advice and wisdom continue to uplift; and Robert Matz, a compatriot to whom I've turned for support when most stressed about teaching and writing.

Generous awards from the Ford Foundation and the University of North Carolina provided crucial financial support at watershed moments during my tenure as a graduate student and junior professor. I am particularly appreciative of my home institution, George Mason University, for granting me release time, which enabled me to complete several projects.

I am especially and inexpressibly grateful to two scholar-friends who read and reread portions of the manuscript, often at the eleventh hour: Hilary Holladay at the University of Massachusetts at Lowell and Sheila Smith Mc-Koy at Vanderbilt University. Both assiduously pored over my prose, forcing me to clarify, elaborate, and rethink when I'd assumed I had already done so.

Thanks to Cambridge University Press and the journal *Callaloo* for permitting me to reprint brief portions of the introductory sections of chapters 2 and 3, which originally appeared under their auspices in slightly different forms: "Baldwin, Communitas, and the Black Masculinist Tradition," in *New Essays on "Go Tell It on the Mountain,"* ed. Trudier Harris, 127–56 (Cambridge: Cambridge University Press, 1996); "Re-(W)righting Black Male Subjectivity: The Communal Poetics of Ernest Gaines's *A Gathering of Old Men,*" *Callaloo* 22.1 (1999): 195–207.

Finally, I am blessed to have a cadre of friends who are family. Though to many I'll remain a perpetual student, their love for me and confidence in my endeavors have remained steadfast: Kimberly and William Hall, Yasmine Hamlett, Willie DuPree, Zandra Thompson Relaford, Lola Singletary, Monica Perry, Jacob Wilson, Trenis Jackson, Lisa Green, Jewell Parham, Mariefrance Desrosiers, Gayle Jupiter, Joy Myree, and Kenyatta Dorey Graves.

Introduction

TAKEN TOGETHER, the words "black masculinity" evoke a plethora of impassioned, conflicted, and often contradictory responses:

> This battle with Mr. Covey was the turning-point in my career as a slave. It rekindled the few expiring embers of freedom, and revived within me a sense of my own manhood. (Douglass 113)

> The one thing they [whites] will not stand for is for a black man to be a man. And everything else is worthless if a man can't be a man. (Killens 180)

> Furthermore, most of us will be men in spite of white men and women who only publish books by black women or homosexual black men with degrading themes or passive attitudes—and then make them into movies of "the black experience." (Brown 225)

These quotations bear out that in the minds of many African-American men, their struggle for masculine status has been a pitched battle against an intractable, well-girded foe. From Frederick Douglass's psychically liberating confrontation with his overseer, Edward Covey, to the cabal of "white men and women" the political commentator Tony Brown casts as co-conspirators committed to "degrading" them, many black men have seen their social, gendered status as men as something fiercely contested and persistently withheld. The exclamations of Douglass, Killens, and Brown reflect a consistently uniform discourse of black masculinity that evolves from a paradoxically complex and simple belief: African-American men have been historically denied the power and privilege that should accrue to them based on their gender. In other words, all the men are white, all the faux men are black;

homosexuals and women only impede black men's ascension to the vaunt-
ed though elusive realm of manliness.

In critical and literary studies, the terms "masculinity" and "subjectivity"
sometimes seemed in the 1990s what "discourse" and "Other" were in the
1980s—the au courant language used to gauge the currency of one's scholarly endeavors. Often these words are bandied about so cavalierly that they
become obfuscated and ambiguous. However, my primary critical aim is to
investigate black male representation in selected short stories, novels, and
plays from the 1940s through the 1990s by taking into account the multiple
components of black men's subjectivities. As Marcellus Blount and George
P. Cunningham conclude in their introduction to *Representing Black Men,*
"The irony, as well as the danger, in contemporary discussions of African
American masculinities lies in the borders separating the critical discourses
of race, gender, and sexuality from one another and often from black males
as subjects" (ix–x). Rather than stratifying different discourses, my interdis-
ciplinary method melds conventional critiques of literary characters; contemporary theoretical modes of interpretation that investigate the tropic
function of voice and narrative in literature; the discourse of cultural studies that teases out the connections between myriad popular and academic
narratives; and germane theories of gender and sexuality. This approach allows me to navigate critical borders that stifle discussions about points of
convergence and divergence regarding literary, social, and cultural configurations of black masculinity. I see my project in conversation with recent
works such as *Representing Black Men* and Phillip Brian Harper's *Are We Not
Men? Masculine Anxiety and the Problem of African-American Identity,* studies that utilize a similar methodology by synthesizing literary, social, cultural, and gender criticism and theory in their investigations of black male subjectivity.

When I use the terms "subjectivity" and "masculinity," I am not conflat-
ing these words, nor am I making rigid distinctions. My conceptualization
of masculinity is based on a socially oriented conception of gender informed
by society's obdurate figurations of manhood—ones rooted in strength,
power, authority, and heterosexuality. Though perceptions of masculinity and
subjectivity overlap, my interpretation of the latter involves the degree of
agency one exercises in self-definition and identity formation. In differenti-
ating subjectivity, I take into account not only a protagonist's socially defined,
gendered identity but the degree to which he reconfigures and refashions
definitions of self that may counter conventional constructions and tenets.
Aside from encompassing issues surrounding personal agency, the location
of an individual voice within a collective milieu constitutes another facet of

subjectivity. Subjectivity transcends limiting and orthodox notions of male power and dominance. Furthermore, *black* subjectivity is not merely an inverted version of hegemonic patriarchal masculinity. I will argue that James Baldwin, Ernest J. Gaines, and August Wilson depart from Wrightian and protest figurations of the black male by problematizing a uniform conception of subjectivity. This sometimes occurs through the demythologizing and often dismantling of a sacrosanct master-narrative that equates an almost fanatical independence and the ability to dominate others with subject status.

Throughout this study I employ the term "masculinist," an often maligned and ostensibly critically incorrect word. Ann duCille's observation reflects the frosty response this word usually elicits: "Phallocentrism and masculinism are pejoratives that make men jumpy in the same way that accusations of racism make white people defensive" (64). This is repeatedly and painstakingly made clear when I attend lectures in which the speaker—irrespective of his or her sex—routinely uses the words "patriarchy," "misogyny," "hegemony," "racist," "heterosexist," and "masculinist" interchangeably. These terms become shibboleths, a sanctioned language that reductively equates "masculine"—the inflected "masculinist" variation notwithstanding—with whatever historical atrocities and social scourges one cares to dredge up. Such tendentiousness, regrettably, glosses over their uniqueness, their distinctiveness, and their currency in different discourses. Echoing what duCille specifies as her "practical" use of the term, I use "masculinist" in a specifically literary and theoretical context: it refers to a body of texts by African-American male authors that thematically and narratologically foreground black men. Thus my critical aim is to investigate how authors have grappled with questions surrounding voice, gender, sexuality, community— in essence, subjectivity. Though discussions of *Native Son* as a misogynistic work are de rigueur, and while that novel may be deemed masculinist, so too are Gaines's multivoiced and multigendered fictions of community and Wilson's polyphonous dramas of inter- and intragender conflicts, both of which I explore in this study.

The discourses of literary and critical theory sometimes partition language to the extent that some terms and concepts become the purview of a specific gender. For instance, words like "community," "healing," "ritual," and "space" often function metonymically, as they are associated with a distinctly gynocritical discourse that engages epistemological questions deemed unique to women's literature and theory. A comment by the black feminist theorist Karla F. C. Holloway reinforces this point:

> However, where the place of complexity is extraterritorial for black women writers, texts by black males often isolate the word, circumscribe its territory,

and subordinate its voice to expressive behaviors. The province of the word for black women commands a perspective that does not isolate it from its community source. Black male writers' texts claim the power of creative authorship but do not seem to share the word with the reader, or among the characters, or within narrative structures of the text. Instead, the word is carefully controlled and its power is meagerly shared. Black women writers seem to concentrate on shared ways of saying, black males concentrate on individual ways of behaving. (7)

Holloway's point is simultaneously incisive and thorny. She accurately pinpoints the pervasive discursive feature of scores of novels by black men. *The Autobiography of an Ex-Coloured Man, Native Son,* and *Invisible Man* are marked by a restrictive conception of voice and self, where black men assiduously attempt to position themselves within society's dominant narrative of male subjectivity via "expressive behaviors"—hence the deeply symbolic function of racial violence in works like *Native Son* and *If He Hollers Let Him Go* in the 1940s. Holloway legitimately concludes that language is bound and guarded, evinced, for instance, in Wright's and Ellison's devotion to naturalism, urban realism, and white postmodernism—discourses that often subsume their characters and stymie their characters' quests for voice.

However, I would question the notion that black male writers have been unable to fashion more inclusive, more communally grounded narratives and a broader conception of narrative voice. Contemporary authors such as Wilson, younger ones such as the late Melvin Dixon, and even venerated ones like Baldwin have challenged the circumscribing conception of language and community evident in their predecessors' works. These authors have attempted to suture the black male voice to its communal fabric and have insisted on its symbiotic relationship to other black people. I will explore how notions of community, space, and healing—the lexicon of intimacy—permeate contemporary African-American men's works, thereby countering the gender-fixed connotations often inherent in these terms.

When I use the term "community," I am attempting to claim it as part of the discourse of a re-envisioned black male literary subjectivity. Like masculinity and subjectivity, the word is circulated so incessantly in academic and nonacademic contexts—the "black community," the "gay community," the "Asian community," the "AIDS community," the "international" community—that its potency has been severely diluted.[1] Consistently, though regrettably, discussions of community vis-à-vis black men conjure the most pejorative images. Gangs, gangsta rappers, what Angela Davis accurately labels the "prison industrial complex," for some even the Million Man March—these are the composite images that gatherings of black men signify for many.

Though this may be partially attributed to the fact that "we lack even the rudiments of a language to discuss community and connection" (Rotundo 285), the thought of a community of black men is for many at once oxymoron and menace. *Black Manhood in James Baldwin, Ernest J. Gaines, and August Wilson* attempts to interrupt the baleful notion that black maleness and thereby black male subjectivity are circumscribed by a type of hypermasculine ethos and performance, engendered by America's historical demonization of black men and some men's attendant internalizing of that demonization (i.e., some forms of rap and/or contemporary incarnations of the "baad nigga" archetype).

Throughout this study, I examine the intersections between black masculinity and community. Specifically, I describe and deconstruct textual situations that dramatize black men *collectively* challenging and reconfiguring the conditions of subjectivity. In other words, my use of the term has a specifically gendered connotation. When the characters in Baldwin's or Gaines's works gather into different communities—artistic, sexual, pedagogical—they often disturb and counter the hegemonic fiction of black men as predatory and bestial. Thus, community often precedes and inaugurates communitas, which the anthropologist Victor Turner conceptualizes as an augmented form of community. In the works under examination, these male-centered communities become spaces that promulgate spiritually and psychically intimate connections between black men and constitute collective acts of resistance and regeneration. One can even detect a budding male community in the *über*-narrative of black male subjectivity, Douglass's 1845 *Narrative*. Despite Douglass's extolling of the valorized patriarchal masculinity, we also glimpse the flowering of a communal conception of black maleness as well. While his primordial battle with Covey embodies what Jerry H. Bryant calls the narrative's "supreme symbolic moment" and demonstrates Douglass's inscription of his life as "one of the basic stories of Western civilization" (29), often overlooked are Douglass's inchoate albeit imperfect male communities. Recall, for instance, the men with whom he plans to escape and those he teaches to read at his clandestine Sabbath school. Even though his autobiography ultimately upholds the culturally enshrined though prescriptive narrative of maleness, an alternative form of black subjectivity is still discernible.

Though the preponderance of novels and plays by black men has inculcated the "official" text of hegemonic masculinity and subjectivity, I identify a discursive reconfiguring in the 1950s, beginning with works such as Baldwin's *Go Tell It on the Mountain*[2] and "Sonny's Blues." While I concur with what Henry Louis Gates Jr. calls the "signifying" relationship between *Native Son* and *Invisible Man*,[3] I think that in different ways both novels epito-

mize black masculinist protest, which situates black men in diametric opposition to other cultures and communities—including African-American ones.
For all of their technical and even taxonomic distinctions—naturalism versus realism and surrealism, modernism versus postmodernism—these supreme texts overwhelmingly apotheosize Anglo-American constructions of
gender and selfhood, *Native Son* being a black boy's American Dream fantasy and *Invisible Man* a sable Huck Finn–inspired picaresque. In their relatively symmetrical representations, these texts often conflate racial freedom
and masculinity, which are narrowly considered the benchmarks for black
subjectivity. Often absent in such representations of black men, however, is
a critique of the interstices in the accredited narrative of masculinity, an interrogation of how the sanctioned discourse of maleness is often anathema
to black subjectivity and eclipses alternative ways of *being* black men. In
Native Son or *Invisible Man,* for instance, issues concerning sexuality are
usually (though not always) restricted to questions surrounding miscegena-
tion; absent is an attendant discussion of issues such as sexual orientation
and homosocial relationships.[4]

Though William Andrews justifiably accuses white writers such as Harri-
et Beecher Stowe and William Styron of rendering the black man invisible
because his "individual humanity has been for the most part veiled by an
abstracted identity projected onto him by the white author's notions of what
a Black man represents, or ought to represent" (61), I would add that Wright
and Ellison themselves frequently abstract their characters. Both authors
superimpose upon their protagonists a desire to locate their subjectivity
within the dominant patrinarrative of American manhood, which predictably esteems marginality and a pathological desire for personal freedom at
the expense of intragender or communal relationships. Dislocation—from
others, from self, within the narrative discourse—becomes the sine qua non
in this conceptualization of black manhood, a mimetic double of patriarchal
masculinity. The fictive project of many writers since the 1950s has been the
investigation and fictionalization of the intricacies of black subject formation. Of course, it would be critically disingenuous to suggest that Baldwin's
reconceptualization of black male subjectivity went uncontested. Perhaps
most notorious is Eldridge Cleaver's scabrous assault on him in *Soul on Ice,*
emblematic of the rigid, anachronistic configuration of maleness that characterized 1960s Black Nationalist ideology.

Recent critics have often used the term "shift" to mark nodal points in black
literature and culture.[5] There is no single explanation for the re-evaluation of
male representation that Baldwin inaugurated in the 1950s—a movement

from the sanctioned, Western master-text of male subjectivity to a more complex rendering that probes black men's relationships with self, community, and, especially, each other. Perhaps Baldwin's prescient literary vision anticipated the watershed Black Arts Movement of the 1960s. As Houston A. Baker Jr. points out in his examination of Amiri Baraka vis-à-vis the playwright-poet's predecessors, "The brilliantly projected conception of black as a country—a separate and progressive nation with values antithetical to those of white America—stands in marked contrast to the ideas set forth by Baldwin, Wright, Ellison and others in the fifties" (*Journey* 106). Though I will argue that Baldwin himself departed measurably from Wright and Ellison's literary and cultural aims, Baker's point is nevertheless well taken: the 1960s marked a profound sense of collective upheaval reflected in the period's artistic production. However, this explanation is less convincing in light of the corrosive and ubiquitous sexism, misogyny, and homophobia that too often tainted this counterhegemonic notion of blackness. One could just as easily contend that the male authors and aestheticians in the 1960s inculcated and practiced the very patriarchal principles that they were decrying in whites.

The Black Arts period promulgated the notion of a communal art and aesthetic that at least allowed black men to begin reconsidering the belief that subject/identity formation was an isolated endeavor, one removed from the shared concerns of black people. But inconsistencies and fissures within this thinking were quite real—witness the implacable phallocentrism and homophobia underlying much of the movement's literary and political tracts. Harper articulates the attendant exclusivity of such discourse—its essentializing of blackness in ways that castigated and abjured those African Americans who were deemed insufficiently black or militant. In a section aptly entitled "Blacker Than Thou," he exposes the disjunctures inherent in Black Nationalist dogma, using Baraka's poetry as cultural metonym:

> Thus the project of Black Arts poetry can be understood as the establishment of black nationalist subjectivity—the forcible fixing of the identity of the "speaking" I—by delineating it against the "non-I person," the *you* whose identity is clearly predicated in the poems we are considering. So the *you* in Baraka's "Poem for Half White College Students" is the African American who identifies with the Euro-American celebrity, against which the speaking I of the poem is implicitly contrasted. . . . It is this intraracial division on which the Black Arts project is founded, and not any sense of inclusiveness with respect to the African-American community that we might discern in Baraka's "SOS," which fact greatly problematizes the possibility of effective communal action after the issuance of Baraka's call. (48)

I quote Harper at length to illustrate the contradiction that is embedded in the benignly halcyon idea of community: community, by definition, is as exclusive as it is inclusive.

Sadly if not inexplicably, the same black men at the vanguard of calls for black solidarity in the 1960s would venomously denounce and exclude Baldwin. Cleaver's apotheosizing of Wright, whom he deemed a "rebel and a man" (106), emblematizes the contradictory and often myopic demands inherent in Black Nationalists' calls for a unified "Black Nation." Ignored is the fact that the effete Baldwin, dismissed as a counterfeit and testosterone-challenged version of manhood, immersed himself in the volatile civil rights struggle not merely by attending the celebrity-strewn 1963 March on Washington but by embarking upon potentially life-threatening trips to a rabidly racist American South. Meanwhile, Wright forsook "the cause," choosing to live and travel abroad—oceans away from the "The Horror and the Glory" of American life, which he vivified and vilified in *Black Boy*. Baldwin's own life incarnates what I see as the shift in both lived and artistic black male subjectivity, notwithstanding the stentorian voices that championed disturbingly mimetic forms of white patriarchal, hegemonic masculinity. Ultimately, the late 1950s and 1960s are not a monolithic moment in terms of black male subject formation. On the contrary, writers during this period paradoxically celebrated reinvigorated forms of black community while trafficking in hackneyed notions of maleness. For the purposes of this study, I concentrate on what I consider the affirmative part of Black Nationalist male discourse: its insistence on a black malehood–black community nexus.

Baldwin's artistic production and personal life, in contradistinction to Wright's, provide a map for reinterpreting black male subjectivity.[6] As critics and the author himself have documented, Wright's life was marked by an agonistic relationship with family and nation. "Flight," the fitting moniker for book two of *Native Son*, became the major leitmotif in his art and his personal creed. Baldwin's life and work, conversely, reflect a lifelong concern with relationships—filial, fraternal, sexual, national, global. His wrenching private flights, like those of his characters, were always marked by a return, for the journey to selfhood invariably involved a renegotiation of his relationships with others. The same unresolved familial conflicts depicted in a work such as *Black Boy* are clearly restaged in *Go Tell It on the Mountain*, but, unlike Wright, Baldwin would not only continue to grapple with questions of self and its relationship to family and community throughout his fictive and nonfictive corpus, he would even reach a tenuous reconciliation (if not rapprochement) in works such as his last novel, *Just Above My Head*. As I will argue in the second chapter, his life and art mediate black masculinist protest and a broader conceptualization of the black literary subject.[7]

Black Manhood in James Baldwin, Ernest J. Gaines, and August Wilson investigates how three African-American male authors since the 1950s have attempted to open up and frequently counter the discourse surrounding black masculinity and subjectivity. Baldwin, Gaines, and Wilson have expanded the literary landscape with respect to masculine depiction, contesting atavistic portraits of African-American men in literature. These authors' portraitures often involve a more complex and inclusive rendering of subjectivity not exclusively tied to gender and gender privilege. Reimagining black men, their diverse artistic strategies and multifaceted portraitures have radically dislodged our dwarfing conceptions of black men and opened a discursive space for more expansive fictive and critical praxes.

1 Countering the Counterdiscourse: Subject Formation and the Aesthetics of Black Masculinist Protest Discourse since 1940

THE 1995 MILLION MAN MARCH in Washington, D.C., grew out of what many African Americans perceive as the nation's concerted efforts to demonize blackness and black maleness. Thousands of men gathered to respond to years of denigrating, sometimes relentless and bellicose efforts to erase the black self. Ostensibly the aims of the march were not new: Martin Luther King Jr., Bayard Rustin, and other civil rights stalwarts laid the groundwork for collective struggle, for the 1963 March on Washington evolved from a fervent desire to end generations of social, economic, and political extirpation. But the 1995 gender-exclusive march, with the "endangered black man" as its raison d'être, serves as a cultural and critical touchstone for my exploration of three prominent African-American male writers: black men acting collectively and communally speaks to the issues this study addresses.

The history of African Americans reflects individual and communal replies to attacks on their personhood. A perusal of the original Constitution—which Ralph Ellison in *Shadow and Act* calls one of the "sacred papers" (163) codifying American identity—exposes America's quantitative and psychic evisceration of the black self. No wonder, then, that the primary function of African-American literature, from its inception through the 1960s at least, has been to further the political and social aspirations of African Americans collectively. One need only glance at the titles of contemporary literary studies to gauge African-American authors' extensive attempts to construct a centered and whole self. Scholarly investigations such as Robert B. Stepto's *From Behind the Veil: A Study of Afro-American Narrative*, Valerie Smith's *Self-Discovery and Authority in Afro-American Narrative*, and Farah Jasmine Griffin's *"Who Set You Flowin'?": The African-American Migration Narrative* investigate authors' attempts to formulate an identity in a society that would obstruct such attempts at self-definition.

The artistic mission of generations of black men and women writers has been the configuring of an authentic African-American self—a task that clearly hearkens back to W. E. B. Du Bois's "double-consciousness." Douglass, the nameless Ex-Coloured Man, Janie Crawford, Milkman Dead—all represent archetypal black questing figures. My work interrogates how the novelists James Baldwin and Ernest J. Gaines and the playwright August Wilson have reconstructed masculinity in portraying and positioning the literary subject. Because the subject "itself is the effect of production, caught in the mutually constitutive web of social practices, discourses and subjectivity; its reality is the tissue of social relations" (Henriques 117), I aim to examine what informs the production of the contemporary African-American literary male subject. What is the relationship between the array of competing discursive and social practices and the narratives that give the subject its contours?

Figurations of the Black Male Literary "Subject"

I deliberately foreground the notion of subjectivity in my study, for its multifariousness captures the difficulty of achieving selfhood, identity, and wholeness. The word "subject" contains somewhat discrepant denotative meanings, ones that inform my conceptualization of the term. Steven Cohan and Linda M. Shires outline these multiple definitions in *Telling Stories: A Theoretical Analysis of Narrative Fiction:* the term can delineate "(1) who performs the action—doing, thinking, feeling; (2) who apprehends him- or herself as an identifiable agent of action, the grammatical subject of a predication; and (3) who finds a signifier of that identity in discourse, I as opposed to *you*. But *subject* is also a term of passivity, as when one is subject to a monarch or law, or the subject of an experiment. Falling within these two poles of agency and passivity, *subjectivity* is the condition of being (a) subject" (136). These distinctions iterate several basic questions that this study will examine. How have African-American male authors portrayed their protagonists' attempts to exercise agency and authority? With respect to the "grammatical" subject, what is the connection between subjectivity and narrative discourse? Has language—written and oral—served as a vehicle for centering the self, or has it hindered black protagonists' quests for subjectivity? And to what extent has the desire for subjectivity been a negative endeavor, one resulting in being "subject" and powerless, "object" and other?

Given the merits of the French linguist Emile Benveniste's claim that "It is in and through language that man constitutes himself as a *subject*, because language alone establishes the concept of 'ego' in reality, in *its* reality which is that of the being" (729), it is no wonder that language figures so integrally in black male literary subject formation. For instance, one can discern a distinct discursive and lexical intertextual relationship between works such as Douglass's 1845 *Narrative* and Richard Wright's revisionist "slave narrative" *Black Boy,* published exactly one hundred years later. Assuredly, Douglass's transformation from abject object to articulate hero,[1] from the object of psychophysical violence to the subject of his own spoken and written narratives, demonstrates the connection between subjectivity and the ability to inscribe and orate one's self into existence. Young "Dick" Wright's Herculean attempts to wrest literacy from his abnegating cultural environment—black and white—certainly foreground the link between identity, voice, and subject status. Put another way, the struggle for language and voice emerges as one of the central components of the black male protagonist's identity formation.

My critical task, therefore, is to extrapolate the intersection between subjectivity and masculinity, exploring how male writers have negotiated and critiqued constructions of gender in formulating and depicting black male literary subjects. The black feminist critic bell hooks identifies the standard scholarly approaches to African-American men and masculinity in *Black Looks: Race and Representation:*

> This work [scholarship on black masculinity] conveyed the message that all black men were tormented by their inability to fulfill the phallocentric masculine ideal as it had been articulated in white supremacist capitalist patriarchy. Erasing the realities of black men who have diverse understandings of masculinity, scholarship on the black family (traditionally the framework for academic discussion of black masculinity) puts in place of this lived complexity a flat, one-dimensional representation. (89)

I focus on the idea of a resituated black male subject to address the issue of narrative and textual positionality and the concomitant centrality of gender. Though earlier studies have privileged the subject's cultural dislocation and psychic paralysis, I problematize the notion of subjectivity. I concur with Linda Hutcheon's assertion that "to situate it [the subject], as postmodernism teaches, is to recognize differences—of race, gender, class, sexual orientation, and so on" (159). Of particular relevance for this study is the intersection between race, gender, and sexual orientation with respect to black male subjectivity. Moreover, as Hutcheon notes, the archetypal "universal" subject has tended to be "bourgeois" and "white" (159); I would add "heterosexual" here as well. Given this standard conception of the subject, I construct a paradigm of literary subjectivity that demonstrates the significance—but not necessarily centrality—of race and how contemporary writers have appropriated and demythologized American constructions of masculinity in literature featuring black male protagonists.

This study concentrates on three writers whose works vividly represent the evolution of the male subject and black men's discursive praxes since the mid-twentieth century. The writings of Baldwin, Gaines, and Wilson encompass a wide range of themes, narrative strategies, and genres (the novel, short story, drama, and literary/cultural criticism). However, the 1940s, which marked the publication of two of black literature's most pathbreaking works, warrant some discussion. I want to establish a context for exploring the three writers on whom this study concentrates by briefly discussing Richard Wright's aesthetic concerns and how they are manifested in his work. I'll comment on *Native Son* (1940), because its inscription of the black male captured the Zeitgeist. Incontestably, Wright influenced male and female writers in the 1940s and 1950s such as Chester Himes, Ann Petry, and Ralph Ellison (despite Ellison's protestations). The year 1940 provides an appropriate benchmark for my examination, since Bigger Thomas incarnated the desires of so many African Americans from the 1940s through the 1960s to be recognized as native sons and daughters, with the same inalienable rights and access to the mythic American Dream enjoyed by their white counterparts.

Wright's life and work emblematize protest discourse, a literary categorization that best describes black men's (and some women's) writing in the 1940s and 1950s. His depictions emanate from a conceptualization of blackness in contradistinction to whiteness, a binary in which the black self seeks to be absorbed by and integrated into the larger Anglo-American milieu. The male subject in *Native Son* embodies the fragmented black self, one physically and psychically maimed by racism and classism. Contrapuntally, the works of Baldwin, Gaines, and Wilson re-envision and reconceptualize black men, constituting aesthetic interventions that expand the parameters of black literary subjectivity. Their artistic endeavors are *recursive*, for they contest earlier constructions of black literary masculinity, and *revisionist*, for they fictivize a rejuvenated subject and inaugurate what might be regarded as the communal, polyphonous model of African-American masculinist writing.

As I mentioned at the outset, linguistic self-definition forms the matrix of this study—the quest for subjectivity through voice. The need to find one's voice, as Douglass does, has been the primary narrative goal of black protagonists, regardless of gender. But an equally important part of voice is the quest for audience. Peter Brooks perceptively captures this reciprocity—the aural and oral undergirdings of what I term "voicedness": "It is my premise that most narratives speak of their transferential condition—of their anxiety concerning their transmissibility, of their need to be heard, of their desire to become the story of the listener as much as of the teller, something that is most evident in 'framed tales' (such as Conrad's *Heart of Darkness*) which embed another tale within them, and thus dramatize the relations of tellers and listeners" (50–51). Notwithstanding the fact that framing recurs throughout African-American literature—consider the formal configuration of Charles W. Chesnutt's *The Conjure Woman* or Zora Neale Hurston's *Their Eyes Were Watching God*—the central point here is that audience plays an equally important role in the search for voice, story, and, therefore, subjectivity.

Hence, voice and community are the primary vehicles for black male authors' reconceptualization of subjectivity. Whereas Wright's foredoomed heroes dismiss the black community as a potential witness to the black subject's plight and perhaps the source of his renewal, the protagonists in Baldwin, Gaines, and Wilson harness the resources of the black speech community, situating themselves squarely within its vernacular/performative traditions. Conversely, the protest text dramatizes the black male subject's—and author's—desire for approbation from a larger cultural and literary sphere, an environment that is largely white and male. Beginning with Baldwin, many of Wright's and Ellison's literary descendents began to re-evaluate the discursive relationship between their subjects and their environments. The writers in my communal paradigm foreground and privilege the black subject's overall relationship to a black speech community—a nurturing, embryonic environment that gives birth to the black male voice.

In constructing a schema that puts forth a sort of binary relationship between groups of writers, I am aware of the problems inherent in such divisions. Terms like "protest," "community," and "polyphonic" can be as knotty and indeterminable as "modernism" and "postmodernism." My critical aim is not necessarily to chart a progression from protest to polyphonic or communal discourse; established writers such as John A. Williams and recent ones like Randall Kenan certainly depict disengaged and liminal male subjects, ones estranged from both blacks and whites. Baldwin, Gaines, and Wilson at the very least conceptualize a different type of protagonist, one whose primary aim is not to be absorbed into and validated by a larger Anglo-American culture but who comes to realize the empowering effect of immersing oneself in his own community—a place with like-minded, black native sons and daughters. This shared space is an alternative to the fictive worlds where Bigger Thomas and Invisible Man reside, worlds where chaos and, predictably, self-erasure were natural outcomes.

"Protest" Discourse, Wright/White Spaces, and the Problem of Being Black

The 1940s do not mark the origins of the black literary self or even the beginning of black masculinist protest; Sutton Griggs and Chesnutt, for example, predate Wright.[2] However, I concentrate on Wright because he is recognized as the indisputable patriarch of black literary protest and naturalism, a cardinal figure who trumpeted a belief in art as innately political and social. That he has become synonymous with the black protest novel bears out Michel Foucault's position on the synecdochic situation that arises when one author drastically alters the contours of a specific literary discourse: "the author's name characterizes a particular manner of existence of discourse. Discourse that possesses an author's name is not to be immediately consumed and forgotten; neither is it accorded the momentary attention given to ordinary, fleeting words" (142). Wright's fiction, especially the works he published in the late 1930s and 1940s (*Uncle Tom's Children* [1938] and *Black Boy* [1945] in addition to *Native Son*), stands as the definitive narratives of black men's protest. The synonymous relationship between *Native Son* and black protest literature attests to Wright's prominence as that discourse's major proponent and leading practitioner.

The year 1940, with the publication of the incendiary *Native Son*, marked extreme social upheaval in the nation's racial consciousness. As the historian Manning Marable observes, "In a real sense, the watershed of Afro-American history occurred during the 1940s. Thousands of black men working as sharecroppers and farm labourers were drafted into the army with the outbreak of World War II" (14). Furthermore, he notes, "In the months immediately following World War II, blacks made decisive cracks in the citadel of white supremacy" (15). The period preceding and following World War II marks a major flex point on America's racial axis, as the country—even if out of political expediency—began adhering to the tenets outlined in its amended "sacred papers," the Constitution. Many black Americans began to believe that "equality" and "pursuit of happiness" would no longer ring as spurious, hollow catchwords.

Not surprisingly, racial discourse from the 1930s through the 1950s and 1960s centered on the so-called Negro problem, a referent that informs the literary construction of the black male subject. Not only did white authors such as Gunnar Myrdal (*An American Dilemma: The Negro Problem and Modern Democracy* [1944]) and Robert Penn Warren (*Who Speaks for the Negro?* [1966]) invoke this terminology, but black writers employed it as well.

Indisputably, the problem was *being* "Negro," which connoted otherness and difference. Juxtaposed with cultural shifts, literary incarnations of the black male subject similarly reflected a desire to become a part of the American cultural landscape, one that would allow blacks a place at the table, their slice of the American pie. Hence, the term "poetics of integration"[3] is apposite in evaluating Wright's texts. Using Wright's 1957 nonfiction collection *White Man, Listen!* to articulate the "dominant cultural perspective" of African-American literature during the 1950s as well as 1960s, Houston A. Baker Jr. writes,

> Wright optimistically predicts that Afro-American literature may soon be indistinguishable from the mainstream of American arts and letters. The basis for his optimism is the Supreme Court's decision in *Brown vs. Topeka Board of Education* (1954), in which the Court ruled that the doctrine "separate but equal" was inherently unequal. According to Wright, this ruling ensures a future "equality" in the experiences of black and white Americans, and this equality of *social* experience will translate in the literary domain as a homogeneity of represented experience. . . . When Afro-American writers have achieved such equality and homogeneity, they will stand at one with the majority culture—in a relationship that Wright terms "entity." (3)

As the critical reception of his works demonstrates, Wright stood at the vanguard of black writers who sought to emulate and inculcate the standards of American literature. But in its mimetic relationship to American literature and culture, protest discourse proffered a deformed black male subject, one based upon a white masculinist, modernist literary discourse that privileges individuals at odds with their cultures (Twain, Hemingway, et al.). Hence, black subjects' marginality and silence are reflected in their antipathetic relationship with the black community in addition to the hostile white one. Given the accuracy of William Andrews's claim that "The two genres of American literature in which the Black male has figured most importantly are the novel and autobiography" (60), one cannot understate the significance of both *Native Son* and *Black Boy* as master-narratives that shaped and continue to inform the critical discourse surrounding writing by and about black males.

Of course, the interdiscursive relationship between black and white male writers is neither new nor incomprehensible. Wright's texts, especially, look back specifically to black men's slave narratives but also interface with Euro-American writers and texts.[4] The Marxist critic Georg Lukács's important essay, "The Ideology of Modernism," offers an insightful assessment of the construction of a modernist subject—one that surfaces in African-American literature: "Man, for these writers, is by nature solitary, asocial, unable to enter into relationships with other human beings. . . . *Man, thus imagined, may establish contact with other individuals, but only in a superficial, accidental manner; only, ontologically speaking, by retrospective reflection. For the others, too, are basically solitary, beyond significant human relationships*" (20; emphasis added). Albeit culturally "neutral," this description of modern man approximates my conceptualization of the disfigured black protest subject. Wright's protagonists embody a conflicted notion of subjectivity, alternatively occupying positions of agency and passivity. Bigger Thomas is a centered subject, for Wright privileges him in terms of action and, arguably, point of view—but not voice. But, ironically, the author's conceptualization of the subject comes closer to the definition of object, for his protagonist lacks agency and is the object of a plethora of definitions, identities, and discourses that others impose upon him. Therefore, Bigger emblematizes the prototype of the deformed subject that populates masculinist protest discourse.

First and foremost, protest discourse foregrounds an image of the black male as fragmented and disfigured—a pathological and perpetual victim. Be it white society's withholding of the American Dream and its attendant accoutrements or the black community's inability to comprehend the depth of his suffering, the black male is defined solely by his victimhood. Psychically and physically deracinated by a venal American "system," he exists as a *subject* in the most pejorative sense, lacking autonomy and being subjected to the vagaries of a capriciously belligerent environment. Of course, black male victimization is not imagined: the Constitution's infamous three-fifths clause, the vile lynching ritual, the Slave and Black Codes of the nineteenth century, and their twentieth century counterpart, Jim Crow edicts in the South all reflect attempts to eradicate the black self. But Wright centers a prostrate black male subject who has few—if any—outlets for his blues. His subjects exist as perpetual outsiders whose voices reverberate in a cultural and metaphorical wilderness, a Wrightian no-man's-land or an Ellisonian underground that offers little sustenance or opportunity for renewal.

This configuration of the black male subject precisely conforms to the modernist notion of subject-as-pariah that Lukács outlines. One of the salient features of protest discourse is the authors' insistence that their protagonists inculcate exogenous—that is, Anglo-American—definitions of masculinity. Since the sanctioned construction of American masculinity traditionally is rooted in "dominance, competitiveness, violence, homophobia, sexism, and misogyny" (Franklin, "Men's Studies" 18), the connection between the purveyors of African-American protest discourse and white American male writers is clear. The distinguishing features of works such as Mark Twain's *Adventures of Huckleberry Finn* or Ernest Hemingway's *The Sun Also Rises* involve what I consider a dysfunctional notion of maleness: fear of intimacy or involvement with community and the tendency toward physical movement or flight. Witness how Twain and Hemingway (or James Fenimore Cooper, Henry James, or William Faulkner, for that matter) apotheosize physical action, dislocation, and violence as the cornerstones of maleness. The way to become a *gendered*[5] subject is not to be *subjected by* family or community. It is not a coincidence that Jack Kerouac's 1957 novel *On the Road,* a book whose very title denotes flight, has achieved legendary status as a paean to the American male's de rigueur code of conduct.

African-American male subjects—fictitious or actual—invariably are influenced by Western or American men's constructions of masculinity and, thereby, subjectivity. Witness, for instance, how Clarence Thomas's ascension to the Supreme Court has been elevated to mythic proportions, a testament to the belief that the black man's determination, analogous to that of "The Man," vanquishes shibboleths like "racism" and "discrimination." Thomas's sepia rags-to-riches story is transmogrified into a quasi slave narrative, chronicling a Georgia-born black boy's self-willed deliverance not so much from the bowels of a racist southern society but from a primitive, diabolic black one.

In describing Thomas's ascension, I use the word "narrative" rhetorically, for it conjures up a primordial story, the birth of the articulate hero, Frederick Douglass. Douglass's narrative is the template for subsequent literary representations of black masculinity, for it positions him as a towering figure whose ingenuity and brawn almost singlehandedly extricate him from the peculiar institution called slavery. Douglass's rebirth is tantamount to an immaculate conception, at least to the degree that it fits so securely into the mythic American male story, an Adamic narrative that centers and privileges the individual and his infinitesimal fortitude. The feminist critic Nina Baym sheds further light on this mythic male ideal:

> The myth narrates a confrontation of the American individual, the pure American self divorced from specific social circumstances, with the promise offered by the idea of America. This promise is the deeply romantic one that in this new land, untrammeled by history and social accident, a person will be able to achieve complete self-definition. Behind this promise is the assurance that individuals come before society, that they exist in some meaningful sense prior to, and apart from, societies in which they happen to find themselves. (71)

Scores of African-American men's narratives—be they actual (Douglass, Wright, and Thomas) or fictional (Bigger Thomas and Invisible Man)—share an insistence upon narrow and myopic perceptions of individuality and masculinity.

If the black male protest subject's quest for Western subjectivity renders him a pathological victim, if his oppression by hegemonic institutions appears almost foreordained, then his native black community represents yet another destructive entity. The black men in these narratives of disunity, having subscribed to a counterfeit American Dream that excludes blacks, foreclose any opportunity to create an identity within their native environment. On the contrary, the black community, itself so long-suffering and traumatized, becomes an extension of the perfidious white culture. If the community does not directly collude with the hegemonic culture, it offers no healing balm to its lacerated native sons, no outlet for their voices. Wright's protagonists must negotiate not only a nefarious white society, they must also overcome an antagonistic black one.

Especially relevant here are the protagonists' relationships with other black men. Not only is the subject consigned to a veritable no-man's-land with respect to white society, he maintains few if any connections with black men. Wright's black males, so mesmerized by American notions of masculinity and selfhood, bypass any opportunities to resituate themselves within a collectivity of black men. The word "intimacy" might aptly connote what is so painstakingly absent in black men's relationships with each other. Being relegated to the position of the Other by an intractable white environment, these protagonists subsequently impose this distinction upon themselves and their counterparts. The late critic Michael G. Cooke's unequivocal declaration that Chesnutt's late nineteenth-century folk trickster, Uncle Julius, was "simply put . . . not cut out for the rigors of intimacy" (59) is equally applicable to the black men Wright imagines in the 1930s, 1940s, and 1950s. These subjects' marginal place within their own community mirrors their own socially and psychologically limited space within the white one.

Ironically, the placelessness connoted in Wright's no-man's-land trope becomes a central metaphor for the black protagonist's tortured desire for subjectivity. This protagonist's psychic isolation and marginalization are reflected in the setting he inhabits. Just as the pastoral text—be it Shakespeare's or Twain's—contains an amalgam of politically and socially encoded meanings, so too do the authors' choices of physical locations in black protest discourse. Contemporary theoretical and feminist discourses speak of the liberating effect of literary subjects constructing their own "space" (think of Virginia Woolf's *A Room of One's Own* or Ntozake Shange's *for colored girls,* for example). Space functions metaphorically, signifying a psychic and spiritual freeing of oneself from enshackling definitions of self, whether from inside or outside one's cultural milieu. However, in male protest discourse concepts such as place and space function either denotatively or symbolically, for they merely concretize the characters' truncated social and psychological conditions. Writing within the confines of the naturalistic and realistic tradition, Wright (along with Ellison) employs setting to reify social and personal abnegation. It is no accident that protagonists in protest discourse often retreat to enclosed edifices[6]: the Wrightian jail and the Ellisonian underground become physical manifestations of the characters' internal malaise. Put another way, the physical holes these characters occupy emblematize their inability to achieve wholeness. If the American self is predicated on mobility, then entombment re-emphasizes the black male subject's failure to reconstruct himself as an integrated, Americanized subject.

One might think of confinement solely in spatial terms. But the notion of black protest texts as "narratives of confinement" refers not only to the protagonists' physical containment and dislocation within the story or plot but also to their difficulty in attaining voicedness in terms of narrative space. Earlier I spoke of the importance of language as a key component of subjectivity; the archetypal American novel, *Huckleberry Finn,* accentuates the importance of speaking one's own story in one's own tongue. Moreover, given African Americans' demoralizing experiences in a country that has historically denied them access to education and language, voice functions literally and metaphorically. Contemporary cultural criticism has spoken of the importance of "finding one's own voice" to tell one's own story, but the protest narrative of confinement mitigates the saliency of speech acts and voicedness. To varying degrees, black male subjects in these texts find their voices mediated, muted, and often silenced.

What might be termed the "paradox of voice" occurs in *Native Son,*[7] a narrative situation in which ostensibly centered subjects are denied the power to shape and determine their stories and how those narratives are inscribed. This dialectic is the natural outgrowth of the protagonist's tenuous position as centered subject. Consider Peter Middleton's notion of the decentered subject to describe protagonists in black masculinist protest narratives: "Poststructuralism has presented a decentered, a kind of subjectivity-less subject: interpellated by ideology, constructed by discourses, constituted by the desire of the other" (117). As a decentered subject, the black male in protest discourse is a tabula rasa upon which different entities—including and especially the authors—impose identities. Stated another way, *Native Son* reflects a certain "double voicedness," not necessarily in the Bakhtinian[8] sense

to imply the novel's vocal heterogeneity, but mainly with respect to the narratological tension that emerges between author and subject.

Consider this poem from Wright's cultural-critical tract *White Man, Listen!* dedicated to "The Westernized and Tragic Elite of Asia, Africa, and the
West Indies." One of the book's epigraphs, Wright's poem is a meditation
on black men's global and existential homelessness:

> the lonely outsiders who exist precariously
> on the clifflike margins of many cultures—men who are
> distrusted, misunderstood, maligned, criticized
> by Left and Right, Christian and pagan—
> men who carry on their frail but indefatigable shoulders
> the best of two worlds—and who,
> amidst confusion and stagnation,
> seek desperately for a home for their hearts:
> a home which, if found,
> could be a home for the hearts of all men.

Wright's paean to psychically and globally displaced black men encapsulates
the defining trait of his construction of the black male literary subject. The
marginality that the poem's subjects experience certainly resonates vis-à-vis
black men's historical, national, and international dislocation—their pressing sense of an existential or, more specifically, Diasporan homelessness. The
poem's language transmits the malaise that engulfs the deformed subject, the
black man forever engulfed in the no-man's-land that Bigger Thomas inhabits—the "lonely" black men, on the "clifflike margins of many cultures,"
seeking a "home." Wright conceives of black male subjects, be they fictional
(Bigger) or biographical (Dick Wright in *Black Boy*), not merely as archetypal
victims but as culturally and spatially dislocated. His deformed subjects occupy a liminal space between cultures, one white and impenetrable, the other
black, bereft, and uninhabitable.

Wright's consistent configuration of the black community as alien is also
a definitive component of his fiction and criticism. His black males' quests
for subjectivity are grounded in two problematic premises. Wright renders
the plight of the black community invisible and ahistorical, casting it as an
abject, feral atmosphere that fails to nurture; concomitantly, his lone, "lonely"
black hero is invested with the Herculean task of getting whites to "listen"
(see the title of his 1957 treatise) because only they can acknowledge his pain
and validate his existence. In the context of the empowering potential of
uniquely gendered communities in Baldwin, Gaines, and Wilson, Wright's
inscription of black males' anticommunal proclivities illuminates another key

facet of protest discourse: the black male subject's conception of his male counterparts as Other, men whose presence is as threatening as the hegemonic culture that oppresses them collectively without distinction.

Critics often and rightly assail Wright's execrable representations of black women; his figurations of men's intragender dynamics merit pique as well. To cast Wright's insistence that black male community and black male subjectivity are incongruous and irreconcilable in a slightly different way, I turn to the work of Chenjerai Shire, who has researched "linguistic and spatial representations of masculinities in Zimbabwe" (147). He explores the effects of colonialism, specifically how the British disrupted and redefined native Zimbabweans' conception of masculinity by affixing to geographic locations gender-specific connotations. Examining the Shona peoples of the country's southern region, he discusses how colonialism forced many men into the city to seek temporary, menial work to support their families and pay colonial taxes. Shire's deconstruction of the colonialism-masculinity nexus reveals how non-Western peoples internalized Western notions of masculinity and subjectivity:

> The city was a space inhabited by migrant labourers. As migrants, they were travellers who expressed their masculinities by identifying with the ideals which privileged roving. In "Shona" nomenclature, a man who disappears to the city is referred to by the same term as one who is broke: *muchoni*. Rural men addressed men born in cities or towns as "*mabhonirokisheni*" ("born in locations"). The plural prefix "*ma*" communicates a negation of cultural authenticity, defining them as "objects" and devaluing the manner and place in which they were born. *The masculinities of urban "Shona" men were constructed from their wage-earning power and through the assimilation of colonial definitions of masculinity. . . . Stripped of their totemic masculinities, urban males inhabited a masculinity that regarded women as* mahure *(whores) whose presence in male spaces, such as beerhalls, evoked extreme forms of misogyny. Any form of violence was legitimized within the male space of the beerhall.* (152–53; emphasis added)

Given Wright's concerns with male subjectivity from Diasporan and global perspectives, which characterized his life as an expatriate,[9] the anthropological signs Shire interprets elucidate male interactions in *Native Son* in provocative ways. The novel portrays the south side of Chicago, where the Thomas family inhabits a rat-infested flat owned by wealthy whites, as a squalid wasteland, an objective correlative for black hopelessness and white rapaciousness. Shire's configuration of the city as a no-man's-land, masculinity as a correlative of men's economic success, male-dominated spaces as arenas in which men display pugilistic, parochial notions of masculinity—

all of these cultural situations particularize what I see as Wright's flawed portraiture of black men individually and collectively.

Shire's specification of the beerhall resonates especially when pondering the absence of male community in the novel. Just as the beerhall provides a site for untrammeled male violence, the pool hall in *Native Son* functions comparably. It is transformed into a hypermasculinized arena that facilitates what might be labeled "cool-posing" in contemporary black male youth culture.[10] Not only does it serve as the strategic center for young black men's sociopathic behavior (Bigger and his friends mastermind an ill-fated robbery there), but more crucially, it fosters black men's estrangement and the enactment of socially legitimized behaviors like competitiveness and violence. This is dramatized most clearly when Gus, one of Bigger's cohorts, exposes Bigger's frail masculine identity by accusing him of being afraid to follow through on the gang's plan to rob a store. Bigger subsequently pins Gus and brandishes a knife: "'Get up! Get up and I'll slice your tonsils!'" (40). While the pool hall might represent a debased form of male community, it reiterates how Bigger's combustible relationships with other black men become nothing more than testosterone-sodden competitions in which he defines himself by standards of patriarchal masculinity; such performances substantiate what Thadious M. Davis calls Wright's consistent depictions of "aggressively masculine subjects" (126). Wright forecloses the possibility of Bigger's insinuation of himself within a black male community (though white men such as his lawyer, Boris Max, claim to "witness" on his behalf as a sort of amanuensis for the silenced Bigger). Perhaps Wright himself best articulates both the failure of community and his own—and his characters'—intragender and intraracial dislocation: in a 1945 interview he declared, "I most emphatically deny belonging to any group. I suppose it's the critics who put you in those categories but it's nothing to do with me" (Kinnamon and Fabre 240). Interrupting this discursive situation, the works of Baldwin, Gaines, and Wilson reimagine black masculinity and the exacting process of forming same-gender relationships in a society that renders black male intimacy unattainable and taboo.

Resituating the Black Literary Masculine

While protest discourse engenders a maimed, decentered subject, African-American male writers have, over the past forty years, drastically re-envisioned constructions of the black male protagonist. On this topic, Charles Johnson, the winner of the 1990 National Book Award for his neo–slave novel *Middle Passage,* has made some provocative claims about post-1970s men's writing in his critical meditation on African-American literature, *Being and Race: Black Writing since 1970*. Johnson contends that, with few exceptions, black writing has been summarily static and jejune. The protagonists in works by writers such as John A. Williams, Clarence Major, and David Bradley are "people deformed by their lack of power in a racially Divided Landscape. Many hate themselves and whites, fear homosexuals, are drawn powerfully to women for release yet fail to sustain healthy relationships, feel a deep revulsion for the black middle class and its values, and accept, or at least give lip service to, the politics of black power, but sometimes in a half-hearted way, tilting toward Negritude but knowing its shortcomings" (93). Johnson concludes that the black male literary canon, despite a few "technical advances," has remained a "literature of tragedy" mired in the protest tradition. Though this position is valid, Johnson regrettably views post-1970s black masculinist writing as homogeneous. I cite Johnson not as a convenient straw critic but to illustrate how even the most astute interpreters of African-American literature can espouse shortsighted assessments.[11] There is merit in Johnson's core assertion that black men's literature often has engaged in the business of protest; this discursive formation constitutes a substantial portion of black masculinist writing. However, African-American male writers since the 1950s—Baldwin, Gaines, and Wilson constituting an emblematic triumvirate—have critiqued, revised, and transcended earlier, more prescriptive parameters of literary subjectivity.

These three authors' works represent the recursivity of much black male literary discourse. The umbilical cord linking Douglass, Wright, Ellison, Baldwin, Gaines, and Wilson is undeniable, but the latter three writers have also spawned multifaceted versions of black men whose notion of subjectivity is much more complex and thereby more liberating. To be sure, "subjectivity is not a unified or transcendent psychological essence but a process. The subject, continually (re)activated and (re)positioned in the multiple discourses of culture, is an effect of signification" (Cohan and Shires 149). In black men's writing, therefore, there has been a marked repositioning or resituating of the subject, reflected in several writers' attempts to retrieve and recenter the decentered subject—to rescue him from the terra incognita between black and white. The reimagining of the black male subject links the writings of Baldwin, Gaines, and Wilson, which I explore in separate chapters. Though Baldwin is usually included in the triptych of "great" black male writers (alongside Wright and Ellison), I place him within the communal model of black male writers because he animated a departure from the constricting lexicon of protest and mediated the two discourses with varying degrees of success.

More specifically, the balance of my study investigates what I identify as the narrative process in which the authors negate their characters' deformation in order to stimulate their reformation. This process involves a type of healing ritual or ceremony in which the authors allow their protagonists to renegotiate and reclaim their status as subjects—not simply in terms of narrative centrality but as agents who envision themselves as members of a collectivity of black people who acknowledge the historical and psychological ties that bind African Americans. In this reconnection, black male subjects recover a heretofore erased collective history, and the process of revoicedness becomes regenerative. The ritual of transformation, characterized by some element of African-American performance traditions, becomes a liberating event, for the authors de-emphasize hegemonic spaces and institutions and accentuate the gendered, black male community and its potential to resuscitate the individual and, by extension, the collectivity.

Critical to my discussion of the ceremonial process of negation and reclamation are the anthropological studies of Victor Turner, which were influenced by Arnold van Gennep.[12] Turner and van Gennep have written widely on the function of rituals and ceremonies in diverse cultures, and some of their insights buttress my discursive rubric. Turner draws upon van Gennep's *rites de passage* in locating three stages of the "drama" of "symbolic action in human society": "separation, margin (or limen, signifying 'threshold' in Latin), and aggregation" (*Ritual Process* 94). He expounds on the "ritual process" further:

> The first phase (of separation) comprises symbolic behavior signifying the detachment of the individual or group either from an earlier fixed point in the social structure, from a set of cultural conditions (a "state"), or from both. During the intervening "liminal" period, the characteristics of the ritual subject (the "passenger") are ambiguous; he passes through a cultural realm that has few or none of the attributes of the past or coming state. In the third phase (reaggregation or reincorporation), the passage is consummated. The ritual subject, individual or corporate, is in a relatively stable state once more and, by virtue of this, has rights and obligations vis-à-vis others of a clearly defined and "structural" type; he is expected to behave in accordance with certain customary norms and ethical standards binding on incumbents of social position in a system of such positions. (94–95)

Turner goes on to adduce that the liminal stage ushers in communitas, which he defines as "a relationship between concrete, historical, idiosyncratic individuals" (131–32). Of final significance is the anthropologist's assertion that communitas "has an existential quality; it involves the whole man in his relation to other whole men" (127). His model offers an instructive method-ological framework for illustrating the role of the healing ceremony in fostering black male subjectivity—communitas being an analog of community that connotes male-to-male engagement on a deeper, psychospiritual level.

While the black men in Wright's texts occupy common physical places, they fail to erect intimate spaces that might facilitate the healing process—spaces connoting not mere physical edifices but emotional and spiritual realms that stimulate resubjectivication. Thus, setting emerges as a crucial part of the empowering and healing process, as Baldwin, Gaines, and Wilson expand the definition of place and space beyond the boundaries of geography. Setting does more than simply symbolize cramped social and psychological positionality. It represents a nurturing, nascent habitat that is conducive to the curative, ritual activity of finding one's voice—and simultaneously that of other black men. The authors who re-envision the black male literary subject may use settings reminiscent of their literary precursors—Gaines appropriates Wright's tropological prison in his 1968 short story "Three Men" and in his 1993 novel *A Lesson before Dying,* for instance—but these venues represent far more than tactile, physical places. In the communal configuration of black men's writing, physical place fosters not fragmentation but communitas, a space where the black subject reclaims his story, which becomes that of his black male counterparts. Moreover, the reciprocal nature of storytelling and other performative acts stimulates the revitalization of the black subject in contradistinction to the disfigured one that populates protest discourse.

Within this framework in which authors reconceptualize black male subjectivity, voice functions as integrally as community and setting. The polyphonic textual model revises the constricted notion of voice promulgated in black masculinist protest discourse: the movement from deformed to reformed self occurs primarily through the subjects' ability to find and define their own voices. The problematical paradox of voice in the protest narratives is dismantled, for authors of the polyphonic texts revoice their protagonists by letting them tell their own tales through the formulation of speech communities. The storytelling act maintains a central place in the process of subject reformation. Hence, I will also elaborate on the function of story not simply as it relates to plot, but how storytelling functions reflexively. The potency of dual storytelling events emerges through the narrative the author weaves for the reader and the parallel performance of black men within the text who speak through, to, and for each other. Ultimately, the act itself as much as the content of the story revivifies the deformed protagonist. In this context, storytelling maintains especial salience, as story-listeners or witnesses assume a paramount role in the reaffirmation process. A distinct difference that emerges between protest and polyphonous discourses is how the former concentrates on the written word while the latter privileges voice and orality. Consider, for instance, Bigger Thomas's obsession with having the newspaper corroborate and validate his transgressive behaviors or Invisible Man's persistent misreading of written texts, even as he proclaims that his inscribed narrative "speak[s] for you" (58).

The authors in this communal framework emphasize the importance of African-American oral traditions, which is especially significant given the re-emergence of vernacular discourse—spoken-word poetry and hip-hop/rap culture—in the 1990s. One might legitimately recall the fundamental claim of the sociolinguist Geneva Smitherman's groundbreaking study *Talkin and Testifyin: The Language of Black America,* where she observes that for African Americans, the oral tradition "preserves the Afro-American heritage and reflects the collective spirit of the race" (73). She also remarks that "The persistence of the African-based oral tradition is such that blacks tend to place only limited value on the written word, whereas verbal skills expressed orally rank in high esteem" (76). In foregrounding orality and vernacular performance, many polyphonic texts creatively employ first-person narration and thereby de-emphasize authorial voice, creating what might be called a more "speakerly text," as the author functions less as a mediating (and editorial) force between his subject and the reading audience.[13] The plurivocality[14] of Baldwin's "Sonny's Blues," Gaines's *A Lesson before Dying,* and Wilson's *Seven Guitars* reflects how community and thereby a refashioned type of subjectivity are attainable through interactive events such as storytelling, story-listening, and musical performance.

The privileging of voicedness in relation to subjectivity is the most distinguishing feature of the communal, polyphonic schema. The potency of performance—jazz, blues and gospel, storytelling—resuscitates protagonists and becomes the basis of their renewal. The polyvocal texts that emerge through this foregrounding of the speaking voice reflect, to some extent, what Alessandro Portelli articulates in *The Text and the Voice:* "Anonymous and polymorphous, orality shatters the identity of the author and explodes the very idea of a 'text' into a multiplicity of discourses engaged in a perpetual, hopeless search for one another, and into a myriad of equally 'authentic' variants" (18). To varying degrees, Baldwin, Gaines, and Wilson concentrate on centering their protagonists' voices while being less concerned with normative literary discourses (Wrightian naturalism or Ellisonian realism/postmodernism, for instance). These authors attempt to de-emphasize their authorial presence and confer upon the protagonists the position of speaking, centered subjects. Ultimately, a panoply of black male voices emerges, voices not in what Portelli deems a "hopeless search" but voices that find one another and formulate authentic speech/performance collectives. Not coincidentally, Baldwin, Gaines, and Wilson were reared in and influenced by black vernacular cultures that esteemed the power of performance and the spoken word.[15] Baldwin's use of jazz, blues, and gospel; Gaines's palimpsestic narratological method; and Wilson's innovative commingling of blues and spirituals, testimonials, and folk biographies all represent ways in which voice and community catalyze the regeneration of the black male and the renegotiation of his subjectivity.

Ultimately, the idea of communal, polyphonic narrative discourse has implications for both the form and content of black men's literature. The multilayered and multivoiced works of Baldwin, Gaines, and Wilson reflect a new wave of African-American writing, where characters and authors background racial oppression and move beyond protesting the sanctity and superiority of whites and whiteness. I locate these authors as key proponents of what the novelist Trey Ellis has termed the "NBA" (New Black Aesthetic), artists whom he feels "are now defining blacks in black contexts—so we are no longer preoccupied with the subjects of interracial dating or integration. And these artists [Spike Lee, Toni Morrison, August Wilson, Living Colour et al.] aren't flinching before they lift the hood on our collective psyches now that they have liberated themselves from both white envy and self-hate" (238). Implicit in the notion of protest is a valorization of the dominant culture, for protest reflects on some level a desire to embrace the very culture that oppresses and eviscerates. The post-1950s trend in black men's literature represents a discursive interruption that transports black men's literary art into another country, where its subjects cultivate psychological, emotional intimacy and bear the burden of restoring their emotionally maimed selves. Countering the counterdiscourse of protest has been the artistic endeavor of the three authors under investigation. I will deconstruct the fallacious idea that the works of postmodern black male authors "often seem to be the *same* story recycled or sliced into different angles" (Johnson 74) by exploring how performing the "same story" transforms the damaged black male Other into the communal Brother.

2 The Perilous Journey to a Brother's Country: James Baldwin and the Rigors of Community

IN EVALUATING and situating James Baldwin's career and life, one encounters several complexities and paradoxes. It is no wonder that the word "conundrum" recurs in his writings and interviews. His life and work reflect a spate of conflicting and sometimes binary oppositions—Europe/America, heterosexual/homosexual, political/personal, black/white. Because he was defined by so many oppositions, Baldwin experienced the angst of an artist at once self-isolated yet craving community. The writer's ambivalence toward community frequently surfaced during the last decade of his life, as evidenced in this 1984 *Paris Review* interview: "No. I've never *seen* one [a community of writers] in any case . . . and I don't think any writer ever has" (Elgrably and Plimpton 247). However, the poet Quincy Troupe's description of Baldwin's St. Paul de Vence farmhouse suggests a more communal spirit:

> Many articles in the house caught my attention, most notably the many paintings and pieces of sculpture, among them the colorful paintings of the late African-American expatriate painter Beauford Delaney, who had been one of Jimmy's best friends. There were two other pieces that I believed said very much about the political commitment of the man. One, a black pen-and-ink drawing of Nelson Mandela against an orange background, accompanied by a poem, was framed and hung over the dining-room fireplace, the most prominent place in the house. The other was an assemblage created by Jimmy's brother David in his honor. ("James Baldwin" 289)

What ultimately emerges is a portrait of an artist who publicly bristled at the notion of "literary" community but privately occupied a living space that renders a cosmic link among an eclectic group of black men—brother artists and blood brothers among them.

One cannot read Baldwin's oeuvre without placing him squarely within a tradition of black masculinist writers. Baldwin's place in a literary male coterie is unequivocal but problematic, for his works certainly counter limiting constructions of the black male self. Beginning with Douglass's 1845 autobiography, black masculinist writers have narrativized the quest for wholeness in a society in which black men are constantly under siege. This quest—as indicated by novels and autobiographies such as James Weldon Johnson's *The Autobiography of an Ex-Coloured Man*, Richard Wright's *Black Boy*, and Ralph Ellison's *Invisible Man*—is the binding motif in the tradition. Although Baldwin is connected inextricably to the black masculinist canon, he nevertheless perambulated the framework established by Wright and Ellison. The tenuous and often ambiguous relationship between Baldwin and his literary cohorts approximates the complex vision of male community he depicts in the short story "Sonny's Blues" (1957) and in his last published novel, *Just Above My Head* (1978). These works, spanning over thirty years of Baldwin's artistic life, painstakingly examine black males searching for and ensconced in different forms of community—sexual and artistic as well as fraternal and familial.

The cadre of native sons and invisible men who permeated black men's writing through the 1950s became the bane of Baldwin's aesthetic vision. His contestation of such parochial representations of black men informs my interpretation of his fiction. The author's own comments about the character who most vividly embodies the antinomies that defined his own life, the tortured jazz musician Rufus Scott from the novel *Another Country* (1962), underscore his refiguration of black subjects vis-à-vis protest discourse:

> A lot of people in that book had never appeared in fiction before. People overlook this fact. And there's an awful lot of my experience which has never been seen in the English language before. Rufus, for example. There are no antecedents for him. He was in the novel because I didn't think anyone had ever watched the disintegration of a *black boy* from that particular point of view. Rufus was partly responsible for his doom, and in presenting him as partly responsible, *I was attempting to break out of the whole sentimental image of the afflicted nigger driven that way (to suicide) by white people.* (Standley and Pratt 104; emphasis added)

Baldwin positions Rufus uniquely within the black literary landscape while simultaneously signifying on the Wright school, a tradition often located under the rubric of American naturalism and protest. Baldwin's use of the term "black boy" to describe Rufus is noteworthy, for Baldwin critiqued and reconfigured Wright's portrait of black masculinity that—for Wright at least—was the literary countersign for America's irremediable, toxic racism.

Baldwin's sustained and occasionally acrid criticism notwithstanding, Wright's influence on his literary heir is well documented. Though forty years have elapsed since his death, the latter's work remains the quintessence of black protest fiction. As Paul Gilroy points out, Wright represented "a new kind of black author, one whose open political affiliations and demand and fearless projection of anger released new creative possibilities and changed the terms in which the racial politics of literary expression were articulated" (147). Wright's work represented the touchstone for Baldwin's own aesthetics; for Baldwin, Wright represented a towering presence that threatened to negate the power of his work. This explains Baldwin's "slaying" of Wright in essays such as "Many Thousands Gone" and "Alas, Poor Richard"—the older writer standing as a leviathan artistic presence who must be destroyed for Baldwin to carve out his own artistic space. But what transpires here is more complex than a Freudian struggle in which a neophyte writer metaphorically vanquishes his literary father. Baldwin vehemently repudiates an aesthetic of literature that privileges black male victimization. Simultaneously, however, his own work protests black men's emotional and spiritual displacement, a condition often—though not exclusively—engendered by white America.

Baldwin's portrait of Rufus Scott, a distinctly different type of black character, signals the writer's disavowal of the black masculinist protest fiction that preceded *Another Country*. Baldwin's primary concern was not so much with how white society deformed and destroyed black men but how these men participated in their own demise. Thus, most of his writings counterpoise the prevailing masculinist discourse that insists upon the black man's physical and mental erasure as a fait accompli. Baldwin's pointed critique of *Native Son* further elucidates his critical and theoretical position:

> What the novel reflects—and at no point interprets—is the isolation of the Negro within his own group and the resulting fury of impatient scorn. It is this which creates its climate of anarchy and unmotivated and unapprehended disaster; and it is this climate, common to most Negro protest novels, which has led us all to believe that *in Negro life there exists no tradition, no field of manners, no possibility of ritual or intercourse*, such as may, for example, sustain the Jew even after he has left his father's house. (*Notes* 35–36; emphasis added)

Baldwin rejects Wright's effacing of the black community, his disregard for entities and institutions that have allowed black folks to "make a way out of no way," be they extended family, the church, civic clubs, or fraternities and sororities. His appraisal of Wright recalls Ellison's comments about popular configurations of the black subject, comments Ellison published in the late 1950s, but which are equally apposite at the dawn of the twenty-first century: "In the Anglo-Saxon branch of American folklore and in the entertainment industry . . . the Negro is reduced to a negative sign that usually appears in a comedy of the grotesque and the unacceptable" (*Shadow* 48). Black masculinist protest, with "grotesque" Bigger as its cultural metonym, an incarnation of the "negative sign," forms the point of discursive departure for Baldwin and his refiguration and recentering of the black literary male. Baldwin's fictive project has been the reconstruction of whites *and* blacks' equation of blackness with absence, otherness, and difference. In "Sonny's Blues" and *Just Above My Head,* he excavates and depicts what he designated as the "field of manners" and varying degrees of "intercourse"—artistic, verbal, and sexual—that comprise black men's lives.

"A Beat beneath the Beat, Another Music beneath the Music": "Sonny's Blues" as Brotherly Panegyric

As a literary interloper and iconoclast, Baldwin fervently challenges a narrowly defined construction of black male subjectivity. Throughout his work one finds a concern with black men's relationships with each other; of less interest are black men engaged in internecine conflicts like Bigger Thomas and his delinquent cohorts or Invisible Man and his perpetual struggle with a battalion of black men. Baldwin goes to great lengths to penetrate the relationships *between* black men—a topic that had been underexamined in black fiction. His protagonists, locked in an inexorable struggle to love one another, search for common emotional and psychological ground and attempt to forge identities beyond the confining parameters of white-imposed definitions of black maleness.

Even more prominent in Baldwin's fictive discourse are black men's internal family dynamics. Specifically, he privileges the seemingly insurmountable task brothers face in trying to overcome social barriers that devalue and stigmatize men's relationships. Baldwin's depiction of brotherly relations is not hewn from a Cane and Abel scenario counterpoising the Manichean forces of good and evil, although he infuses all of his work with the cadences and rituals of the black church. Additionally, however, he examines *why* black men within families consistently view each other more as Other than Brother. This conflict surfaces in several novels—from John and Roy Grimes's demonic psychological struggles in *Go Tell It on the Mountain* to Hall and Arthur

Montana's wrenching attempts to overcome social prohibitions based on sexual orientation in *Just Above My Head*. However, "Sonny's Blues" is arguably Baldwin's most eloquent statement on black brotherly love as well as his most successful representation of black men whose family relationships are defined by their spiritual and emotional closeness.

The notion of the homosocial is apposite in discussing "Sonny's Blues" because it allows one to mediate the knotty problem of men's nonsexual relationships in a culture where men are habitually sexualized. As Eve Kosofsky Sedgwick maintains, "In fact, it [homosocial] is applied to such activities as 'male bonding,' which may, as in our society, be characterized by intense homophobia, fear and hatred of homosexuality" (1). I invoke the homosocial not because of its euphonic relation to the word "homosexual" but because it offers a referent for men's nonsexual relationships—their modes of contact that are decidedly nonsexual and, in some instances, more emotionally and psychologically fulfilling. This fact is particularly relevant to my discussion of "Sonny's Blues" because the author resists his tendency to apotheosize same-sex relationships without adequately situating them within a socioracial context. Uncharacteristically absent are Baldwin's sometimes turgid depictions of homosexual love (e.g., *Giovanni's Room* or *Another Country*) or the anachronistic representations of black men so terrorized by society that they implode and destroy themselves and other black men. Alternatively, "Sonny's Blues" meticulously interrogates and dismantles the superficial, socially imposed aspects of men's relationships precisely because the story is uniquely asexual.

As in most of his fiction, Baldwin foregrounds performance, voice, and community as the vehicles through which black men wrestle with and renegotiate their identities and relationships. As students and teachers of Baldwin's work would expect, blues, jazz, gospel, and confessional narratives— witnessing and testifying—recur as the foremost modes for exploring black men's pain and inability to connect. Though this is not discursively revolutionary in black masculinist writing (think of Ellison or Toomer, for example), Baldwin breaks new ground because he refuses to portray black males as long-suffering, perpetually victimized by and longing for white society. Instead, Baldwin's black male subjects seek the approbation of their fellow black men and community. His narrative strategies foster a convergence of black men's stories, a closing of the chasm that divides them. Through the narrative tropes of voice and space, Baldwin shifts the quest for subjectivity from the external to the internal, from the political to the personal, and from the social to the spiritual.

Baldwin invests Sonny's older brother with the task of narrating the "blues" of his brother, seven years the narrator's junior. Throughout the story, the author uses doubling and reversal to illuminate cyclical patterns in blacks' personal histories, and the repetition is evident in his representation of the brothers. Though the narrator embodies black middle-class life and Sonny the prototypical drug-addicted jazz artist of the 1950s, the two men's lives are mirror opposites. Both subscribe to hegemonic definitions of masculinity, ones that Richard Delgado and Jean Stefancic concisely identify when they assert that "the social construction of men of color is even more troublesome and confining than that of men in general. *Men of color are constructed as criminal, violent, lascivious, irresponsible, and not particularly smart*" (211; emphasis added). A brief look at the men's respective backgrounds reveals that though superficially different, they both inculcate crippling conceptions of Western/American masculinity that black men have historically used as the basis of their self-definition.

Baldwin encodes the men's acceptance of this construction of black maleness spatially, concretizing the nexus between one's personal geography and the environment he occupies.[1] Note the narrator's camera-eye description of his and Sonny's drive "between the green of the park and the stony, lifeless elegance of hotels and apartment buildings, toward the vivid, killing streets of our childhood":

> Most of the houses in which we had grown up had vanished, as had the stores from which we had stolen, the basements in which we had first tried sex, the rooftops from which we had hurled tin cans and bricks. But houses exactly like the houses of our past yet dominated the landscape, boys exactly like the boys we once had been found themselves smothering in these houses, came down into the streets for light and air and found themselves encircled by disaster. Some escaped the trap, most didn't. Those who got out always left something of themselves behind, as some animals amputate a leg and leave it in the trap. It might be said, perhaps, that I had escaped, after all, I was a school teacher; or that Sonny had, he hadn't lived in Harlem for years. Yet, as the cab moved uptown through streets which seemed, with a rush, to darken with dark people, and as I covertly studied Sonny's face, it came to me that what we both were seeking through our separate cab windows was that part of ourselves which had been left behind. (94–95)

This description of the brothers' first meeting in several years (Sonny has spent time in jail and a halfway house for recovering drug addicts) reveals the extent to which black men seek refuge by escaping and renouncing community to reconstruct the self—a darker version of the mythic "road" that scores of American male protagonists and authors have traveled, from Huck Finn and Joe Christmas to Chester Himes and Jack Kerouac. But Baldwin insists that this black flight is merely transitory and physical. His fictionalized black community—in this instance the same "Harlem ghetto" he vivified in *Notes of a Native Son*—is the nucleus of black life: for black male subjectivity to be renegotiated and reclaimed, black men must first make the mythic, eternal return. As the author himself has noted about his own journey from Harlem to Paris and back, "You never leave home. You take your home with you. You better. Otherwise, you're homeless" (Thorsen). Corresponding to his own personal vision, Baldwin imbues home in the story with a gravitational pull that draws black men to their native environments regardless of the physical distances they travel.

Baldwin's innovative use of spatial influences as markers for black men's gender formation evinces itself throughout the narrative. Though the narrator attempts to change his environment, he and his wife, Isabel, still inhabit a "housing project," where the big windows "aren't big enough to make space out of no space" (95). Additionally, the senior brother's participation in the Korean War and Sonny's stint in the navy bear out Delgado and Stefancic's comments on "militarism."[2] Black men have traditionally regarded the armed forces as another benchmark for masculinity. As Chester Himes, John Williams, and Charles Fuller have done in their writings, Baldwin suggests the failure of military service to confer subject status upon African-American men. Though it provides access to violence, a component of patriarchal masculinity that our society venerates, it ultimately proves to be spurious and ephemeral.

The senior brother's problematic conceptualization of masculinity is finally driven home when he and Sonny debate the merits of the jazz legends Louis Armstrong and Charlie Parker. In a bit of literary signifying, Baldwin invokes "Satchmo" not as Ellison does in the prologue of *Invisible Man*—as the quintessential trickster, a testimony to the black man's ability to outwit a culture that would beat him "black and blue"—but as a conflicted version of black masculinity that distorts and dismembers self to fulfill whites' expectations. During a conversation between the fifteen-year-old Sonny and the narrator about Sonny's choice of career, the latter responds to Sonny's desire to become a jazz artist by offering Armstrong as a potential career model. Brother's subsequent question, "'Can you make a living at it?'" (104), exposes his privileging of what Cornell West has referred to as "market values,"[3] which measure men's worth solely by economic yardsticks.

Sonny's own life reflects a desire to conform to the debilitating limitations of hegemonic masculinity. Brother relates an anecdote in which an adolescent Sonny had "been all hipped on the idea of going to India. He read books about people sitting on rocks, naked, in all kinds of weather, but mostly bad, naturally, and walking barefoot through hot coals and arriving at wisdom" (94). While this adolescent episode may seem fairly pedestrian and typical (further reinforcing the narrator's superciliousness), it portends Sonny's belief that the self exists hermetically isolated from community. Moreover, Sonny's precocious thoughts presage his view that flight animates the reconstitution of self—a flight that ends in drug addiction, the ultimate form of self-absorption and estrangement.

Paradoxically, Sonny's adolescent experiences epitomize the birth of the tortured Baldwinian artist who pays in terms of self and communal, homosocial intercourse. While Isabel and her family provide Sonny with a home during Brother's military service, the budding artist is so obsessed with playing the piano that the narrator divulges, "*They began, in a way, to be afflicted by this presence that was living in their home. It was as though Sonny were some sort of god, or monster.* He moved in an atmosphere which wasn't like theirs at all" (107; emphasis added). Note how Baldwin shapes the idea of conformity through Sonny's desire to embrace the limitations of hegemonic masculinity. Though Baldwin conveys the inexorable difference between the artist's conception of art as life-sustaining and the sometimes disdainful attitudes of those around him, he also suggests that Sonny's solipsistic approach to art and life is potentially corrosive both personally and communally. In the search for artistic subjectivity, Sonny metamorphoses into a "monster" whose artistic narcissism threatens to destroy those with whom he lives.

Baldwin approximates the configuration of male protest subjects by having Sonny devalue potentially nurturing black spaces in lieu of white ones that appear to buoy his artistic pursuits. We eventually learn that he has been skipping school and spending time "in Greenwich Village, with musicians and other characters, in a white girl's apartment" (108). Sonny's search for a short-sighted form of subjectivity eventually leads him down the same path as his brother—to the armed forces—but eventually back to Greenwich Village. Though they have been estranged, the narrator locates Sonny and tries to reconcile, but in the young pianist's Greenwich Village room,

> there were lots of people in the room and Sonny just lay on his bed, and he wouldn't come downstairs with me, and he treated these other people as though they were his family and I weren't. So I got mad and then he got mad, and then I told him that he might just as well be dead as live the way he was living. Then he stood up and he told me not to worry about him any more in life, that he *was* dead as far as I was concerned. Then he pushed me to the door and the other people looked on as though nothing were happening, and he slammed the door behind me. (109)

Baldwin's representation of Greenwich Village anticipates Rufus Scott's geospiritual displacement in *Another Country:* Rufus similarly ensconces himself in an Anglo-bohemian enclave and abandons his native Harlem. Also reminiscent of Bigger's cell or Invisible Man's underground, Sonny's physical milieu concretizes his social and spiritual deaths, his acceptance of a form of masculinity that undervalues familial relationships. Though Baldwin himself cut his artistic teeth in "the Village," he also exposes how this Anglo-centered countercultural space vitiates black men's connections to potentially empowering black people and spaces. Just as Brother's attempts to refashion himself according to proscriptive definitions of masculinity fail, so too does Sonny's journey to another country, an alien terrain where communal values and relationships are foreclosed and forfeited.[4]

Given the brothers' parallel conceptualization of masculinity, "Sonny's Blues" requires us to look beneath the beat to glean Baldwin's narrative strategies and how he contests standard constructions of the black literary and cultural masculine. Though critics and Baldwin himself talk about his use of the Jamesian "indirect method,"[5] he crafted his own signature group of signs that pervade his fictive performances: his foregrounding of gospel, blues, and jazz music, his emphasis on storytelling and story-listening—or, to use his biblically tinged lexicon, testifying and witnessing—and his focus on the potency of black speech acts. Baldwin's interlarding of different forms of voicedness and community distinguishes him from many of his literary forebrothers, as he attempts to forge a "field of manners" (his phrase from *Notes of a Native Son*) to transmit the complexities of blacks men's lives.

Baldwin recasts the first-person mode of narration in the story to center the notion of double- or polyvoicedness. Though the older brother narrates the story, it is far from monologic. Sonny is granted voice throughout the text, either verbally or through other expressive means—first through a letter and later via musical performance. Thus, the narrator does not merely interpret the ostensible "subject" of the story; the act of narrating in and of itself does not automatically confer power and agency. Baldwin roots his story in polyphonic narrative discourse, which captures the story's multiple voices and layered vernacular performances. Each linguistic and musical utterance in "Sonny's Blues" reflects individual characters' unique discursive style. Mikhail Bakhtin's comments about language in novelistic discourse further elucidate the story's narratological strategies: "The language used by characters in the novel, how they speak, is verbally and semantically autonomous; each character's speech possesses its own belief system, since each is the speech of another in another's language; thus it may also *refract authorial intentions and consequently may to a certain degree constitute a second language for the author*" (315; emphasis added). The notion of multiple autonomous languages within the narrative correlates to Baldwin's polyglot—the array of voices and experiences of black men and women at different historical moments that he includes within the brothers' stories.

An exchange about superficially different jazz artists exposes the link between characters' speech utterances and their belief systems. After the narrator asks Sonny to "'name somebody—you know, a jazz musician you admire,'" the following exchange occurs:

> "Bird."
> "Who?"
> "Bird! Charlie Parker! Don't they teach you nothing in the goddamn army?"
> ". . . You'll have to be patient with me. Now. Who's this Parker character?"
> (103)

The narrator's language exposes an ignorance of black vernacular culture, accentuated by his pejorative reference to Sonny's artistic mentor as a "character." Sonny's curt, monosyllabic utterances in this stichomythic exchange reveal his contempt for the supposedly unhip, Anglicized middle-class values that he feels have deracialized his brother. But Baldwin hasn't simply pitted the conservative, "assimilated" older brother against his culturally grounded, "authentic" younger sibling. On the contrary, Sonny's self-absorption, reflected in his drug use and escape into white bohemian culture, parallels his brother's myopic, conformist attitudes. The characters' value systems are evidenced through their language, which "refracts" the author's own speech. In other words, the meaning that Baldwin intends to convey lies somewhere between the binary oppositions, constituting a sort of second (or third) language—one that connects disparate conceptualizations of self, masculinity, and art. Baldwin moves beyond Bakhtin's dialectical conception of voice: Baldwin's is rooted in polyphony, because it takes into account not merely characters who are linked dialogically but includes extra- or transverbal modes of African-American communicative discourse.

Given that the jazz artist–as–prophet conceit pervades Baldwin's writing, he does privilege Sonny from an epistemological standpoint—the story is, after all, *Sonny's* blues. The narrator, in his constant attempts to "read signs," is removed from vernacular culture and even denigrates such culture. Berndt Ostendorf's delineation between "oral" and "literate" cultures is instructive here: "Oral cultures are dramatic, literate cultures epistemic in their focus of attention, the first develops the resources of spontaneity, style, affective performance, and catharsis, the second scrutiny, contemplation. . . . *Literacy also puts a brake on semantic freedom and development;* semantic ratification and adoption into usage are slow and laborious processes. *Innovations, adaptions, and neologisms are treated as intruders, and subcultural improprieties run into a small wall of purists*" (224; emphasis added). These distinctions shed light on the characters' opposing life philosophies. As the narrator and shaper of the tale, the senior brother is naturally logocentric; thus, he privileges the written or "literate." Sonny's identification with "Bird" links him to a volatile, fertile period in black art—the emergence of bebop jazz in the 1940s—that Parker helped to inaugurate. Parker's connection to oral and performative culture can be located in his creation of this "neologistic" jazz idiom that was anathema to Armstrong's mode of performance, which sometimes seemed manufactured for white audiences' consumption.

The opening of the story, where he learns of Sonny's drug arrest and addiction, reveals the narrator's valorizing of the written word: "I *read* about it in the paper. . . . I *read* it, and I couldn't believe it, and I *read* it again. Then perhaps I just stared at it, at the newsprint spelling out his name, spelling out the *story*" (86; emphasis added). That the narrator depends on another medium to retrieve Sonny's story exposes a spatiocultural gap between the narrator and Sonny specifically and black culture generally. This point is amplified when he subsequently reveals: "I was trying to remember everything I'd heard about dope addiction and I couldn't help watching Sonny for signs" (96). Throughout the story, the narrator engages in the hermeneutical process of textualizing Sonny's body, reducing it to a negative sign or set of behaviors.[6] Furthermore, he interprets Sonny metonymically as representative of a generation of young black men who abjured the brand of male subjectivity he advocates. Baldwin suggests that the narrator's vocation as an algebra teacher has eroded his ability to distinguish between abstract mathematical symbols and the signs encoding black men's experiences in America—an audible holler that is far removed from Anglo-American semantics and ways of knowing.

The narrator's use of the term "story" is rhetorically cogent in terms of voice and reconfigurations of black male subjectivity. Anticipating writers like Ernest Gaines, Baldwin saturates the short story with multiple stories, which strategically foregrounds the exchanging of personal narratives. He imbues the text with a metafictive quality; it is a short story that concomitantly conveys the value of shared history as cultural artifact and personal currency. As a result, the text revolves around the exacting but unavoidable task of not merely speaking the unspeakable but of doing so within a collective of culturally, psychically, and spiritually bound persons. Baldwin does not privilege black men haunted by an irrepressible need to be recognized as "men" according to the austere dictates of American masculinity. His characters exist in symbiotic relation to each other, and their fates are complex and interwoven.

Thus, Baldwin's narrative frame is deceptive: though the narrator ostensibly shapes the tale, he is as much a witness or hearer throughout the story. I correlate this amorphous narrative positioning to what Turner designates as the "liminal" stage in his ritual rubric, where the "characteristics of the ritual subject (the 'passenger') are ambiguous; he passes through a cultural realm that has few or none of the attributes of the past or coming state" (*Ritual Process* 94). Baldwin structures the story around a series of performances, both verbal and nonverbal, which constitute ritualistic acts that transport both protagonists from a realm of uncertainty and tenuousness into a state of communitas. I will examine a few of these speech acts in order to elucidate Baldwin's polyphonous poetics.

A proleptic exchange occurs after the shocking newspaper account of Sonny's arrest. The narrator encounters one of Sonny's childhood friends, a drug addict whose self-destructive path parallels what the narrator sees as his brother's own profligacy (he even initially confuses him with his younger sibling). This meeting reveals the narrator's cultural isolation and myopia, but Sonny's double penetrates the narrator's heretofore impenetrable mien. The narrator's initial reaction to the young man's pathetic suicide wish, however, reveals the depth of his own spiritual stagnation: "'Look. Don't tell *me* your sad story, if it was up to me, I'd give you one [a pistol with which to kill himself].' Then I felt guilty—guilty, probably, for never having supposed that the poor bastard *had* a story of his own, much less a sad one" (89). While the narrator's intransigence is palpable, equally significant is a native recognition of the algebra (his vocation) or complexity of black men's lives. The narrator grudgingly acknowledges the interiority of this young man's life— and therefore the possibility of Sonny's and his own, a region that black men have abandoned to conform to a prescribed form of masculinity that precludes black men's spiritual and psychological reunification. This moment establishes the narrative's three most resonant storytelling and performative acts, which, taken together, represent a tripartite figuration—a ceremonial exorcism—that catalyzes black men's healing through voicedness and connectedness.

The first speech act involves a heretofore hidden story surrounding the death of the protagonists' father's brother, a guitar-playing uncle who was callously run down by a group of drunken whites. Again, Baldwin effectively uses doubling, as the pairs of brothers are linked thematically if not temporally as musicians. Though the story does not elide the omnipresent racism, Baldwin prefigures works such as August Wilson's *Ma Rainey's Black Bottom* and *Seven Guitars* by decentering it. The most cogent dimension of the tale is not racial violence in and of itself but the ways in which it devitalizes black men collectively. When his mother reveals to the narrator that "'Your Daddy never did really get right again'" (100), she articulates an element of black men's lives that often remains cloaked or denied—their emotional, homosocial need for each other. Her story contests a construction of masculinity that valorizes men's independence and vitiates their interdependence. Baldwin effectively conveys black men's cosmic connections, their generational ties that transcend time and space.

The critical point elucidated here is not only thematic but narratological: the author foregrounds the importance of story—storytelling, story-listening, and story transmission. The narrator's question, "'What happened to his [his father's] brother?'" induces his mother's speech act, a tale that he mindfully absorbs and processes. Baldwin's free indirect discourse shifts the power of narration from a single controlling consciousness to another figure, thus moving the narrator from teller to hearer and witness. His mother becomes a conduit for invaluable cultural information that heretofore had been suppressed. One could argue that Baldwin's portrait conforms to a prescriptive and atavistic view of women as emotional fulcrums who willingly sacrifice selfhood to fulfill their consecrated roles as "wife, companion, and comforter."[7] However, the mother simultaneously transcends this role by maintaining a pivotal role in the male-centered speech/performance community. Unlike the monodimensional women who populate black masculinist protest literature, she vitally deconstructs and revises her sons' blemished definitions of subjectivity. By situating her within the constellation of male figures, Baldwin envisions the black woman as a central part of the nascent speech community, for she bequeaths to her older son the spiritual legacy that binds suffering brothers—father, uncle, Sonny's friend, the narrator himself.

The second important performance, the middle passage in the brothers' progression from liminal to voiced subjects, occurs after the rehabilitated Sonny has moved in with the narrator and his family. An "old-fashioned revival meeting," held on the street "near the entrance to a barbecue joint," becomes a galvanizing event, one that joins the brothers spiritually (110). Though they remain psychologically distant (a fact buttressed by their positions during the revival, as Sonny stands on "the edge of the crowd" while his brother watches from his living room window), the gap between the two has begun to recede, and their simultaneous witnessing of the revival presages their journey to each other's emotional space. The quasi church service, conducted by "three sisters in black and a brother," reflects not only Baldwin's inversion of sacred and secular spaces but, more crucially, the potentially empowering role of vocal and musical performance:

All they had were their voices and their Bibles and a tambourine. The brother was testifying and while he testified two of the sisters stood together, seeming to say, amen, and the third sister walked around with the tambourine outstretched and a couple of people dropped coins into it. Then the brother's testimony ended and the sister who had been taking up the collection dumped the coins into her palm and transferred them to the pocket of her long black robe. Then she raised both hands, striking the tambourine against the air, and then against one hand, and she started to sing. And the two other sisters and the brother joined in. (110–11; emphasis added)

This scene is Baldwin's signature, for it reflects his keen and intimate grasp of black oral culture's spiritual underpinnings. It also captures cathartic qualities of black performance rituals and the potentially curative effects of finding and privileging one's own voice.

Baldwin's ordering of performers' "instruments" reveals his privileging of the secular and oral: the human voice precedes both the religious artifact and synthetic instrument. Stated another way, voice takes on a primordial significance that supersedes even God's word. The showcasing of testifying and singing reflects black culture's tendency to favor the vernacular, destabilizing the narrator's hyperinterpretive propensities. Baldwin also effectively uses doubling and revision in this scene. After Sonny places money in the tambourine and leaves, he joins the narrator and both witness the remainder of the revival, which is marked by the singing of *"If I could only hear my mother pray again!"* (112). Subtly and indirectly, Baldwin has traversed spatial, temporal, and gender boundaries by rhetorically and thematically linking this scene to the earlier "confession," where their mother pled and prayed for the narrator to watch over his brother. While he may have been ambivalent when his mother initially placed this burden on him, he is now equipped to "hear" her prayer anew. The brothers' concurrent witnessing of the revival becomes a watershed moment, for it compels Sonny to confess his own self-destructive experiences; reciprocally, the narrator begins to unlock his own epistemological prison. His revelation about his complicity in Sonny's disintegration—"I realized, with this mocking look, that there stood between us, forever, beyond the power of time or forgiveness, the fact that I had held silence—so long!—when he had needed human speech to help him" (114)—sets the stage for the final phase of the movement toward the evolution of artistic and linguistic community.

The story's rendering of the brothers' emotional reconnection reaches its apex in its concluding scene, which might be thought of as the point of "reaggregation" or "reincorporation."[8] The final ceremony in the story, Sonny's performance in a jazz bar attended by his narrator-brother, inaugurates community. Signifying on the Western bildungsroman, where a single figure such as Huckleberry Finn or Stephen Dedalus undergoes a transformation that subsequently marginalizes him, Baldwin's polyphonic narrative strategy brings a convergence of the central figures within a communal context. An array of stories and performances—Sonny's letter, the mother's wrenching remembrance of past men's relationships, the impromptu outdoor revival—coalesce in the final scene. Baldwin's men move from self-imposed personal prisons to the hallowed ground of intimacy and connectedness.

Countering the discourse of black masculinist protest, Baldwin concludes "Sonny's Blues" not with black men decrying their mistreatment by white society—their failure to be recognized as native sons—but with them immersing themselves in the power of collectivity and voicedness. In a reversal of the earlier outdoor revival, Baldwin moves his characters into the womb-like internal confines of a bar; not to be lost is the irony of Baldwin's ascribing of sacred and even Christian traits to an ostensibly secular and disreputable space. The final performance conveys the potency of the author's narrative of immersion, conversion, and renewal. At this juncture, Baldwin decenters the narrator's authority by centering Sonny's artistic flowering, a quasi-religious awakening for both brothers.

Sonny's jazz quartet consists of Creole, his bandleader and artistic mentor, a drummer, and a horn player, all of whom perform "Am I Blue." The jazz group becomes the crucible for the wordless telling and hearing of common stories, the ways in which black men gather and communicate *transverbally*. The jazz group's voiceless voicings, their reciprocal riffing, replicates the story's narrative strategy, which foregrounds each character's personal story amidst a larger, shared history. The multilayered performance reinforces the ostensibly antinomic nature of jazz, its seemingly irreconcilable rendering of individual and collective, personal and group identity. As Ralph Ellison asserts in *Shadow and Act*, "true jazz" is a "cruel contradiction" because it is "an art of individual assertion within and against the group." Ellison concludes that "each solo flight, or improvisation, represents . . . a definition of his identity: as individual, as member of the collectivity and as a link in the chain of tradition" (234). Baldwin's afflicted brothers ultimately realize that their quest for selfhood—their solo-ness, their desire to resituate themselves as subjects—does not eliminate their need for intimacy.

The consummation of the performance invigorates both Sonny and his brother—testifier and witness. As Ronald Bieganowski observes about the story's vernacular moorings, "Talking, telling, and playing the blues require a reciprocal understanding that starts with one's sense of self" (73). The title of the song itself, "Am I Blue," is both statement and question; it becomes a musical analog of the narrator's earlier question to his mother about his uncle, which stimulated her remembrance of the men's concealed past. Located within Sonny's piercing confession is his brother's own suppressed story, which allows him to see that their lives are interwoven and that Sonny's suffering mirrors his own:

> He [Creole] hit something in all of them, he hit something in me, myself, and the music tightened and deepened, apprehension began to beat the air. . . . He and his boys up there were *keeping it new,* at the risk of ruin, destruction, madness, and death, in order to find new ways to make us listen. *For, while the tale of how we suffer, and how we are delighted, and how we may triumph is never new, it always must be heard. There isn't any other tale to tell,* it's the only light we've got in all this darkness. . . . Then they all gathered around Sonny and Sonny played. Every now and again one of them seemed to say, amen. Sonny's fingers filled the air with life, his life. *But that life contained so many others.* (121–22; emphasis added)

The male artistic community, which like Ellison's idea of "cruel jazz" abounds with contradictions (light and dark, tell and tale, suffering and delight), rejuvenates and reconnects both men. Sonny's artistic subjectivity gives birth to the narrator's newly conceived linguistic subjectivity, where he realizes the value of reciprocity—of telling and hearing, of testifying and witnessing. The narrator articulates the fusion of black men's histories and engages in some literary signifying as well. Just as Baldwin's multivoiced discourse contests black masculinist protest, his narrator offers a veiled critique of white male modernist discourse as well: he re-envisions Ezra Pound's dictate, "make it new." The narrator insists that the black man's story is "contradictory" because it is simultaneously made new with each performance but paradoxically "never new." The story itself is constructed around this dialectic: though black men may not exist contemporaneously (recall the generations of tormented black men throughout the story), their collective stories connect them cosmologically and suture heretofore fragmented black male subjects. Oral and aural are conflated, as the men's voices and the attendant community of listeners transcend time, place, and space.

The story's denouement marks a synthesis of different types of performance communities. The narrator's linguistic/narrative authority becomes part of his brother's musical narrative. The older sibling has overcome his limiting conceptualization of narration as a purely hermeneutical enterprise and now forges a connection with his brother, a communion evinced in the narrator's epiphanic confession: "Freedom lurked around us and I understood, at last, that he could help us to be free if we would listen, that he would never be free until we did. . . . I heard what he had gone through, and would continue to go through until he came to rest in earth" (122). The brother's narrative space, from which he distanced, judged, and interpreted his brother, becomes an inclusive, curative one that cements their connection. The linguistic prison-house, which Keith Byerman feels causes the narrator to "misread" Sonny because of his insistence upon "proper verbal expression" (368), is actually shattered; Brother's language allows him to articulate the ecclesiastical experience he and Sonny share. Though Baldwin does not attempt to replicate an unmediated oral text, the narrator is now able to articulate—to witness—both his own blues as well as his brother's. Whereas the narrator had accepted Western culture's "text" of Sonny as indicative of black men's innate turpitude, the fusion of the linguistic and jazz performances paves the way for a reconstructed black male subject, one who rejects culturally binding constructions of gender.

Not coincidentally or surprisingly, Baldwin suffuses the final scene with religious undercurrents, most ostensibly the confessional and the baptismal. The barroom ceremony, a masculine ritual in which black men face and exorcise their common demons, becomes a healing event that approximates the vestiges of traditional Christian practices without what Baldwin considers the pungent and alienating ideology; here, the secular is converted into the sacred. Upon Sonny's completion of "Am I Blue," his brother procures for him a scotch and milk, which Baldwin describes quasi-religiously: "it glowed and shook above my brother's head like the very cup of trembling" (122). Baldwin's ritual appropriates but subverts the book of Isaiah in order to impart the sacredness of the brothers' acts of immersion and expiation; scotch and milk is a far cry from the wine and wafers of traditional Christian iconography.[9] The author invests setting—black men's emotional and physical spaces—with healing properties. Moreover, Baldwin's tropological use of space bears out the African scholar Malidoma Patrice Some's thoughtful observation about "ritualized space" as the locus of regeneration and healing: "The more ritualized our space, the more ritualized our lives. . . . a space (cultural space or community space) in which ritual is the yardstick by which life is measured puts the people living in it in a constant state of ritual energy that sanctifies their lives" (60). The story's configuration of space and place conveys the necessity of black men reclaiming their stories and voices, finding their shared spiritual space but also claiming a safe place where they can engage in spiritually intimate acts of confession and reunification.

In black masculinist literature, space is usually represented in purely realistic or naturalistic terms. In *Native Son*, the Thomases' tenement flat, for instance, functions as an objective correlative for their economic and racial oppression. Setting is usually symbolic, a physical synecdoche for African Americans' historical violation and victimization. Bars have a particularly ignominious history in black men's writing. In *Black Boy,* for instance, the bar is the incubator for six-year-old Richard's downward spiral into drinking, profanity, and sociopathic behavior. His "performance" of salacious words and phrases does not foster communal relations but turns him into a spectacle, the object of the adult bar patrons' derision and laughter. In *Invisible Man,* the Golden Day, a scurrilous parody of the Judgment Day, becomes a site for untrammeled bacchanalian behavior where black men can enact a revenge fantasy on their patriarchal white father, Mr. Norton, who is rechristened "Thomas Jefferson" (76). In these texts, black male subjectivity is represented either as the black community's own pathological "initiation" of black boys, or it becomes a grotesque version of white American males' historically misguided sense of masculine privilege.

However, in his interruption and reconstruction of protest discourse, Baldwin reinscribes and re-encodes space so that it doesn't only signify pathology or victimhood but also potentially occasions restoration and regeneration. Throughout the story he revises the tropic function of space and place, challenging their association with different forms of gender oppression or black men's stunted socioracial lives. As a sacred and ritualized zone, the bar is a restorative and metaphysical realm where black men free themselves from the asphyxiating constructs of Western masculinity that devalue intimacy and reduce black men to pariahs, phalluses, or predators. The symbolic tombs that psychically and physically eviscerated Bigger Thomas and Invisible Man are transformed into a communal, spiritual womb that facilitates black men's exploration of their own complex interiority. In Baldwin's revisionist world, this transformation allows them to renegotiate their subjectivity.

The texts that saturate "Sonny's Blues"—written, spoken, musical—make it the quintessence of communal and polyphonic narrative discourse. Though "the final proposition of the aesthetics in the story 'Sonny's Blues' is that the blues functions as an art of communion" (Reilly, "'Sonny's Blues'" 169), Baldwin's narrative discourse embraces the cadences of the black church—the testimonial and gospel music—and, even more significantly, jazz idioms as well. He published "Sonny's Blues" in 1957, an especially fecund period in jazz history that witnessed the emergence of artists such as Ornette Coleman, the pioneer of free jazz. Coleman and adherents such as Don Cherry and Pharaoh Sanders re-envisioned the contours of jazz by infusing it with freer modes and structures that promoted improvisation, riffing, and multi-instrumentality (e.g., Coleman's inclusion of the trumpet and violin as part of his on-stage repertoire alongside his native instrument, the alto saxophone). Each member of the group configured his own musical design, which simultaneously contributed to the larger composition; therefore, collaboration was dialectical in that each member played within and outside of the group. This structural rubric parallels the narrative methodology in "Sonny's Blues," where each person's solo is at once a self-contained confession and an integral part of black men's collective and common history. Baldwin doesn't jettison black men's social selves, but he insists that the personal is the locus of selfhood; interrogating homosocial relationships offers a constructive vehicle for exploring the diverseness of their reformation as subjects. Presaging Hall Montana's profound observation in *Just Above My Head*, "There is always a beat beneath the beat, another music beneath the music, and beyond" (542), "Sonny's Blues" explores not merely black men's otherness—their internal pain—but the restorative power of the performance community, the witnessing and testifying in the company of psychically, historically, and spiritually bound brothers.

Disturbing the QC Discourse—and Turning the Other Cheek?: *Just Above My Head* and the Conundrum of Baldwinian Homopoetics

If "Sonny's Blues" seems an aberration in Baldwin's oeuvre for its lack of psychosexual conflict, then his last novel, *Just Above My Head,* marks a return to familiar fictive terrain. The labyrinthine text's thematic and aesthetic concerns are the cornerstones of Baldwin's art: the self's arduous and elusive quest for love; the black church's harsh dictates that preclude unconditional and unmediated love; the vertiginous internal and external journeys individuals embark upon in their search for love; and the astronomical price both whites and blacks pay for America's baleful racial tenets. The book's narrative arc connects it to *Another Country,* while the confluence of religious ideology and sexual difference recalls Baldwin's first novel. *Just Above My Head* is Baldwin's most "confessional" book since *Go Tell It on the Mountain,* which appeared twenty-five years earlier. However, though it interfaces with earlier novels, *Just Above My Head* forthrightly treats the black man as a sexual subject. The latently homosexual adolescent John Grimes is reincarnated as the indisputably gay gospel performer, Arthur Montana. Baldwin spoke to the novel's recursiveness: "So in a sense the novel is a kind of return to my own beginnings, which are not only mine, and in a way of using that beginning to start again. In my own mind I come full circle from *Go Tell It on the Mountain* to *Just Above My Head,* which is a question of a quarter of a century, really" (Standley and Pratt 191).

One of the reasons I've paired "Sonny's Blues" and *Just Above My Head* is because of their intertextuality; the short story and the novel address each other structurally and thematically. Baldwin re-employs the narrative device of an older brother narrating and negotiating his younger artist-brother's conflicted existence. Again, the older brother must confront his younger sibling's alternative life path that places him at odds with black and American cultures, and art and performance engender explorations into fraternal intimacy and mutual pain. As in "Sonny's Blues," the demons that haunt the artist must be confronted and exorcised before the narrator can empower and heal himself. The gospel singer, Arthur, catalyzes the narrative act of storytelling. As in "Sonny's Blues," the novel accentuates different types of performance and their generative power vis-à-vis black men's relationships. In the words of Hurston's redoubtable Janie Starks, Hall must "go there to know there."

The novel demonstrates how reclamation functions as a life-giving and affirming act for black men, a mandatory act in Baldwin's figuraton of the black male self. Baldwin again uses as his narrative scaffolding the process of an older brother reconstructing and interpreting his younger sibling's life, which in turn stimulates his own interior journey and reinvigoration. Hall, heretofore unwilling or unable to revisit Arthur's disjointed life, has been struck silent; that two years have passed between Arthur's death and Hall's inscribed remembrance of his life underscores the difficulty of being his "brother's speaker." Hall's admission, "I know I'm wrong to trap them [his and Arthur's family and friends] in my silence" (16), exposes his complicity in marginalizing his brother's reality, rendering it unspeakably separate from his and his family's existence. The question the narrator of "Sonny's Blues" poses to his mother about his father's life adumbrates Hall's narrative performance, which is set in motion when his teenage son asks, "'What was my uncle—Arthur—like?'" (36). The call that binds black males across generations stimulates Hall's speech act. Baldwin emphasizes not merely the content of Arthur's tortured life as singer and seer but also the exacting but imperative act of excavating that life through storytelling. Just as Sethe Suggs in Toni Morrison's *Beloved* must "rememory" the wrenching details of a dis(re)membered past—a heretofore ineffable tale of sexual and racial violence and infanticide—so too must Hall revisit, respeak, and reconcile Arthur's story.

The salience of plurivocality and community as they relate to black male subjectivity is conveyed early in the text. Baldwin's acute grasp of vernacular culture makes *Just Above My Head* his most speakerly novel, for it centers the different ways black men hear—and don't hear—each other, whether these ways be verbal or musical. To paraphrase the conclusion reached by the narrator of "Sonny's Blues," the tale of how they suffer must be heard at all costs. In the novel's opening refrain, Hall recalls how his brother suffered a stroke in a London pub and his unbridled reaction to the news of his death:

> Arthur. Speak. Speak. Speak. I know, I know. I wasn't always nice to you, I yelled when I shouldn't have yelled, I was often absent when I should have been present, I know, I know; and sometimes you bored the shit out of me, and *I heard your stories too often,* and I knew all your fucking little ways, man, and how you jived the people—but that's not really true, you didn't really jive the people, you sang, you sang, and if there was any jiving done, the people jived you, my brother, because they didn't know that *they* were the song and the price of the song and the glory of the song: you sang. Oh, my God my God my God my God my God, oh my God my God my God oh no no no, my God my God my God my God, forsake me if you will and I don't give a shit but give me back my brother, my God my God my God my God my God! (14–15; emphasis added)

This opening lamentation demonstrates black men's irrepressible bonds and how speaking the unspoken can impel reconciliation. Perhaps more so than in other novels, Baldwin foregrounds the centrality of confessing and witnessing, calling and responding. The conversational and exhortative opening lines recall "Sonny's Blues," where black men were linked irrespective of time and space; here, Hall tries to contact his brother posthumously. This passage also establishes the novel's blues form—its repetition, reversal, and revision of key phrases and ideas and the underlying pathos. Also evident is Arthur's centrifugal role as singer and prophet—Sonny's gospel counterpart—who sings not merely *of* himself but *for* those who have insulated themselves from the pain of self-exploration and potential of self-discovery. Baldwin transcribes the orality and lyricality of Hall's voice by using commas and dashes before he abandons punctuation altogether; Hall's and Arthur's lives, like the thoughts in this passage, converge and are inevitably bound. Eleanor Traylor sums up the narrative schema concisely: "*Just Above My Head* is a gospel tale told in the blues mode" (95). The blues is at once about individual and collective pain, and this novel examines the interdependence of black men's lives, even in death.

Even more noteworthy than Baldwin's transcription of blues and gospel idioms into fictive discourse, however, is the novel's treatment of sexuality,

especially its candid rendering of homosexuality. *Just Above My Head* represents a melding of the homosocial and the homosexual—a coalescence of
black men's interrelationships in emotional and sexual contexts. Baldwin is
often considered a literary crusader (irrespective of race) who dared to openly
depict the love that dare not speak its name in black men's literature. To be
sure, he is without peer, notwithstanding Audre Lorde's pathbreaking explorations of lesbianism or the recent spate of young black gay male writers (e.g.,
Randall Kenan, Melvin Dixon, Essex Hemphill, E. Lynn Harris) who have
uncloseted black men's intraracial and intrasexual relationships. However,
before exploring the novel's representation of black men's identity formation and negotiation, it is imperative to investigate the underpinnings of
Baldwin's "homopoetics," a term I use to describe his aesthetic position on
and literary representations of men who love each other sexually.

Several critics, especially within the last ten to fifteen years, have delved
into this taboo terrain. Its treatment in African-American literature has been
sparse. However, most of Baldwin's fiction—if only a scant number of his
essays—tackles a subject that many scholars of African-American literature
have peripheralized or ignored.[10] Just as the homosexual silences that per-
sisted throughout the Harlem Renaissance have recently come under critical scrutiny, several younger African-American literary scholars have begun
to hypothesize and theorize about Baldwin's homosexuality and its impact
on his literary representations of men's relationships.[11] I am not suggesting
that critics have heretofore ignored homosexuality in Baldwin's work. Early
interpreters such as Robert Bone in the 1960s noted its presence without
engaging in protracted discussions of its centrality to Baldwin's literary aesthetics. Also, scholars such as Georges-Michel Sarotte, in his groundbreaking *Like a Brother, Like a Lover: Male Homosexuality in the American Novel
and Theatre from Herman Melville to James Baldwin*, have attempted—if
rather parochially—to extrapolate the same-sex dimension of the writer's
work. Moreover, Queer Studies has embraced Baldwin as one of its most
revered and propitious *subjects*. I italicize this word to foreground its multiple connotations, especially the pejorative ones that suggest a lack of agency, voicelessness, and appropriation. I share Bryan R. Washington's skepti-
cism about the queer critical gaze being turned toward Baldwin: "In a new
era of radical chic [criticism], reading Baldwin is de rigueur" (98).

The so-called gay community's claiming and heralding of Baldwin is paradoxically understandable and ineluctably problematic. Witness, for instance,
Mark Lilly's summation of Baldwin's life and work, the impact of which he
feels was diminished because Baldwin was "generally secretive and closed
about his sexual life in public, and took no part in gay rights campaigns"

(144). This comment reflects oppressed communities' tendency to engage in a sort of seize-and-apotheosize mentality. Regrettably, recalcitrant or ambivalent artists are thrust into the foreground for political expediency and exigency; recent incidences of "outing" are perhaps the most notorious manifestation of this phenomenon. Therefore, I am incredulous when a black homosexual artist as multifaceted as Baldwin is claimed, for such ownership can result in the erasure of essential portions of the artist's self. Specifically, questions of race, gender, and culture are potentially subordinated or excised altogether. I would be remiss in suggesting that only self-proclaimed gay activists and theorists engage in this self-serving behavior. For instance, in "'Ain't Nothing Like the Real Thing': Black Masculinity, Gay Sexuality, and the Jargon of Authenticity," Kendall Thomas assails some Black Nationalists' efforts to downplay and even efface Baldwin's sexuality in the name of an unencumbered racial and masculine "purity."[12] Querying Baldwin's queer critics, I will discuss Baldwin's unique version of homopoetics—his aesthetics of homosexual representation that presciently opened a space for inquiry between a lived experience of sexual and racial difference and "theories" of queerness. I will address how his sometimes quixotic but unflinching positions on homosexuality contest a sort of homonormative discourse, which frequently privileges sexual difference as the self's single most significant component.

Critics routinely exaggerate and assail Baldwin's early ruminations on homosexuality, especially his assertions that the French novelist Andre Gide's homosexuality was "his own affair which he ought to have kept hidden from us" (Baldwin, *Nobody* 128) and that "*Giovanni's Room* is not really about homosexuality. . . . It's about what happens to you if you're afraid to love anybody" (Goldstein 176). One critic misinterprets these statements as indicative of Baldwin's "horror" about his own sexual orientation; another regrettably concludes that they expose Baldwin's "discomfort with the subject."[13] However, these rather precipitous extrapolations belie the much more complex philosophical positions that Baldwin takes, all of which are reflected in the scope of his writings. Though I would grant some credence to Thomas's comment that Baldwin's position on homosexuality is "often equivocal, but always articulate" (61), I would argue that Baldwin has been agonizingly discomfiting for those trying to reduce him to an ambivalent *gay* black writer or a recalcitrant *gay* literary iconoclast—a moniker that makes racial identity ancillary.

Though Baldwin's much chronicled "French Connection"—Paris is often considered the cradle of his professional career—makes comparisons with the gay French playwright Jean Genet inevitable, Baldwin's unique aesthetic and personal position on same-sex relationships render such comparisons suspect. Genet, whose sensational life included forays into the subterranean prison enclave as well as encounters with sailors and other stock gay-delineated experiences, has been elevated to the revered sphere of literary outlaw and martyr, a writer who made homosexuality the cornerstone of his art and life. Equating homosexuality with a catalogue of decadent, salacious experiences seems emblematic of gay identity politics. Hence, this becomes an essentialistic endeavor that not only designates sexual orientation as the most prominent component of one's identity but sanctions a particular type of homosexuality where the self heroically and often willingly embraces estrangement from society, family, and community. Bruce Bawer's observation in his review of a queer scholarly interpretation of Walt Whitman is particularly apropos here: "Yet what is reflected here is the lamentable tendency, all too familiar in queer cultural and political circles, to reduce gay life and identity to gay sex, and to equate openness about sexual orientation with explicitness about the details of sexual behavior" ("Poet Out" 10).[14] In light of this, Genet's experiences are deemed "authentic," the official narrative of *all* gay artists' lives. One need only look at the sordid lives of Hart Crane and Tennessee Williams or the mythological status that locales such as Fire Island (where the gay poet Frank O'Hara died) or Key West have assumed in gay literature and culture. The artist as sexual outlaw is another conceit; he languishes as the sick rose who nevertheless blossoms in the "alternative lifestyle" and community that white gay culture cultivates.

In "The Black Boy Looks at the White," Baldwin deftly deconstructs Norman Mailer's pseudoliberal hipsterism of the early 1960s (see *Nobody Knows My Name*). The title of this essay aptly describes Baldwin's persistent interrogation of "gayness" and by extension a "queer" cultural and literary politics that delineates sexual difference as sacrosanct. His theorizing of same-sex relationships in the 1980s is neither ambivalent nor indeterminate: he fervently resists critics' attempts to superimpose a "queerly correct" (or QC) identity. Baldwin's 1984 interview with the *Village Voice* writer Richard Goldstein captures his ability to resituate himself as a subject; he proffers a *multi*subjectivity that encompasses racial, sexual, cultural, and national identities. Responding to Goldstein's question, "Do you feel like a stranger in gay America?" Baldwin unswervingly rejoins, "*The word 'gay' has always rubbed me the wrong way.* I never understood exactly what is meant by it. I don't want to sound distant or patronizing because I don't really feel that. *I simply feel it's a world that has very little to do with me,* with where I did my growing up. *I was never at home in it*" (Goldstein 174; emphasis added). Baldwin's bristling at the term "gay," perhaps a seemingly benign dismissal and one possibly explained by his age (he was sixty when the interview occurred), represents an unmitigated rejection of Anglo-American homosexual discourse.[15] Baldwin cannily inverts roles here, extricating himself from the confining position of interviewed *subject*—the *object* of the white interlocutor's gaze and lexicon. By deconstructing Goldstein's tendentious and leading question, Baldwin eludes his attempts to define—and confine—him as a *gay American* subject by not allowing his racial identity to be subsumed within Anglo-American queer discourse, which obviates racial and other realities. In one eloquent response, Baldwin deromanticizes Greenwich Village, the ostensibly secure space for white gay artists (Henry James, Allen Ginsberg, et al.), the lexicon of gayness, and the "strangeness" that is supposedly an inherent trait of racial difference. The interview hearkens to the performances of Sonny and his brother, who freed themselves through voicedness; analogously, Baldwin's "performance" allows him to abrogate imposed definitions of sexuality and to transform himself into a speaking subject.

Thus, the writer ardently thwarts attempts to recolonize him, to abstract and objectify his life for a "gay rights" agenda, one that some might argue is anathema to black people. Further, I conjecture that Baldwin, like many of his black counterparts, would have concurred with Ian Barnard's assertion that "Any U.S. politics, no matter how coalitional its compass, that identifies itself in terms of gender and/or sexual orientation only ('lesbian separatism,' 'Queer Nation,' 'Lesbian and Gay Studies') will be *a white-centered and dominated politics, since only white people in this society can afford to see their race as unmarked, as an irrelevant or subordinate category of analysis*" (77; emphasis added). In the Goldstein interview, Baldwin dissects the white-centered discourse of homosexuality by attacking the primacy of sexual identity itself. Not only does he further dismantle QC discourse, but he lucidly articulates black gays' indisputable multisubjectivity:

> A black gay person who is a sexual conundrum to society is already, long before the question of sexuality comes into it, menaced and marked because he's black or she's black. The sexual question comes after the question of color; it's simply one more aspect of the danger in which all black people live. I think white gay people feel cheated because they were born, in principle, into a society in which they were supposed to be safe. The anomaly of their sexuality puts them in danger, unexpectedly. Their reaction seems to me in direct proportion to the sense of feeling cheated of the advantages which accrue to white people in a white society. There's an element, it has always seemed to me, of bewilderment and complaint. Now that may sound very harsh, but the gay world as such is no more prepared to accept black people than anywhere else in society. It's a

very hermetically sealed world with very unattractive features, including racism. (Goldstein 180)

Baldwin does not merely debunk the idea that racism and homophobia are equivalent forms of oppression (another edict of "queer rights," since African-American civil rights is always the touchstone for other liberation movements), but he exposes how whiteness itself is not fixed or static but reproduces its own set of hierarchies.

In Karen Thorsen's evocative film *James Baldwin: The Price of the Ticket*, Amiri Baraka cuts to the heart of Baldwin's sexual politics: "Jimmy Baldwin didn't go around proclaiming homosexuality, nor did he deny it." For Baldwin, the homosexual and homosocial were inextricably bound. This, coupled with Baldwin's own vigorous attack on the hermetically sealed world of white homosexuals, has made him a strange icon, a figure who did not deny being gay but who also insisted that race be a part of any queer discourse. Baldwin spiritedly dissects Western binary epistemological thinking by insisting that race, gender, gender orientation, and culture not be fragmented and prioritized (a point articulated most eloquently in *Another Country*). His blues voice, his worrying the line by making race and racism part of any discussion about sexual difference, is something that critics have seemingly ignored or even repudiated, exposing their own "racialism" in the process. Sarotte is guilty of this, and Lilly and David Bergman epitomize the very sexual myopia that Barnard decries.[16] Critics such as Goldstein and Bergman do a grave disservice to "queer" discourse/rights by superimposing upon the black artist their own distinctly different cultural/gender lexicon—an unequivocal derivative of Anglo-American ethnocentrism. To his credit, Goldstein subsequently acknowledges to Baldwin that "I'm imposing these terms on you" (Goldstein 185).

Countering Western constructions of identity that are rooted in oppositions (white versus black, or gay versus straight), Baldwin engages in a radical act of self-definition, not only by recalling Audre Lorde's well-grounded caveat that "the master's tools will never dismantle the master's house" (112), but by challenging the very terms of Western/American sexual discourse. As a black gay artist, Baldwin does not take refuge in the marginalizing discourse of "queerness," which centers sexuality at the expense of one's otherness, the black self's multiple subjectivities. In Baldwin's discursive other country, homosocial and homosexual are not divorced from one another but are invariably wedded.

When reading *Just Above My Head* within and against black masculinist protest literature and the author's own precepts surrounding homosexuality, innumerable paradoxes and irreconcilable conflicts emerge. As I have noted throughout this chapter, Baldwin's fiction enters and disrupts canonical black male writing, which might be accused of underrepresenting black men's sexuality—alas, his charged claim that "There is a great space [in Wright's fiction] where sex ought to be; and what usually fills this space is violence" (*Nobody* 151). The paucity of violent episodes in his work reflects his attempts to reverse this discursive trend. Moreover, heterotextuality has been the de rigueur mode of black men's literary discourse. Black men are represented usually in antagonistic and predatory relationships with white women (Chester Himes's *If He Hollers Let Him Go*), or as perceived despoilers of chaste white womanhood (*Native Son*), or as incarnations of the "Mandingo" archetype (the infamous "Sybil" episode in *Invisible Man*). Whereas earlier works such as *Go Tell It on the Mountain* and *Tell Me How Long the Train's Been Gone* performed a crucial discursive task by suggesting the possibility (if not viability) of black men's same-sex relationships—*sexual community*—*Just Above My Head* marks the fictive coming out of such relationships.[17]

However, Baldwin's configuration of the novel and his representation of black men's relationships are profusely problematic, fraught with a sort of ambivalence that runs counter to the lucid and unambiguous black gay subjectivity he articulated. Nevertheless, I am posing an altogether different question from the one that debates the author's sexual authenticity. Baldwin's ambivalent figuration of a *black* gay subject in terms of narrative voice and sexual community subverts the text's potentially nuanced and corrective rendering of black male intimacy. In exploring narrative voice and authority alongside the thematization of black men's interrelationships, *Just Above My Head* becomes a textual and sexual conundrum, a conflicted representation of sexual difference that raises as many questions as it answers. Ultimately, a tension emerges between the author's resolute articulation of black gay subjectivity and his presentation of black male homosexuals.

Toni Morrison has spoken about the semantic potency of her novels' opening lines; they function as a gateway to the novels' distinctive ethos and serpentine representation of black life. The first line of Baldwin's last novel is equally revelatory: "The damn'd blood burst, first through his nostrils, then pounded through the veins in his neck, the scarlet torrent exploded through his mouth, it reached his eyes and blinded him, and brought Arthur down, down, down, down, down" (13). The passage fixes Arthur Montana's life as a textual catalyst by describing his demise so graphically. From this one might conjecture that his life will propel the narrative machinery and function as the enigma we must unravel in order to grasp his and the other characters' lives. In this respect, his premature though proleptic death recalls Rufus Scott's early suicide in *Another Country,* which becomes the crystallizing event thematically and narratologically. Nonetheless, the passage also speaks volumes about Arthur in terms of narrative positionality. It clearly posits him as a *spoken,* not *speaking* subject, for his voice and life are consigned to someone else's province; we quickly learn that Hall will narrate his brother's story. Also, Arthur is literally disintegrating physically, emblematic of the subjectivity-less subject of protest discourse who is under constant physical erasure; the difference, of course, is that illness, specifically a stroke, is responsible for Arthur's unraveling. *Just Above My Head* begins with the black gay subject literally and metaphorically *subjected*—his story is in his brother's mouth (to paraphrase Hurston), and his body has imploded in "a men's room in the basement of a London pub" (13).

But to what extent does this word-picture dilute Arthur's voice and narrative presence? The opening sentence not only conveys his physical rupturing but also textual gaps that taint his representation. Though the device Baldwin employs—bequeathing an older brother the wherewithal to capture the life of a younger, tormented artist-brother—renders "Sonny's Blues" an intricate, jazz-hued mural of verbal, written, and musical voices, the narrative frame in the novel raises several gnawing questions. One relates to the rather pedestrian issue of length: the short story form allows Baldwin to modulate and control the multiple stories, but the unwieldy *Just Above My Head* often subjugates the black gay character to the verbal authority of the straight brother/narrator. Though Arthur's life and death spawn Hall's narrative act of extro- and introspection, Arthur's narrative becomes distorted in the hands of a brother who expresses at various times an anxiety about homosexuality—an anxiety exemplified when he clarifies for his son, Tony, that Arthur may have been homosexual but that he was "nobody's faggot" (37).

Baldwin represents Hall as the apogee of American masculinity. Like the narrator of "Sonny's Blues," he served in Korea, returned home, married, and settled into the culturally sanctioned world of heterosexuality. Notwithstanding his earlier sexual escapades—for instance, he "had fucked everything I could get my hands on overseas, including two of my drinking buddies" (309)—Baldwin depicts him as the archetypal Western and American male. As Trudier Harris points out, "Hall has seduced or envisioned seducing every significant black woman in the novel" (*Black Women* 191). In Hall's hands, Arthur's multifaceted story as a black man, artist, and homosexual is mediated and, at times, reduced to the stereotypical realm of the sexual. Perhaps most emblematic of this is Hall's recapitulation of Arthur's ostensibly most life-sustaining relationship, a union with another black man named Jimmy.

Hall and, more tellingly, Baldwin relegate this relationship to a few pages toward the end of the novel.[18] The late critic and novelist Melvin Dixon succinctly articulates how Hall's narration becomes a subterfuge that muffles his brother's voice: "Hall's heterosexuality seems a poorly constructed shelter in his retreat from the moral 'wilderness' of Arthur's life and sexuality. No haven, not even the narration of the novel, seems without its contrivances, its device" (138). Sure enough, Hall's filtering, phallocentric presence blurs and eclipses key dimensions of Arthur's existence.

Again, a disconcerting question arises from Baldwin's circumscription of Arthur's voice and story through the novel's formal strategies. One could conjecture that such narratological defects reflect the author's own anxiety of masculinity, which Eldridge Cleaver crudely addressed in *Soul on Ice*. Though Cleaver's comments have been roundly dismissed as phallocentric and self-aggrandizing, it is also significant that Baldwin's next novel, *If Beale Street Could Talk* (1974), is deafeningly silent on issues of same-sex love. The book mawkishly extolled the virtues of heterosexual love and the black man's ability to endure virulent white racism.[19] Though a young black woman, Tish Rivers, narrates the story, it is nevertheless a paean to anachronistic constructions of black manhood, what black feminist critics such as Michele Wallace and bell hooks have delineated as "Black Macho" and "fierce phallocentrism," respectively. This excessively flawed novel reflects the black gay author's attempt to valorize an accepted version of black male subjectivity: hypermasculinity and hypersexuality. Fonny Hunt, Tish's lover and the novel's protagonist, becomes a younger, more virile composite of Bigger Thomas and Invisible Man. A comparable narrative gap emerges in *Just Above My Head*, where the black gay subject's story is submerged beneath the normative, "official" narrative voice.

What results is a sort of narrative transvestism, reminiscent of works such as Willa Cather's *My Ántonia*, in which the author camouflages prolesbian sentiments via her use of a white, straight, male narrator.[20] Perhaps Baldwin could not translate his resonant, uncompromising conception of his own gay subjectivity into his fiction. Stated another way, the black gay writer does not grant his black gay subject the narrative voice to articulate his own unique history of racial and sexual difference. In a perversely ironic way, Baldwin's erasure of portions of Arthur's life mirrors his own critique of what he perceived as Wright's monolithic presentation of Bigger as violated "nigger" and sociopath. Though I would refrain from labeling this dynamic "internalized homophobia," I would contend that this narrative cross-dressing may reveal Baldwin's desire to legitimize his role as race man, which to many staunchly precludes sexual difference.[21] Hall's heteronormative text blots out Arthur's homosocial *and* homosexual text; as his name suggests, Hall leads us to Arthur's story but leaves the interiors of Arthur's sexual self largely unexamined.

The contours of Arthur's life, however, are clearly delineated; he is in fact Baldwin's fictive doppelganger. Recalling his autobiographical portrayal of John Grimes in *Go Tell It on the Mountain,* Baldwin makes recognizable connections between his and the characters' lives. Arthur's adolescence, in which he performed with a male gospel quartet, recalls the precocious Baldwin's formative years, when he entered the pulpit at fourteen. His adolescence was marred by acute sexual angst, as the young minister's nascent homosexuality, like that of his fictive counterpart, collided with biblical and church dogma. As an adult artist-activist, Arthur covers the same geographic terrain as Baldwin by journeying to the South during times of racial upheaval and violence (one of the members of Arthur's gospel quartet disappears in Alabama and is presumed murdered). And Arthur, like Baldwin, becomes an international celebrity who spends much of his life abroad. In terms of the author's much dissected representations of and positions on homosexuality in his fiction, Arthur's self-conception is quite revealing, as Hall recalls an adolescent experience: "I told my brother that the way he wore his hair made him look like a sissy, and that may be the first time I ever really looked at my brother. He cracked up, and started doing imitations of all the most *broken-down queens* we knew, and he kept saying, just before each imitation, '*But I am a sissy*'" (29; emphasis added). Though one could dismiss this scene as both brothers' parodying of jaundiced American constructions of sexual difference, I think it reveals a great deal about the author's sexual taxonomies and his flawed conceptualization of an African-American, homosexual subject.

Baldwin encodes Arthur's life as recognizably "gay" in that the church defines his existence. Most people are aware of standard perceptions about the presumed homosexuality of many black male church musicians, a subject upon which Philip Brian Harper expatiates in a chapter entitled "Eloquence and Epitaph: AIDS, Homophobia, and Problematics of Black Masculinity." Writing about the "flamboyant" disco star Sylvester, who died of AIDS in 1989, Harper critiques *Jet* magazine for the way it reported his death:

> If it is true that, as *Jet* . . . put it, "The church was . . . the setting for Sylvester's first homosexual experience," it is also true that "Sylvester learned to sing in churches in South Los Angeles and went on to perform at gospel conventions around the state." *That is to say that the church-choir context in which Sylvester was groomed for a singing career has stereotypically served as a locus in which young black men both discover and sublimate their homosexuality,* and also as a conduit to a world of professional entertainment generally conceived as "tol-

erant," if not downright encouraging, of *nonnormative sexualities*. In Sylvester's case, this was particularly true, since he was able to help create a disco culture—comprising elements from both black and gay contexts—in which he and
others could thrive as openly gay men. Thus the black-church milieu, though
ostensibly hostile to homosexuality and gay identity, nevertheless has traditionally provided a means by which black men can achieve a sense of themselves
as homosexual and even, in cases such as Sylvester's, expand that sense into gay-
affirmative public personae. (13–14; emphasis added)

Perhaps Baldwin chose to situate Arthur in an arena where "nonnormative
sexualities" are tolerated because it may have been easier for readers to accept as culturally accurate. Put another way, it gave Baldwin the artistic space
to safely portray a black gay man without challenging American and African-American verities that resoundingly condemn homosexuality. Just as the
gospel-disco environments fostered Sylvester's construction of a different
sexual subjectivity, so too does Baldwin's representation of Arthur as a "sis-
sified" gospel artist conform to culturally approved vehicles for black male
difference.

However, Hall's generally deprecatory description of Arthur as well as
Arthur's self-image suggests that Baldwin harbors irreconcilable anxiety
about fictionalizing black sexual difference. As critics such as John Lash have
pointed out,[22] Baldwin explicitly distinguishes "sissies" from men who happen to love other men; recall his vilification in *Giovanni's Room* of "*les folles*"
(38–39), the grotesque denizens of Paris's transvestite underworld. And while
I take issue with Donald B. Gibson's assertions that *Giovanni's Room* is
"against homosexuality" or that *Another Country* represents a forum for
Baldwin's "conservative values" (108), there is something inherently disconcerting about Baldwin's representation of the black gay male artist whose
sexual identity is characterized by both narrative veiling and sexual stereotypes. If Arthur is Baldwin's incarnation of the queen/sissy, which he has
ardently rebuked as the epitome of a deformed masculinity, then his consigning of Arthur's story to Hall's narrative domain is problematic but consistent. Just as there is a tension between Baldwin's unwavering cultural stance
on homosexuality and his own propensity to be, as his biographer David
Leeming puts it, "drawn not to other homosexuals but to men who were
sometimes willing to act homosexually, temporarily, in response to a need
for money and shelter or to what can only be called his personal magnetism
and persuasiveness" (76), there is also a textual ambiguity in his portrait of
Arthur Montana. Baldwin's ostensibly gay male subject is paradoxically a
character from whom subjectivity—voice, community, and selfhood—is
ultimately withheld.

Baldwin's apparent ambivalence is clear from the first page of the novel, where Hall remembers receiving a telegram specifying how Arthur died in a "men's room in the basement of a London pub" (13). In what seems to be a re-envisioning and reversing of the final scene of "Sonny's Blues," the London pub concretizes Arthur's physical and communal estrangement. Moreover, his basement death rhetorically underscores his confinement in terms of voice and agency in the novel. Finally, that Baldwin sets Arthur's demise in a men's room raises questions about whether the author felt some disdain for the character most clearly patterned after himself, since men's rooms evoke some of the most corrosive stereotypes about gay men; such venues are viewed as sanctioning a licentious form of "community." According to these provincial perceptions, they are sexually voracious and predatory—think here of the social lore surrounding "t-rooms," public toilets where gay men "loiter" for sex. At best, Baldwin's resituation of his black gay subject is inconsonant, for the author impedes the character's quest for voice and community not only narratologically but thematically as well. Perhaps Baldwin felt at least some authorial anxiety about rendering sexual difference textually if not personally, reflected in his portrayal of Arthur as a flawed and often invisible gay subject.

In interpreting *Just Above My Head* as a textual and sexual conundrum, I realize that I am lauding Baldwin's disruption of heterocentric black masculinist discourse while criticizing his depiction of the novel's central gay character. This is a bit of a critical double-bind, for as Charles I. Nero has pointed out, "The image of gay men in black writing is complicated by homophobic values in society that make homosexuality unspeakable and gays invisible" ("Gay Men" 312). Not to be downplayed is how Baldwin's fiction has audaciously spoken the sexually unspeakable. *Just Above My Head* may be his most substantive, uninhibited presentation of black gay men attempting to form a different type of community rooted in sexual difference. Significantly, Arthur's sexual experiences with other black men are described explicitly. In essence, Baldwin reinterprets and revises the unconsummated relationship between John Grimes and the older Elisha in *Go Tell It on the Mountain* by portraying Arthur's adolescent lovemaking with Crunch, another member of the Gospel quartet (203–9); what remained latent and implied in his first novel is celebrated in his last. Baldwin's detailed description of their lovemaking is revolutionary, for sex between black men had remained one of the last literary taboos. The room Arthur and Crunch share during one of the group's tours becomes a hallowed space reminiscent of the Edenic albeit ephemeral garden inhabited by the white male lovers Eric and Yves in *Another Country*. In this idyllic space, the older Crunch—a play on *church?*—simultaneously witnesses to Arthur about his own tragic life while anointing him through the act of lovemaking. Baldwin convincingly melds the curative function of voice and the possibility of sexual community when Arthur "realizes, for the first time, conclusively, that Crunch listens to him, responds to him, takes him seriously" (188). At this moment, their union transcends the sexual, affording both young men the vestiges of an intimacy uncharacteristic of black men's relationships, gay or straight.

Baldwin describes the subsequent lovemaking in quasi-religious terms, elucidating the cleansing, regenerative, and transformative power of the corporeal: "the terror of someone in the water," "anguish," "joy," "Crunch's eyes were wet and deep *deep like a river*" (208–9). That this relationship flowers in the South, a region traditionally hostile to racial and sexual difference, is both ironic and audacious. By way of emigration and defamiliarization, Crunch and Arthur abandon the "liberal" North and their native Harlem and enter a figurative other country, a region where religious and familial prohibitions against homosexuality can be abrogated.[23] Just as he subverted the biblical "cup of trembling" image in "Sonny's Blues" through Sonny's scotch and milk, Baldwin similarly undermines biblical tropes to convey the burgeoning power of black same-sex relationships. The bisexual Crunch becomes a sepia version of Eric Jones, the bisexual Everyman of *Another Country* who transports both men and women into the other country sans sexual baggage and cultural condemnation. However, the bower of bliss offers only a temporary respite. After all, Crunch has relationships with women, gets drafted, and eventually goes insane, while Arthur becomes an international star whose global bed-trotting includes relationships with black and white men. While Baldwin's unrestrained inscription of black same-sex desire disrupts an intractably heterocentric black literary discourse, his representations, like his depiction of Arthur, are not without their discomfiting aspects.[24]

Given that, as Sedgwick notes, "Our own society is brutally homophobic; and the homophobia directed against both males and females is not arbitrary or gratuitous, but tightly knit into the texture of family, gender, age, and race relations" (3–4), one can only conjecture the degree to which such social realities impacted Baldwin's fictive imagination. The litany of pathological behaviors society equates with black masculinity—violent, hypersexual, sexually predatory, bestial—denies black men's interiority. Though Baldwin's fictions witness against the notion that black men are unable to fashion intimate connections with each other, his final novel nevertheless raises several vexing questions. The brevity of Arthur and Crunch's relationship and the scant attention devoted to Arthur and Jimmy's allegedly fruitful union suggest a certain anxiety about black-on-black male love, almost as though Baldwin accepts a cultural ethos that might not necessarily embrace white men's sexual relationships but completely disdains black male intimacy, sexual or otherwise.

If society is guilty of phallusizing black men, then Baldwin's emphasis on sexual contact without adequate investigation of the complexities and pressures unique to black men's unions contributes to their hypersexualized image. In this context, Crunch becomes a *homoeroticized* Mandingo whose braggadocio and virility emblematize the stereotypical "b-boy" who permeates popular 1990s black sexual and popular discourse.[25] Are we then to conclude that black men's sexual engagements are at best unstable or should remain invisible and largely underscrutinized? Ultimately, we return to the question of voice, authority, and authenticity: Hall narrates and splices Arthur's life, rendering it a fragmented, second-hand tale. How ironic that within this ostensibly gay-framed text—a gay writer uses a straight man as the amanuensis for a gay artist—the issue of black men's multiple subjectivities, including the prospect of same-gender/race relationships, gets obfuscated. While Baldwin could conceive of the viability and simultaneity of the homosocial *and* the homosexual in his own life, perhaps something in his fictive imagination prevented him from ascribing such complexity and roundedness to his representation of a black gay subject.

The term "aporia" in critical discourse often refers to "a point of undecidability, which locates the site at which the text most obviously undermines its own rhetorical structure, dismantles, or deconstructs itself" (Harmon and Holman 36). Perhaps this best describes the narratological and representational fissures in *Just Above My Head*. This textual self-sabotage forces the reader to look incredulously at something as seemingly pedestrian as the novel's cover art. It is emblazoned with drawings of what appear to be a scantily clad Hall and an even more scantily clad woman (his wife Ruth, perhaps), framed by larger sketches of Julia Miller's and Arthur Montana's faces. Glaringly absent is any hint of Arthur's sexuality. This facade suggests a sultry, heteronormative love story, while "homodeviant" relationships between black men are rendered unfit for public display. Hence, the novel's cover reinforces Arthur's diminution, magnifying his erasure within the pages of the novel.

James Baldwin's "divided mind,"[26] epitomized by his use of his own first and middle names for different characters in the novel (Jimmy and Arthur), evinces itself in his invaluable retrieval of black men from loveless, abnegating places in "Sonny's Blues" and the tenuousness and ephemerality of black male intimacy represented in *Just Above My Head*. Baldwin remains a literary pioneer, for he cleared the literary space—or in his effusively colloquial lexicon, "paid the dues"—for a cadre of young, popular black gay writers such as E. Lynn Harris and James Earl Hardy, who privilege black men's intraracial, same-sex desire. Traversing the limitations of black masculinist protest, Baldwin contested a discursive framework that disregarded black men's irrepressible need not only for voice but for different forms of community—artistic, spatial, sexual. His resituation of black male subjects clearly made the literary terrain fallow for Ernest Gaines's fecund imagination and the blossoming of his Louisiana-hewn voice. Baldwin's urban realism sets the stage thematically for Gaines's bucolic allegories chronicling African-American men's vigilant attempts to negotiate the terms of intimacy.

3 Reimagining Richard: Ernest J. Gaines and the Neo-Masculinist Literary Imagination

WHEN HAROLD BLOOM introduced the phrase "anxiety of influence" to our critical lexicon, he did not have Richard Wright, Ralph Ellison, or James Baldwin in mind. But his incisive observations about "strong" Anglo-American male poets' inclination to write *against* each other transcend racial lines. Hence, the narrative trope of "signifying" takes on especial rhetorical weight, as Henry Louis Gates Jr. observes in *The Signifying Monkey:*

> [Ishmael] Reed has criticized, through Signifyin(g), what he perceives to be the conventional structures of feeling that he has received from the Afro-American tradition. He has proceeded almost as if the sheer process of the analysis can clear a narrative space for the next generation of writers as decidedly as Ellison's narrative response to Wright and naturalism cleared a space for Leon Forrest, Ernest Gaines, Toni Morrison, Alice Walker, James Alan McPherson, John Wideman, and especially for Reed himself. (218)

African-American male writers have waged a battle royal to clear narrative space in particular. The paternal literary tree might read as follows: Frederick Douglass's generative *Narrative* sits atop the genealogy, which begets the voices of Charles Chesnutt and Paul Laurence Dunbar; these turn-of-the-century authors spawn the voices of the Harlem Renaissance luminaries James Weldon Johnson and Langston Hughes; and these two artists' works provide a blueprint for Wright, the literary father of and obstacle for Ellison and Baldwin. However, this literary bloodline has not always flowed so sanguinely.

The concept of literary signifyin(g) illustrates how contemporary authors regard their counterparts. Wright's disparaging comments about the Harlem

Renaissance generally and Zora Neale Hurston specifically are well documented, but even more vehement is both Ellison's and Baldwin's rejection of Wright as a literary patriarch. Ellison's repudiation of his "blueprints" for black writing has become a litany most students and critics can recite: "No, Wright was no spiritual father of mine, certainly in no sense I recognize. . . . It was Baldwin's career, not mine, that Wright proudly advanced by helping him attain the Eugene Saxton Fellowship, and it was Baldwin who found Wright a lion in his path" (*Shadow* 117). The somewhat puerile tenor of these comments belies the fact that they were written by arguably the greatest black American novelist of his time. Not to be outdone in terms of literary patricide and sibling rivalry, Baldwin dismissed his literary benefactor as well. Echoing Ellison, he castigated masculinist protest and its archetypal document, *Native Son,* for effacing the "humanity" of black people. Deeming Baldwin's critique of Wright "extraordinarily derogatory" and "venomous" (*Blues* 140), Houston A. Baker Jr. nevertheless exposes the cankers on the male literary tree, where sons can only find their artistic voices by renouncing the slightest hint of literary influence. Apparently, black male writers have not been able to, as the battered Los Angeles motorist Rodney King opined, just get along.

In evaluating and assessing Ernest J. Gaines's life and career, it should come as no shock that he too disavows any literary consanguinity. His comments about Wright and Ellison situate him securely among the quarreling male voices; of the former he declares:

> *Native Son* would not have had an influence on me, had I read it. It's urban, Chicago. It was not a part of my experience. I didn't know a thing about urban life. If I had come from New Orleans, if I had been there and seen the violence, seen the [French] Quarter, seen that kind of background, maybe I could have tried to write that. But I came from a place where people sat around and chewed sugarcane and roasted sweet potatoes and peanuts in the ashes and sat on ditch banks and told tales and sat on porches and went into the swamps and went into the fields—that's what I came from. (Gaudet and Wooton 36–37)

Though perhaps not as pungent as Baldwin or Ellison's respective denunciations of Wright, Gaines's declaration of artistic independence is nevertheless resolute and unequivocal. He claims that he never even read the quintessential document of black masculinist protest during his artistic apprenticeship. Unsurprisingly, he too extols white male writers as his literary models: Gaines cites Joyce and Hemingway as major influences in the same way that Baldwin claims James and Ellison locates Faulkner and Eliot as his artistic progenitors. Keith Byerman accurately sums up this testosterone-laden one-upmanship: "Yet this very denial of literary fathers . . . has itself become a part of the tradition. Each generation of Afro-American writers seems to need to create a space for itself by claiming kin to no black predecessor or by citing the influence of European and white American artists" (*Fingering* 41). But I would go further and argue that this disremembering of kin is unique to male writers. Consider how Alice Walker, Toni Morrison, and Gloria Naylor, a contemporary distaff version of the Wright-Ellison-Baldwin troika, affectionately claim Hurston and Ann Petry as literary foremothers. These ardent dissings and dismissals are apparently a male thing that critics and readers understand all too well.

Still, Gaines's comments do more than demean Wright's dreaded protest poetics: they convey crucial dimensions of his own aesthetic—his passionate and emphatic concern with voice, place, and story. Perhaps most emblematic is his 1983 novel *A Gathering of Old Men,* which revolves around several elderly black men testifying and witnessing to each other about whites' extirpation of their selfhood and their own complicity in it. The title of that novel provides an apposite starting point for my discussion of Gaines's fictive aims and my reading of his most recent novel, *A Lesson before Dying* (1993): *Gathering* signifies on the grand narratives of black men's writing, *Native Son* and *Invisible Man,* by foregrounding not black men's marginality and absence but instead their solidarity and communality.

As I stated in the first chapter, black male writers have been almost obsessively concerned with manhood and subjectivity. For black men, this quest often involves mimicking their white counterparts and thereby valorizing the rather narrow conceptualizations of masculinity to which American culture pledges allegiance. Such beliefs are derived from standard Western constructions of gender, ones the sociologist Clyde W. Franklin II laments when addressing the inaccessibility of black manhood: "How else is it possible to explain white society's reluctance to extend male power and privilege to Black men?" ("'Aint I'" 275). Regrettably, black masculinity has been conceived as the offspring of white patriarchal masculinity, itself an abysmally flawed construct not worthy of emulation. Gaines contests this myopic view, which limits black men's visions of what constitutes a fully human subject. Structurally, thematically, and representationally, he interrupts a mimetic configuration of male subjectivity that centers white patriarchy and privilege as the touchstones for selfhood—rights and privileges never meant to extend to black boys and native sons.

Several critics have located black masculinity as the driving force behind Gaines's fictive machinery. David C. Estes's comment is representative: "Gaines's most predominant theme comes out of his African-American heritage. It is the search for black manhood" (9). However, Gaines does not merely digest and regurgitate shopworn definitions of masculinity. His re-inscriptions surpass the sacrosanct and ingrained conceptions of masculinity that accentuate violence, power, and sexual dominance, probing the to-tality of the black male self from emotional, psychological, and spiritual perspectives. In Gaines's expansive literary imagination, black men are more than the sum of their socially splintered selves. Perhaps inadvertently, he answers Baldwin's call for black writers to articulate a "field of manners" (Gaines's bucolic settings suggesting an even literal interpretation) by explor-ing black men's complexity not only as individuals but as fathers, sons, hus-bands, and brothers engaged in collective struggle. The broad scope of his portrayals constitutes a radical reconfiguring of black literary subjectivity.

Gaines's responses to both black and white men's literary discourse are cen-tral to any theory of his fiction. The novelist's pervasive concern with how men engage fundamental questions surrounding personal, communal, and existential identity connects him as much to the legacy of Joyce and Faulkner as it does to Wright. Vis-à-vis Wright specifically, works such as the novel *Of Love and Dust* and, more definitively, the story collection *Bloodline* center the experiences of young black males in a racially and economically stratified American society. A comment Gaines made early in his career sheds some light on his central discursive concerns: "My heroes just try to be men; but because the white man has tried everything from the time of slavery to deny the black [man] this chance, his attempts to be a man will lead toward dan-ger" (O'Brien 146–47). His comments could apply to Wright's "Big Boy Leaves Home" as well as to his own stories, but Gaines's fictive praxes involve more than the seemingly angry literary son claiming the mantle of white literary forefathers while simultaneously disclaiming his relatives, Wright and Ellison. He critiques the masculinist tradition, race notwithstanding. However, in my discussion of *A Lesson before Dying,* I will concentrate on the author's signifi-cation on and re-envisioning of black men's literary aesthetics.

Gaines's work interfaces with black masculinist literary discourses, most notably the slave and protest narratives. Though male and female slaves chronicled their lives, Douglass's 1845 *Narrative* remains the benchmark for black male characters' measurement of self-worth. As Deborah E. McDow-ell asserts, "At the heart of all these enterprises [contemporary works such as Alex Haley's *Roots* that attempt to retrieve and reinterpret black history] is a preoccupation with manhood and masculinity, a preoccupation illumi-nated graphically and not surprisingly in the slave narrative. It is well known that the majority of published slave narratives were written by black men" (142). One cannot help but notice the connection between these narratives' thematic concerns and Gaines's: the pervasive quest for voice and literacy and the reconstitution of one's personhood in a physically violent and relentlessly hostile white patriarchal society dominate Gaines's fictive cosmos. However, Gaines does more than mimic or appropriate the conventions of this primordial genre. For instance, whereas literacy, education, and geographic relocation are synonymous with mental and emotional liberation and empowerment, the novelist often subverts this notion, thereby questioning the culturally enshrined definitions of masculinity promulgated in male slave narratives.[1]

Gaines revises the rhetorical and thematic components of the male protest narrative, the fictive descendant of the slave narrative (e.g., Johnson's *The Autobiography of an Ex-Coloured Man* or Ellison's *Invisible Man*). However, his works proffer an alternative vision of black male subjectivity. Challenging the discursive formations of masculinist literature, which turns black men into social subjects menaced by Anglo-American culture, Gaines depicts their lives from myriad angles and points of view. This panoramic representation portrays black men not merely as social victims but as active agents capable of effecting change. What Gates labels "tropological re-envisioning" (xxv) might aptly describe Gaines's intent. Though there are undeniably intertextual connections between slave and protest discourses and Gaines's reconfigurations of black male subjectivity, his fictive modus operandi has been more countertextual, for he radically dismantles the archetypal depictions of black men as tragic racial victims.

In focusing on the multifariousness of black male subjectivity, the author questions the discursive feature most emblematic of black men's writing—the subject circumscribed by a hegemonic American culture. Young male protagonists, the inexorable products of their environments, are perpetual and almost infallible victims defined by financial, sexual, and social exigencies. One recurring thread linking famous black protagonists—the Ex-Coloured Man, Bigger, Clay Williams—is their myopic and limited conception of themselves in relation to their white counterparts. Stated another way, these figures envision subjecthood as something to be wrested away from an intractably malicious culture; the external realm, emblematized by an omnipresent and impenetrable whiteness, becomes the benchmark for self-measurement. Sociological discourse of the 1980s and 1990s surrounding the "endangered black male" contributes to the typecasting of protest subjects: "Many young Black males have come to view themselves as victims, triply disadvantaged by race, poverty, and social isolation, nonachievers in the schools, nonproducers in the labor market, and nonparticipants in the society. Thus, perceived as nonentities in every major social institution, too many

Black males have decided to drop out permanently by literally destroying themselves as they can see no way out of their unendurable situations" (Gibbs 129). This standard narrative of black maleness as synonymous with socio-pathic and pathological behavior echoes the prototypical treatment of black men in literature. However, Gaines poses what John F. Callahan labels "interiority" as the basis for probing the complex black male fictive self.[2] In Gaines's countertexts, he does not efface the scourges of racism, poverty, and violence, but neither does he allow them to eclipse black men's relationships with each other or others in their orbit.

Consonant with his attempt to depict black men finding their voices, Gaines's protagonists express an array of emotions that counter the dominant fiction of masculinity in general and black masculinity specifically. American male culture, steeped in rugged individualism, self-reliance, and stoicism, often prohibits verbalizing the internal, and black men are triply confined: as men, they often don't reveal their frailties and fears; they possess few vehicles for expressing internal desires outside of protesting their social marginality (though black men have often achieved voice in blues and other musical forms); and they have categorically been denied the cultural space—within their own community as well as in the dominant one—to speak and experience their psychic malaise.

Contemporary popular culture buttresses this point: how often are black men allowed to feel and express pain? Think of how tragedies in the 1990s suffered by Michael Jordan and Bill Cosby—the death of the basketball star's father and the murder of the comedian's son, respectively—were minimized amidst a swirl of allegations about the athlete's gambling habit and the entertainer's mysterious "love child." Leland K. Hall accurately assesses America's inattention to black men's inner lives: "The American culture and its subsocieties do not expect the Black male to exhibit emotions and feelings about his or his family's life situation and the dire impact that society may have on him when he tries to live up to these unrealistic expectations" (162). Thus, the confluence of gender and race renders black men's interiority alien and taboo, a veritable terra incognita because of the larger culture's pejorative attitudes. This pain often goes unspoken, consigning black men to hermetically sealed prisons where they cannot seek solace from each other or their community. Thus, another key component of Gaines's aesthetic apparatus has been to inscribe a language capable of transmitting different forms of pain.

To accentuate his centering of black male interiority, the author reimagines the tropological function of space. I do not think it coincidental that two of Gaines's most prominent works, *Bloodline* and *A Lesson before Dying*, have as their primary settings interior spheres—the prison in both "Three Men" (the central story in the volume) and in the novel. These settings stimulate black men's internal probing of how they can counter and re-envision the ways they have attempted to resituate themselves as subjects. Reminiscent of Reed's troping of Ellison, Gaines revises Wright by transforming prisons into curative environments—a stark contrast to Bigger Thomas's tomb-like cell. Interior spaces—traditionally sites for exploring the effects of domesticity on women or as asphyxiating environments that symbolically kill black men—stimulate the characters' spiritual and psychic regeneration. Paralleling the rhetorical strategy in "Three Men," *Lesson* subverts the prototypical depiction of prison as a masculinized space, an objective correlative for America's black male–phobia. Alternatively, the cell engenders the spiritual rebirths of both Grant and Jefferson, the dual protagonists in *Lesson*. Gendered space, so often the purview of feminist literature, emerges as paramount in Gaines's reimagining of black masculinist discourse.[3]

In addition to carving out space, metaphorically and literally, to explore the totality of black men's lives, Gaines's fiction is concerned with a range of black male characters. In another instance of rhetorical self-fashioning, Gaines discards the monologism of protest discourse in which the voice of a lone disembodied, maimed subject predominates. *Native Son* and *Invisible Man* are perhaps best categorized by their microscopic focus on a singular man's trek through the jagged and debilitating American social terrain. These contemporary racialized allegories pit a Bigger Thomas or a Bob Jones (the protagonist of Chester Himes's 1945 novel *If He Hollers Let Him Go*) against an inimical culture committed to his erasure if not outright extinction. On the outskirts of these protagonists' journeys lie black women, black children, and other black men. These narratives fit cozily within the masculinist Western epic tradition, which focuses on an insular, embattled hero or antihero whose journey abounds with hinderers and helpers, trials and tribulations. Odysseus, Gulliver, Leopold Bloom, Jake Barnes, Huckleberry Finn—all represent literary antecedents for black male characters in the 1940s and 1950s, who often situate themselves in diametric opposition to community. The acquisition of voice, be it in Douglass's captivity tale or Ellison's sable picaresque, usually comes at the expense of communal ties.

Responding to this prevailing discursive dynamic, Gaines constructs a multivalent verbal world, one containing a panoply of voices. *Bloodline,* like *A Gathering of Old Men,*[4] showcases Gainesian multivocality, his insistence that black men must renegotiate the terms for selfhood among a collectivity of other black men. In other words, his narratives epitomize the polyphonic quality of much black male writing after *Invisible Man*. Although Valerie

Melissa Babb concludes that "While he breaks with a history that devalues African-American culture, he substitutes in its place a rich communal folk history that validates and celebrates that culture" (252), Gaines seems as much committed to foregrounding a male community as he is to representing an idiosyncratic "folk" one.[5] Thus, his centered subjects tend to be diverse—the multiple storytellers in *Bloodline,* the venerable story-weavers in *A Gathering of Old Men.* Gaines's men are not, ultimately, so inflexibly opposed to each other or community. Voicing their common histories inaugurates the renegotiation and reclamation of subject status. This accounts for Gaines's works being so firmly rooted in orality, his texts unfolding as multitiered verbal performances.

This recentering of black men's collective voices conforms to Gaines's theory of fiction. Though Wright's ubiquitous voice has evoked the most visceral responses from younger authors, Gaines also assails what he considers a glaring weakness in Ellison's magnum opus: "When I come to the omniscient point of view and I create a character, a narrator who's much like myself, I do too much thinking. I don't have the freedom. That's one of the things I criticize *Invisible Man* about. There's too much thinking going on all the time. There's thinking in every goddamned sentence. You don't think. Let the thing flow. Let it go" (Gaudet and Wooton 13). A distinguishing feature of black masculinist poetics is not merely the characters' stymied attempts to recast themselves in terms of white male subjectivity but also the authors' own need to convey a mastery of white masculinist literary aesthetics. What amounts to a battle royal emerges between character and author, and the question of textual subject—whose voice is being centered, whose story is being told—is thrust into question. At times, Ellison and Wright sacrifice their protagonists' voices on the altar of their white literary fathers' aesthetic commandments; we can picture them sparring with Whitman, Hemingway, Faulkner, et al. Though Gaines also apotheosized some of these same writers (most notably Hemingway), he skillfully modulates his authorial voice in his fiction. While one can detect a signifying relationship with Faulkner,[6] Gaines does not muffle his characters' voices or fasten them to any particular ideology. Eluding formal pigeonholing, he has been difficult to situate, as well-worn categories of naturalism, protest, realism, and regionalism ultimately fail to capture his technical dexterity. Gaines does not obsessively try to demonstrate his literary manhood by inculcating and mastering the forms of his male Anglo-American predecessors. Decentering his own authorial presence and voice permits him to foreground black men's spiritual and psychic journeys within a primarily male environment.

"I Am Still Part of the Whole": Disassociation, Reassociation, and the Communal Urge in *A Lesson before Dying*

Gaines's works unquestionably converse with Wright's, making him the literary native son whose father's words are indelibly etched into his literary memory despite his attempts to minimize the kinship. The central narrative event in *Lesson* connects it to *Native Son:* A young black man is standing trial for the murder of a white person, and an ineffectual and patronizing white lawyer speciously defends him by invoking a black-man-as-savage stereotype defense. Once this dubious effort fails, the youth is sentenced to death. Both texts condemn legal and social institutions that ruthlessly strip black men of voice and agency. Notwithstanding Bigger Thomas's guilt and Jefferson's innocence, these superficial similarities belie Gaines's concerns with how black men negotiate, renegotiate, and re-envision the terms of their own subjectification.

One way to differentiate between these two distinctly southern male voices is to consider their structuring of narrative action. Though common themes emerge in *Native Son* and *A Lesson before Dying,* formal differences illuminate Gaines's departure from the structural constraints of protest. I return briefly to the work of Steven Cohan and Linda Shires, who theorize the differences between "plot" and "story" in fiction; though I will subsequently alter their distinctions, their work informs my delineation of Wright's and Gaines's fictions. Using E. M. Forster's *Aspects of the Novel* as the basis for their discussion, they posit that "Plot and story are therefore not interchangeable terms. Plot refers to a type of story structure, one which places events in relations of subordination, not mere coordination. This type of logical order is so familiar a convention of narrative that readers often expect every story to have a plot, but that is not always the case" (58). The central point here is that plot and story are not synonymous, and I use these as rhetorical distinctions to differentiate writers distinctly bound by their shared southern literary heritage.

If we recall the tripartite configuration of *Native Son,* we discern a hierarchy of action, where certain narrative events are subordinated to others. The book's section titles, "Fear," "Flight," and "Fate," serve as rhetorical guideposts that convey the novel's narrative arc, the scope of action involved in Wright's construction of the plot. His Africanized American tragedy follows a fairly conventional line of action: Bigger's threadbare environment animates his downward spiral, first into sociopathic behavior (plotting a robbery) and eventually into murder and extortion. Wright makes it clear that racism is the central culprit, the scourge that accounts for Bigger's subjugation. The text privileges the unraveling of *white* Mary Dalton's murder: this violence propels Wright's recitation of Bigger's asocialization and attendant psychic dislocation. Characteristic of the detective/mystery rubric under which the novel is sometimes placed, the murder of a white person represents the cardinal narrative moment. Hence, a fairly pedestrian, cause-and-effect line of action ensues, as the novel etiologically traces Bigger's psychological and social evisceration. And as several black women critics have argued, *black* Bessie Mears's murder is subordinated, a random act of rage that in and of itself does not provide the impetus or explanation for Bigger's psychosocial implosion. Unsurprisingly, the exigencies of Bigger's own family and surrounding community become ancillary fictive concerns: black male victimization and victimizing and white malevolence dominate Wright's fictive universe and provide the novel's contours.

Conversely, Gaines's fictive cosmos encompasses the worlds of myriad black men who are connected historically, socially, and communally. Less existential than local, his protagonists are distinctly black Everymen, their experiences resonating not in and of themselves but demonstrating how they interact to form a communal narrative. I use the term "storycentric" to describe Gaines's fictive apparatus. As the novelist Gayl Jones has reflected, "When I think of Gaines, I think of voice and story" (Harper 368). For Gaines the term "story" does not relate to the coordination or subordination of events. Instead, it involves personal, communal, and individual histories, that web of experiences that impacts not merely a lone, disfigured black man but a constellation of black men whose fates are intertwined. "Story" thus signifies interiority and history, not external events and the hierarchical ordering of action—what we commonly think of as emplotment. In Gaines's storycentric figuration, social and external events—actions and behaviors—are subordinated to the explorations of black men's collective stories, which may or may not have their bases in cultural phenomena like racism and classism.

To see how Gaines recasts issues of race and class as well as the logistics of action and plot, one need only read the first chapter of *A Lesson before Dying*, where he lays out the central episode. The twenty-one-year-old Jefferson hitches a ride with two young black male acquaintances in search of liquor. The three enter a store owned by Grope, a Cajun (white), who agrees to sell the men alcohol only if they pay in advance. Despite their pleas for credit, Grope refuses and, with Jefferson an innocent bystander, the two acquaintances instigate a gun battle with the store owner that leaves all three of them dead. Jefferson, assumed to have been a willing accomplice, is tried and convicted of the murder by a jury of "twelve white men" (8). As in *Native Son*, a white defense attorney claims innocence by reason of cultural deprivation and genetic bestiality. Not only would a black man lack the mental acuity required to plot a robbery, but his ignorance of the inviolable written artifacts of Anglo-American culture leaves him intellectually bereft: "Mention the names of Keats, Byron, Scott, and see whether the eyes will show one moment of recognition. Ask him to describe a rose, to quote one passage from the Constitution or the Bill of Rights. Gentlemen of the jury, this man planned a robbery? Oh, pardon me, pardon me, I surely did not mean to insult your intelligence by saying 'man'—would you please forgive me for committing such an error? . . . *Why, I would just as soon put a hog in the electric chair as this*" (8; emphasis added). This bombastic performance recalls Bigger's "defense." Mining the same racially incendiary territory as Boris Max, Jefferson's lawyer invokes a comparable culturally sanctioned script: the black man is America's sable curse, the "heart of darkness" who embodies the inscrutable, pathological Other. Ostensibly, Jefferson's designation as "hog" engenders the narrative action.

However, though the novel's agon resembles that of *Native Son*, Gaines immediately shifts the focus away from cultural and social impoverishment as the reasons for black men's psychic alienation. He refuses to characterize them as perpetual victims who in turn victimize. By revealing the plot in the first nine pages of the novel, Gaines telegraphs to the reader his intent to dismantle and demythologize protest discourse. His fictive machinery is ignited not by black men's lack of money or even white perfidy but by a desire to articulate alternative vehicles for black male subjectivity, ones not rooted in financial exigency, misogyny, or patriarchal masculinity. The author maintains that his protagonists can effect their own reconstruction and regeneration if they are willing to do the Herculean work of entering the emotional terrain of both themselves and the black men with whom they share physical and psychic space. To this end, Gaines (like Baldwin in *Another Country*) subordinates the standard plot by foregrounding several interlocking stories and the exacting but mandatory task of sharing those stories, entering into another's complexity, and re-emerging as a communally connected subject, an indisputable part of the whole.

Ellison's prescient observation about Wright specifically and protest discourse generally speaks to my assessment of Gaines's novel: "Wright believed in the much abused idea that novels are 'weapons'—the counterpart of the dreary notion, common among most minority groups, that novels are instruments of good public relations. But I believe that true novels, even when most pessimistic and bitter, arise out of an impulse to *celebrate* human life and therefore are *ritualistic* and *ceremonial* at their core. Thus they would preserve as they destroy, affirm as they reject" (*Shadow* 114; emphasis added). Ellison's more sanguine view of the novel as a genre provides a context for my reading of *Lesson*. The words "celebrate," "ritualistic," and "ceremonial" stand out, for a perusal of black men's writing would seem to render Ellison's use of them puzzling or inapplicable. The men in *Lesson*, like so many of Gaines's characters, undergo a ritualistic process in which they must confront their deformation, where their conceptualization of subjectivity is problematized, interrogated, and finally dismantled. The word "ceremonial" aptly describes the process by which Gaines's protagonists are transformed from maimed, voiceless objects to regenerated, voiced subjects. During this initiation, these characters confront and exorcise a host of demons: antiquated and debilitating constructions of masculinity and their attendant scourges—hypersexuality, violence, and alienation. Moreover, they reconcile their tormented homosocial relationships as well as their place within the entire black community. Writing against the pervasive cultural episteme that insists on black men's otherness and the masculinist protest narrative that concentrates myopically on their victimization, Gaines captures black men in various stages of development. Clearly, he deromanticizes black maleness and portrays his characters as works in progress: they are fallible and scarred, but they also possess the means to forestall their deformation. As Byerman observes, Gaines's stories are "narratives of process rather than resolution," and his "narrators come to understand that the quest, rather than the object of the quest, is of greatest importance" (*Fingering* 74).

Gaines's novels and short stories portray bipartite, tripartite, or multiple figurations of deformed masculinity, evinced by titles such as *Bloodline* and "Three Men." That *Lesson* depicts the lives of multiple black male subjects counters a distinctive feature of men's writing.[7] Gaines's writings depict black men in relation to other black men, what might be considered a same-gender community. In this way, his discursive praxis approximates that of Toni Morrison, who fictivizes communities of black women. McDowell's observation about Morrison's 1974 novel *Sula* also applies to Gaines's conceptualization of black male characters: "Not only does the narrative deny the reader a 'central' character, but it also denies the whole notion of character as static *essence*, replacing it with the idea of character as *process*. Whereas the former is based on the assumption that the SELF is knowable, centered, and unified, the latter is based on the assumption that the SELF is multiple, fluid, relational, and in a perpetual state of becoming" (105). In the same vein, Gaines resists static perceptions that reduce black men to social problems who can be "solved" algorithmically by rote analysis. Depicting multiple figures, he captures the complexity—the otherness—of the black male subject.

As my modal framework for interpreting *Lesson,* I delineate the narratives of disassociation and reassociation. This paradigm elucidates the different phases of black male subject formation while accentuating most clearly the ritualized process through which the author transports his protagonists. The three characters who emblematize these stages are Jefferson, the apparent victim of white injustice; Grant, his recalcitrant mentor who grudgingly accepts the task of transforming him from a "hog" into a "man" before his electrocution; and Matthew Antoine, a quasi "tragic mulatto" who, though limited in terms of narrative space, still conveys most wrenchingly the debilitating effect that internalizing accepted fictions of Anglo-American subjecthood has on black men. The narrative of disassociation[8] locates patriarchal masculinity as the hallmark of black male selfhood. Some of the following dynamics characterize this narrative: a ruptured relationship with the larger black community; a desire to escape (as in Wright's "flight" motif); an enmity toward whites, particularly white males, for denying black men the privileges they believe should accrue to them based on anatomy alone; and a proclivity toward self-erasure. As a corrective, Gaines inscribes the narrative of reassociation, which counters the narrative of disassociation by depicting black men who reconstruct and re-envision themselves as subjects. The key facets of this reconfigured black male subjectivity are storytelling and story-listening; voicedness—reconstructing the self via language within a community of historically connected individuals; and a reconnection or reassociation with other black men and the broader community. I will trace the disassociation of these characters in order to illustrate how Gaines portrays Grant and Jefferson as alternative models for black male selfhood.

Black male subjectivity, with the attendant problems of voice, narrative authority, and silence, is contested ground from the outset of the novel. Starkly reminiscent of the opening line of *Invisible Man,* an enigmatic assertion and denial of selfhood, Grant proclaims "I was not there, yet I was there [at Jefferson's trial]" (3). This incongruous assertion of presence and absence bespeaks Grant's marginality amidst cultural and communal events. As is often the case throughout the novel, his *thereness* is always tenuous. Though he will often inhabit the same physical space as his fellow Quarters denizens, he more often than not remains on the outskirts emotionally and psychically. In this way, Grant resembles countless unreliable narrators—from Marlowe to Nick Carraway to the older brother in "Sonny's Blues," men seemingly estranged from their cultures and whose own malaise impairs their ability to interpret events. The telling of the story emerges as the centered subject, a metafictive technique that permeates his writing.[9] Furthermore, Grant relates the details of Jefferson's trial, a spectacle where black male humanness is disputed. Through Grant, we hear conflicting versions of Grope's murder: Jefferson's version, a tale not narrated by Jefferson himself but by Grant, who has heard it second-hand; the prosecutor's interpretation, where "Jefferson and the other two [Brother and Bear] had gone there with the full intention of robbing the old man and then killing him so that he could not identify them" (6); and finally the attorney for the "defense," who fallaciously argues that Jefferson's native ignorance, deprivation, and social impoverishment account for his client's antisocial behavior.

The text's central event—albeit not its subject—recalls countless fictional episodes that depict black men falsely accused and denied voice: the beleaguered Richard in *Go Tell It on the Mountain,* so distraught over white policemen's brutality after being falsely arrested for a robbery that he slits his wrists, and Bigger Thomas, whose racial horror story is similarly filtered through whites who claim to speak on his behalf, are two such examples in black men's literature. This fictive situation evokes comparisons to the primordial document of black male subjectivity, Douglass's *Narrative.* Recall how the slave-scribe's own voice, at least initially, is deferred, superceded, and "authenticated" by white men who corroborate his tale. However, unlike the slave narrative or the aforementioned novels, Gaines's text does not attempt to "prove" black men's truth or innocence amidst whites' dogged attempts to persecute them. In other words, his novel is not a romanticized or heroic tract in which a multivictimized black male does or does not overcome white men's innumerable attacks on his personhood. Instead, Gaines emphasizes the salience of voice and voicedness, the importance of articulating the self and speaking and/or writing that tattered self into existence as a way to reclaim subjectivity. Articulating the self becomes a resuscitative act, a way to assert one's agency and subjecthood in the context of oppression.[10]

Because Gaines appropriates the fictive situations and strategies of his black literary forefathers while simultaneously revising them, I locate Grant as a counterpart of other disassociated black male subjects, men whose alienation presages their spiritual and emotional paralysis. In this context, Grant is reminiscent not only of the nameless Invisible Man but also of the nameless narrator of "Sonny's Blues." The biographies of Grant and Sonny's brother link them unequivocally: though formally educated, each man eschews communal and familial ties. Reminiscent of Sonny's narrator-brother, Grant is an educator who teaches black children and lives within the community without building emotional and spiritual bridges to its denizens. Grant bluntly confesses his ineffectuality to Miss Emma (the godmother who reared Jefferson) after she asks him to restore Jefferson's personhood: "'Yes, I'm the teacher. . . . And I teach what the white folks around here tell me to teach—reading, writing, and 'rithmetic. They never told me how to keep a black boy out of a liquor store'" (13). One can't help noticing the Wrightian essence of Grant's language: "black boy" and "liquor store" hearken back to a central episode in *Black Boy*, where the miseducated and drunken six-year-old Dick repeats obscenities in a bar and scrawls them onto the neighbors' windows.

Though he has narrative control and is, ostensibly, the speaking subject, Grant is voiceless inasmuch as he lacks an audience. Like the Ex-Coloured Man, Invisible Man, and Sonny's narrator-brother, Grant epitomizes the miseducated black subject, one whose formal training quashes any empathy for his black compatriots. Grant's syllogistic revelation to Miss Emma, where he conveys his own inertness and unwillingness to reach out to Jefferson, exposes a pedantic persona that distances him from the black community, not unlike the educated persona of *Black Boy*, who repeatedly decries his family's and community's ignorance. Victor J. Seidler in *Rediscovering Masculinity: Reason, Language and Sexuality* speaks to the shortcomings of "rationality" and miseducation in gendered terms that help explain Grant's superciliousness: "For men, our very identification with our reason gives us a vantage point of superiority in relation to women outside and beyond our own lived experience, which we can only appropriate in the most abstract of terms. *We are trapped as observers, not only of the natural and social worlds, but also of ourselves. We are left as observers, rather than as participants, in our own lives*" (130–31; emphasis added). Grant's fecklessness cannot be concealed by the patina of educational superiority. He is the articulate antihero who desires to speak for no one, including himself, on higher or lower frequencies. Once he realizes that he has a vested interest in Jefferson's life—a mirror of his own—the transformation from passive object to participating subject can commence.

Grant's cultural disassociation is most evident, ironically, when he shares physical space with other black men. As I have pointed out, Gaines's fictive project has been the reinvigoration not of a sole, fragmented protagonist but a collectivity of black men. Hence, male-specific or gendered communities take on a crucial formal and thematic import. Throughout the novel, the vocally privileged but experientially challenged Grant positions himself on the periphery, his narrative marginality magnified by the psychological distance between himself and other black males. Age notwithstanding, Grant is the perpetual odd man out:

> Standing by the fence, I watched the five older boys saw and chop the wood. Two would saw while another would straddle the wood pole to keep it steady. The other two boys split logs and chopped up small branches with the axes. They laughed and kidded each other while they worked.
>
> And I thought to myself, What am I doing? Am I reaching them at all? They are acting exactly as the old men did earlier. They are fifty years younger, maybe more, but doing the same thing those old men did who never attended school a day in their lives. Is it just a vicious circle? Am I doing anything? (61–62)

Mired within the epistemological hell of himself, Grant devalues the ontological power of black male community—the sense of connectedness that comes with *being* among a group of historically and psychically bound persons. He embodies hermeneutics run amok: in his self-ordained role as interpreter, he underestimates the value of male rituals and reduces black men to texts that he misinterprets, not unlike the attorneys who mischaracterize Jefferson. In his cognitively limited worldview, he can only depersonalize and abstract the experiences of other black males, reading them as signifiers of unfulfilled lives. Reminiscent of Troy Maxson in Wilson's *Fences*, Grant is "fenced in" by his failure to comprehend his place within the African-American community.

This proleptic episode dramatizes how both young and old black men, despite Grant's minimizing of their collective experiences, find ways to affirm and connect. Subsequently, in a scene that recalls both the bar-room conversion Sonny's brother undergoes and the old men's storytelling rituals in his 1983 novel, Gaines shifts the action to the Rainbow Club, the bar and restaurant to which Grant often flees to escape his aunt's demands and Jefferson's moribund plight. During one visit with two old men and the proprietor and bartender, Joe Claiborne, present, Grant witnesses a re-enactment of Jackie Robinson's heroics by one of the men, who transforms himself into a faux Jackie by batting and stealing home plate. After one man acts out Robinson's trademark batting and base stealing, another "nodded his head emphatically, with great pride, and went back to the bar" (88). Though generational differences and self-imposed isolation prevent Grant from fully appreciating the men's reverential performance, associative memory eclipses formal education when he recalls his adolescence and the profound and palpable communal despair that followed Joe Louis's loss to Max Schmeling—"This was a period of mourning" (88). However, upon Louis's subsequent avenging of this defeat, Grant recollects:

Then it was over. And there was nothing but chaos. People screamed. Some shot pistols in the air. There were mock fights. Old men fell down on the floor, as Schmeling did, and had to be helped up. Everybody laughed. Everybody patted everybody else on the back. For days after that fight, for weeks, we held our heads higher than any people on earth had ever done for any reason. I was only seventeen then, but I could remember it, every bit of it—the warm evening, the people, the noise, the pride I saw in those faces. (88–89)

Though it may be transitory, Grant makes the journey back by using memory to relocate himself within the vortex of a black expressive community.[11] Although Gaines employs sports as a metaphor, he subverts its traditionally male-centric underpinnings. Instead of being a venue where men fetishize competition, violence, and hypermasculinity, it inaugurates catharsis and solidarity. Still, despite this brief remembrance of things past, Grant remains a spectator.

Perhaps Grant's discontent stems from his conceptualization of masculinity. As a young man growing up in the South in the 1940s, he was subjected to countless instances of black men being denied access to the culturally approved vehicles for manliness. However, Gaines does not merely protest the withholding of "masculine privileges" enjoyed by black men's white counterparts. He exposes the vacuity of the forms of masculinity that society and black men value, undermining conventional male constructs through his portrayal of Grant. Subsequently, he suggests how Grant and Jefferson can vanquish these debilitating constructions and create a new model of black male subjectivity.

The defining feature of black men's protest discourse is its valuation of patriarchal masculinity, which has represented the normative model black writers emulate while simultaneously contesting white male authority. Black manhood is achieved only by standing up to white men: Douglass's psychospiritual alchemization from *slave* to *man* after his battle with Covey exemplifies this. Wright's and Himes's protagonists often rhapsodize about the advantages of "white boys," who enjoy infinite possibilities in an impenetrably racist culture, where white skin and a penis are unimpeachable currency. Initially, Grant, the apogee of disassociation and liminality, attempts to mimic a form of masculinity that black men have found tenuous at best. One of the most resonant examples of Grant using normative masculinity as a barometer for his own sense of selfhood is when he attempts to secure the time and space to transform Jefferson from "hog" to "man."

This intercession takes him to the home of Henri Pichot, Sheriff Guidry's brother-in-law. After having waited in the kitchen for several hours, Grant finally meets with Pichot and Guidry: he reflects, "I tried to decide just how

I should respond to them. Whether I should act like the teacher that I was, or like the nigger that I was supposed to be" (47). Grant's behavior vacillates throughout the encounter. For instance, responding to the white men's inquiry of how long he had been waiting, he replies "'About two and half hours, sir,' I said. I was supposed to say, 'Not long,' and I was supposed to grin; but I didn't do either" (47). He and Guidry have a brusque exchange:

> "She's old," I said. "She [Miss Emma] doesn't feel that she has the strength to come up there all the time."
> "She doesn't, huh?" Sam Guidry asked me. He emphasized "doesn't." I was supposed to have said "don't." I was being too smart.
> "Yes, sir," I said. "She doesn't feel that she can."
> I used the word "doesn't" again, but I did it intentionally this time. If he had said I was being too smart and he didn't want me to come to that jail, my mind would definitely have been relieved. (48)

Grant's ephemeral manhood vanishes, however, when Guidry accuses him of being "a little too smart for your own good"; a diffident Grant muses, "I was quiet. I knew when to be quiet." Grant's verbal one-upmanship—his momentary "standing up" to white men—becomes a Pyrrhic victory, one where linguistic self-assertion is at best conditional and where he is ultimately rendered silent.

Another common trait of the disassociative black subject is his devaluation and sometimes denigration of black women. Usually they function either as the sexual repositories for black men who experience crushing social discrimination (think of Bigger Thomas or Gabriel Grimes) or as the handmaids in white men's efforts to annihilate black men. Before his epiphanic experience with Jefferson, Grant sees his aunt as a co-conspirator in the white patriarchy's campaign to demasculinize him emotionally and psychologically. Clinging to his miseducation as evidence of his subject status, Grant admonishes his aunt for sending him—again—to Jefferson's cell to help actuate his redemption:

> "Everything you sent me to school for, you're stripping me of it," I told my aunt. They [his aunt and Miss Emma] were looking at the fire, and I stood behind them with the bag of food. "The humiliation I had to go through, *going into that man's kitchen.* The hours I had to wait while they ate and drank and socialized before they would even see me. Now going up to that jail. To watch them put their dirty hands on that food. *To search my body each time as if I'm some kind of common criminal.* Maybe today they'll want to look into my mouth, or my nostrils, or *make me strip.* Anything to humiliate me. All the things you wanted me to escape by going to school. Years ago, Professor An-

toine told me that if I stayed here, they were going to break me down to the nigger I was born to be. But he didn't tell me that my aunt would help them do it." (79; emphasis added)

Grant's agitation is revelatory. Again, he uses white masculinity as the touchstone for his own sense of self. Resisting what he sees as attempts to emasculate him psychically, Grant views his subjectivity as contingent upon being what white men deem unacceptable. White masculinity and its black counterpart exist symbiotically in his mind.

Grant's emotional eruption exposes an even more disturbing condition—an anxiety over his unstable sense of a culturally sanctioned manhood. His graphic description of the events in Henri Pichot's kitchen hearken back to the plights of Douglass's Aunt Hester or Morrison's Sethe Suggs, women abused by omnipowerful masters. Within this context, his erasure becomes sexual as well as spatial: in essence, Grant views his violation as a "rape" that feminizes him not only because he is rendered physically powerless by white men but also because it takes place in the kitchen, a domestic milieu usually associated with black women's subjugation. That he feels that his aunt colludes in his "stripping" is all the more foreboding, for he accuses her of conspiring with white men to eviscerate him. His recapitulation of the "ritual" he must undergo prior to seeing Jefferson further evinces what Grant sees as his own emasculation (consider how authors such as Chester Himes and Jean Genet have depicted the subterranean prison as an incubator for male-on-male sexual and physical violence). Thus, Grant's graphic descriptions synthesize multiple sites where sexual violation has historically occurred: white men's kitchens, the plantation, and the prison. Finally, his position as teacher perhaps intensifies his discomfiture; recall his symbolic imprisonment inside his church schoolroom while his students fraternally chop wood outside. Especially in the black community, the classroom, like the kitchen, is primarily a distaff space that has historically provided black women with economic alternatives to white women's kitchens.[12] In fact, the other teachers in the novel are female colleagues of Grant's lover Vivian, who teaches at a school with a woman principal. Within the circumscribing fictions of American malehood, the educated Grant is liminal in racial and communal terms, and, additionally, he is hard-pressed to carve for himself the hallowed space of the masculinized sexual subject.

If men are socialized to minimize communal and familial commitments, then Gaines's inchoate black male subjects are refreshing aberrations. Two exchanges between Grant and Vivian bear witness to the intersection of geography and space in this reconfiguration of black subjectivity. The first occurs at the Rainbow Club. Vivian reminds Grant that, as teachers, they have a unique commitment to the South, and he caustically rejoins: "'You hit the nail on the head there, lady—commitment. Commitment to what—to live and die in this *hellhole*, when we can leave and live like other people?'" (29; emphasis added). Grant's language here is especially resonant in terms of black cultural and literary discourse. As critics such as J. Lee Greene have noted, the North and South have historically been encoded and symbolic spaces, the latter often (though not always) perceived as a hell on earth, especially for black men who were subject to lynching.[13] Moreover, one can't help but hear in Grant's execration echoes of Quentin Compson's shrill denunciation of the South at the end of *Absalom, Absalom!*

The second encounter takes place in Vivian's classroom, when she and Grant are commiserating over the ties that bind them to their native Louisiana—her pending divorce, his education of Jefferson:

> "I wish I could just run away from this place."
> Vivian shook her head. "You know you can't."
> "Why not?"
> "For the same reason you haven't done it yet."
> "I've wanted to."
> "But you haven't."
> "Why?"
> "You know the answer yourself, Grant. You love them more than you hate this place."
> "Is it love or cowardice? Afraid to take a chance out there."
> "You have your folks in California. You can always go to them."
> "I have thought about it many times."
> "Sure," she said. "You even did it once, but you came back. This is all we have, Grant." (94)

The gender theorist Peter Middleton's observation about men's propensities to "forget [themselves], become oblivious to self-consciousness, and switch off the inward gaze" (192) speaks to Grant's desires to relocate himself emotionally, psychologically, and geographically. Flight becomes a remedy, a palliative for the pain that the "inward gaze" animates. This second ritualistic exchange is salient (perhaps also an explanation for Vivian's last name, "Baptiste"): her refutation of Grant's misgivings is a watershed moment in his ritualistic transformation to communal subject. Vivian's voice is not only the moral counterpoint to Grant's solipsistic wish to abandon his southern community, it illustrates Gaines's discursive interruption of black men's literary discourse, which often vilifies both the South and black women. Thus, Gaines uses geography, as he does space, tropologically to elucidate how black protagonists can (re)claim subject status in their native homeland. Just as Grant must learn that "feminine" sites, while exacerbating his anxiety of masculinity, do not signal his psychic castration, so too must he come to realize that black male subjectivity and the South can exist coterminously.

Thus far I have focused on Grant as the central questing figure, the protagonist emblematic of the black male grappling with different ways to refashion himself. However, another character central to Gaines's tripartite figuration of maimed black masculinity is Matthew Antoine, whom Grant remembers as "the big Mulatto from Poulaya" (62). Antoine looms in Grant's consciousness just as the voices of Wright and Ellison remain inspiriting influences vis-à-vis Gaines's artistic imagination. His ex-instructor represents an indelible, near spectral presence that instills in Grant a sense of disillusionment, despair, and nihilism. Though Antoine occupies scant narrative space (a single eight-page chapter), his foreboding presence conjures up memories of Rufus Scott, the early suicide whose demons haunt the inhabitants of Baldwin's *Another Country*. Antoine, more than any other black male in the novel, personifies the disassociative subject, a figure whose life is so racked with hatred that he atrophies spiritually and physically.

Antoine displays his convoluted racial convictions when Grant visits him prior to enacting the daunting task of transforming Jefferson. Antoine and Grant's exchanges are the antithesis of Grant's encounters with characters like Vivian: theirs is an anticommunal ritual. Grant himself acknowledges this: "There was no love there for each other. There was not even respect" (64). Witness, for instance, Antoine's estimation that "Nothing pleases me more than when I hear of something wrong. Hitler had his reasons, and even the Ku Klux Klans of the South for what they do" (63). This perverted Weltanschauung recalls the "Seven Days" in Toni Morrison's *Song of Solomon*, where the black vigilantes' ideology sanctions vindicatory violence, thereby justifying their cabalistic killing of whites. Antoine's dogma also echoes the beliefs of "Schoolteacher," the fiendish slave master in *Beloved* whose cancerous racial views justify his subhuman treatment of blacks generally and his brutalizing of Sethe Suggs specifically. Antoine's veneration of Hitler and the Klan is especially telling, for they represent white patriarchal masculinity in its most virulent form: xenophobia, which posits blacks' inherent bestiality, justifies the extermination of the dark Other.

Antoine's repudiation of blackness in lieu of a vapid form of Anglo-American subjecthood is amplified during the following exchange, which begins with Antoine's declarations, followed by Grant's remonstrations:

"Where else could I [Antoine] have felt superior to so many but here?" "Is that important?" I [Grant] asked him. "It is," he said. "For everyone. Especially for the whites and the near whites. It is important." "Do you feel superior to me?" I asked him. "Of course," he said. "Don't be a damned fool. I *am* superior to you. I am superior to any man blacker than me." "Is that why you hate me?" I asked him. "Exactly," he said. "Because that superior sonofabitch out there said I am you." "Do you think he is superior to you?" I asked him. "Of course," he said. "Don't you?" "No," I said. "Just stay here long enough," he said. "He'll make you the nigger you were born to be." "My only choice is to run, then?" I asked him. "That was your choice. But you won't. You want to prove I'm wrong. Well, you'll visit my grave one day and tell me how right I was." (65)

Clearly, Antoine's psychosocial numbness stems from his inculcation of white patriarchal thinking and the attendant realization that he is not only "not white" but that his Joe Christmas–like status renders him a cultural orphan or bastard. In his rigid hue-based hierarchy, his white blood—albeit adulterated by the "mighty drop" of black blood—becomes a purifying balm that saves him from the malignant and inferior realm of niggerdom. His racial liminality nonetheless prevents him from being accepted into the white hegemonic social strata he deifies.

Another salient facet of this verbal joust is its syntactic dimension. Whereas Gaines usually differentiates characters' speech utterances by clearly distinguishing who's speaking during dialogues, he alters this standard narrative practice for rhetorical effect. Employing a technique Hemingway perfected in stories such as "A Clean, Well-Lighted Place," Gaines counterpoises and melds Antoine's and Grant's voices in this exchange, which can be read either antistrophically or monologically. The two characters possess markedly different racial philosophies, and Grant refutes his erstwhile instructor's claims. However, since Grant has harbored similar abnegating thoughts about the black community, he shares a tacit kinship with Antoine. Because Gaines inscribes their exchange as a single paragraph, the reader can interpret the voices as a single speech utterance; they in effect echo each other. Perhaps Gaines intends for us to think of these characters as doubles or as dual parts of a single consciousness. Consider this fusion of characteristics in light of Cohan and Shires's observations about "traits":

> In addition to performing functions for a story, characters are also differentiated according to semantic features which readers interpret as *traits*. Seymour Chatman defines *trait* as "a narrative adjective . . . labeling a personal quality of a character, as it persists over part or whole of the story." . . . In spite of the seeming individuation of character through traits, the range of traits in a given narrative and their effect of differentiating among characters are not based on the psychological individuality or essence of a given character's "human

nature"; rather, traits cite a historical culture's assumptions of what qualities are recognizable as "human nature." (72–73)

Gaines jettisons the semantic markers or "traits" that usually differentiate character, mainly dialogic markers, to elucidate not only many blacks' conflicted responses to racial ambiguity but also to expose the proximity of Grant's feelings about the Quarters and his mentor's tainted racial attitudes. Grant's exchange with Antoine underscores how some blacks have internalized the hegemonic culture's septic view of blackness as an act of self-definition. In attempting to cope, Antoine valorizes whiteness to the point of psychological self-erasure.

Grant's own tenuous racial identity is revealed: one could just as easily read this passage as an interior monologue or interpret Antoine as merely a projection of Grant's devitalized psychoracial self. The most noteworthy feature of this exchange is not the men's psychological "differences," which distinguish them as characters, but their acceptance of pernicious conceptualizations of blackness. The antiblack seeds that the Anglo-American culture has successfully sown in Antoine's consciousness are also budding in Grant's psyche, though they ultimately will not germinate. Not only does the Antoine-Grant dialectic demonstrate how some blacks have transferred the culture's xenophobia onto themselves and each other, it also suggests the disassociative black male subject's prospects for renewal and reconnection—reassociation.

The product of this nihilistic dogma is, to revise slightly the title of Elaine Scarry's penetrating study of the historical and cultural dimensions of pain, a "black body in pain," one whose social and cultural disequilibrium engenders his physical deterioration. Grant's physical descriptions of Antoine reveal the material price one pays for engaging in what amounts to cultural suicide. Antoine's lamentation during his visits with Grant, "I'm cold," becomes his mantra, buttressing the idea that his psychosocial death will hasten his physical one. During his final visit before Antoine's premature death at forty-three, Grant observes: "He sat at the fireplace. Summer or winter, he always sat at the fireplace when he was inside. We shook hands. His hand was large, cold, and bony. He was coughing a lot. . . . 'I guess I'm a genuine teacher now,' I said. He nodded, and coughed. He didn't seem to want to talk. Still, I sat there, both of us gazing into the fire. 'Any advice?' I asked him. 'It doesn't matter anymore,' he said. 'Just do the best you can. But it won't matter'" (66). One can't help but speculate that Gaines, like Ellison, is signifying on his white male literary counterpart Joseph Conrad by describing his decaying character in terms reminiscent of the psychically and corporeally atrophied Kurtz. Literal and metaphorical darkness is a scourge to both characters, and each is haunted by the *horror* of blackness. Moreover, Antoine's insistence on pain and victimization and his self-annihilating response exemplify how many protest subjects view their lives: "for the person in pain, so incontestably and unnegotiably present is it that 'having pain' may come to be thought of as the most vibrant example of what it is to 'have certainty'" (Scarry 4). In essence, pain provides at least the remnants of an identity in a culture that equates blackness with absence. Though the novel is not explicitly a roman à clef, Antoine's and Grant's acrid relationship recalls that of Wright and Baldwin, where the older writer both influenced and infuriated his protege by exiling himself from a black American culture he viewed as dysfunctional and barren. The skeletal Antoine and his jaundiced worldview haunt Grant throughout the novel, for his mentor embodies and articulates his own worst fears about the futility of black life. Antoine attempts to bequeath Grant his anemic view of self and community—the lesson he teaches Grant before dying.

That Antoine's cancerous racial doctrines maintain such a core place in his pupil's consciousness as well as in the novel indicates not only their historic resonance but their structural importance as well. Antoine's life becomes refractory, an oblique illumination of the novel's deformed protagonists' tormented lives. Within Antoine's brief life-portrait we can discern Grant's desire for connectedness, his simultaneous desire to repudiate community, and Jefferson's self-loathing—his acceptance of whites' misdesignation of him as a "hog." These three congruent personal histories resemble the formal components of the blues, what Jones calls "worrying the line, repetitions and variations on key lines or phrases, like the blues singer who 'won't leave the line alone'" (196–97). Looking at the narratives of Grant, Antoine, and Jefferson in terms of the blues, we might consider Jefferson's inculcation of whites' misnaming of him—the opening courtroom scene in which he is branded a "hog"—as the statement of the black male subject's distorted view of self; and the accompanying narratives of Grant and Antoine become restatements of the initial scene, for both men's stories reflect a discomfort about blackness and an apotheosizing of hegemonic, Anglo-American constructions of maleness in general and black masculinity specifically. The third movement of this blues triptych—the resolution—occurs when Jefferson pens his "Diary" near the end of the novel.

Gaines delays Jefferson's voice until the twenty-ninth chapter, thus climactically dramatizing the connection between voicedness, community, and subjectivity. The deferral of Jefferson's voice also accentuates a salient point—black men's primary existence as texts that are misread, misinterpreted, and silenced in American culture. Jefferson's text serves a corrective function, representing an antidote for Antoine's poisonous racial precepts. Recall the novel's opening chapter, where Jefferson's lawyer and the prosecutor simultaneously bestialize, demonize, and render him agencyless. The prosecutor portrays him as an "animal" who "'stuffed the money into his pockets and celebrated the event [the murdering of the shopkeeper Grope by Brother and Bear, who are also killed in the melee]'" (6–7). His own attorney similarly argues that Jefferson is no more than "'a cornered animal [who] strike[s] quickly out of fear, a trait inherited from his ancestors in the deepest jungle of blackest Africa—yes, yes, that he can do—but to plan [the murder]? To plan, gentlemen of the jury? No, gentlemen, this skull here holds no plans. What you see here is a thing that acts on command. A thing to hold the handle of a plow, a thing to load your bales of cotton, a thing to dig your ditches, to chop your wood, to pull your corn'" (7–8). Employing what might be deemed a type of "synecdochic inflation,"[14] the prosecutor hyperbolizes what is portrayed as Jefferson's racially specific pathological behavior as representative of all black persons, whether they hail from Louisiana or the "Dark Continent." This prejudiced precis of Jefferson's existence is clearly meant to expose the depth of the white community's antipathy toward black men. But the retelling of Jefferson's involuntary participation in the robbery reiterates how black men have traditionally been hermeneuticized, not only denied the ability to speak for and to define themselves but vilified and misread to corroborate the larger society's scurrilous text of black maleness.

This disparaging configuration of black maleness has its antecedents, most notably in Wright's *Native Son,* where the white press describes the just-captured Bigger Thomas as "look[ing] exactly like an ape" (322). Regrettably, one needn't probe the annals of American history too deeply to locate instances of black men being categorized as subhuman. The latter portion of the twentieth century abounds with atrocities: Rodney King deserved to be brutalized by swarming Los Angles policemen because he was "threatening"; in Boston, Charles Stewart nearly eluded justice by blaming the murder of his white wife on some chimerical but ubiquitous feral "black male"; and most recently, New York City police savagely assaulted and sodomized the Haitian immigrant Abner Louima apparently without fear of reprisal. These actual cases buttress the novel's portrayal of the judiciary system's dehumanizing, viciously pejorative fiction of black maleness that is part and parcel of many whites' historic perceptions. Jefferson's narrative voicelessness becomes part of a larger cultural mindset in which voice and agency are not merely denied but consistently abrogated. Because black manhood—and personhood—has been and continues to be so vigorously contested, Gaines's delaying of Jefferson's voice becomes a rhetorically, historically, and technically resonant act.

In stark contrast to the cerebral Grant's hyperarticulateness stand Jefferson's autobiographical reflections. The dialect and stream of consciousness notwithstanding, his eloquent diary conflates the male characters' conflicted conceptions of self. It stands as a composite text that crystallizes the novel's primary concerns surrounding male subjecthood. The diary addresses these interlocking issues: black men's relationship to God, their relationship to whites, their dealings with the black community, their understanding of women, and perhaps most significantly, their relationships with each other. The author complexifies the black male self in this narrative tour de force, where these multiple selves are depicted in paragraph-like units in which one of the aforementioned relationships is foregrounded. Moreover, Gaines does not use standard paragraph demarcations but only white space, thus imbuing the section with a poetic, lyrical quality. I will not explicate each stanza in Jefferson's journal but will elaborate on those that most clearly elucidate how he and Grant are transformed from disassociative to reassociative subjects.

Several archetypal genres and postmodernist literary techniques inform the stylistic features of Jefferson's pastiche-like diary. Most noticeable is the presence of black dialect with phonetic spellings and the absence of standard grammar and punctuation. Furthermore, it recalls the first section of *The Sound and the Fury,* for both Benjy Compson and Jefferson are presented as mentally deformed, childlike figures whose thought processes are presented associatively. However, Gaines, like Langston Hughes, infuses his work with a distinctively black modernistic symbology. Recalling issues raised by Craig Hansen Werner in his exploration of black writers' responses to Faulkner, Gaines's technique reflects yet another pointed signification on Faulkner's Anglo-American modernism, which consistently effaced blackness. Rather than chronicling an "idiot's" mental deficiencies, Gaines meticulously maps out the process through which black men reclaim their personhood.

In terms of the other voices in the text, Jefferson's stands out not only for what it conveys but also for what it represents. His solecistic self-revelation becomes a counternarrative that challenges Grant's written text and his authority as narrator and interpreter. The diary is both autobiographical and pedagogical in essence, for it serves as a guidepost for the overly cerebral Grant and similarly disconnected black men. Its opening section foregrounds several thematic and formal concerns related to voice, authority, and agency: "mr wigin you say *rite* somethin but i dont kno what to rite an you say i must be thinkin bout things I aint telin nobody an i order put it on paper but i dont kno what to put on paper cause i aint never rote nothin but homework i aint never rote a leter in all my life cause nanan [his godmother, Miss

Emma] use to get other chiren to rite her leter an read her leter for her not me so i cant think of too much to say but maybe nex time" (226; emphasis added). This compact stanza highlights the depth of Jefferson's voicelessness and, by extension, his asubjectivity. Because Grant has impressed upon Jefferson the significance of writing as an act of empowerment and resistance, we can see the nascent stages of a speech community—black men collectively reclaiming a sense of self through shared speech acts. Gaines's use of "rite" suggests that verbal expression, be it written or spoken, is a prerequisite for black male subjectivity, a rite of passage that must occur among men. Writing will allow Jefferson to interrupt and vitiate society's constructions of black men as an act of self-discovery and regeneration. Therefore, writing, which figured so prominently in Douglass's emotional and spiritual unshackling, becomes the catalyst for Jefferson's rebirth and renewal.

Additionally, Jefferson's narrative emblematizes the author's insistence on black expressive culture—written or oral—not only as his artistic source but also as the basis of black selfhood. Many critics have commented on how Gaines mines the story-world of his native Louisiana and his fervent commitment to storytelling and story-listening—what we now rather generically call the oral tradition. But Jefferson's inscription masterfully conflates the written and the oral, as the two modes of communication exist not binarily but complementarily. A condensed account of his physical travails and spiritual renaissance, the diary becomes a blues confession that converses directly with Grant while simultaneously attesting to blacks' collective fortitude. Markedly different from Grant's solipsistic narrative, Jefferson's syncretic text records his transformation from disassociative to reassociative subject.

The emancipatory impact of Jefferson's written/oral performance evinces itself through the effect it has on Jefferson and Grant's relationship. The diary sutures these previously disconnected and psychically deformed black men who were not only estranged from each other but who were, more lamentably, isolated from a community of black people. Jefferson's physical and emotional displacement is reflected in Grant's life; one particularly revelatory instance of the teacher's self-imposed marginalization occurs after his students' Christmas pageant when he starkly declares, "I looked back at the people around the tables, talking, eating, drinking their coffee and lemonade. But I was not with them. I stood alone" (151). However, Jefferson's diary arrests and corrects black men's spiritual and communal alienation. The fact that it facilitates his and Grant's regeneration and reconnection is apparent when Jefferson writes, "im sory i cry mr wigin im sory i cry when you say you aint comin back tomoro im strong an reven ambros gon be yer wit me and mr harry comin to an reson i cry cause you been so good to me mr wigin an nobody aint never been that good to me an make me think im sombody" (232). Jefferson's highly cathartic repentance counters what Scarry calls the "unsharability" of pain, which it ensures "through its resistance to language" (4). Jefferson laments not only his own pain, but he voices a pain that Grant attempts to stifle through his facility with language. In terms of black orality and vernacular traditions, Jefferson's unmediated confession to Grant retains the cadences of the blues: his repetition of the pain that Grant's absence will engender and Jefferson's subsequent resolution of that pain transform him into a blues subject who speaks for both self and others. Furthermore, Jefferson's "roll call" of the novel's central black male characters marks a spiritual if not actual gathering that conveys how black male communitas can foster wholeness. Men with disparate backgrounds—the uneducated Jefferson, the formally educated and secular Grant, and the zealously Christian Reverend Ambrose—can transcend their differences in ways that depart from standard configurations of black male subjects.

Jefferson's lament counters a discursive formation in black men's writing that renders black male intimacy rare, nonexistent, or off-limits. Whether it be the generative black masculinist genre, the slave narrative, or Wright's and Ellison's fictive paeans to black male victimization and invisibility, nurturing relationships between black men have remained taboo. Within the scope of the novel itself, Grant and Jefferson's jailhouse fellowship revises and corrects the earlier exchange between Antoine and Grant, one rooted in antipathy and misanthropy. Jefferson's speech act also marks an inversion of the essential elements of the slave narrative. In contrast to what Robert Stepto has called the male slave narrative's "articulate hero" who "ascends" by speaking and writing himself into being, Gaines foregrounds a superficially inarticulate one who emerges with a song not merely of himself but one for other black men and, by extension, a collectivity of black people. In contrast to Stepto's model, Gaines's disassociated subjects descend into the depths of their self-imposed estrangement on their way to reclamation and rebirth.

The conclusion of A Lesson before Dying, as in most of Gaines's fiction, marks the evolution of the neo-masculinist literary imagination and an innovative reimagining of Richard Wright. Whether it be the repositioning of black men within a community of black men and women or the revising of Bigger's cathartic jailhouse self disclosure to the white Boris Max through Grant and Jefferson's hallowed prison interactions, Gaines deconstructs the conventions of African-American protest discourse. Moreover, by having Jefferson's diary posthumously transmitted to Grant via Paul Bonin, a white prison guard who challenges corrosive attitudes toward blacks, Gaines mirrors his female literary counterparts such as Toni Morrison (Beloved), Alice

Walker (*Meridian*), and Shereley Anne Williams (*Dessa Rose*), who insist that racial and gender barriers are not intractable. Eschewing the main discursive trait of male protest fiction, which fixates on a relentlessly oppressed male subject, Gaines reinvigorates black men's literary discourse and sows the seeds for the fecund artistic imagination of the playwright August Wilson. Like Gaines, Wilson re-envisions black male subjectivity, retrieving it from the constricting and eviscerating fictions proffered by American culture and the psychically destabilizing responses of violence and isolation—roads taken by generations of invisible native sons.

4 Race, Ritual, Reconnection, Reclamation: August Wilson and the Refiguration of the Male Dramatic Subject

VERY RARELY DOES an author articulate his artistic strategy as concisely as does August Wilson in this 1991 interview in the *New York Times:*

> Part of my process is that I assemble all these things and later try to make sense out of them and sort of plug them in to what is my larger artistic agenda. That agenda is answering James Baldwin when he called for "a profound articulation of the black tradition," which he defined as "that field of manners and ritual of intercourse that will sustain a man once he's left his father's house." . . . In terms of influence on my work, I have what I call my four B's: Romare Bearden; Imamu Amiri Baraka, the writer; Jorge Luis Borges, the Argentine short-story writer; and the biggest B of all: the blues. (Wilson, "How" 5)

These comments encapsulate the playwright's "artistic agenda" and his place within the larger context of black male writers. With the production of several plays, including two Pulitzer Prize winners, the degree to which other art forms—the blues being paramount—influence Wilson's writing is well documented. His comments also illustrate the extent to which he situates himself within a twentieth-century black male artistic community. Wilson summons Baldwin's and Baraka's ancestral voices, affirming how they cultivated the cultural and artistic ground on which his feet are solidly planted. Wilson resituates the writer as subject: he claims and mines a fertile artistic heritage without "dissing" those who wrote before—no anxiety about his influences. That he places himself within a collectivity of African-American male writers underscores how his plays chronicle black men's exacting struggle to locate an inspiriting and uplifting environment in which they can realize a radical, authentic subjectivity.

For this chapter's title, I invoke Baraka's 1971 essay collection *Raise, Race, Rays, Raze* to suggest points of convergence and divergence vis-à-vis Wilson and other Black Arts dramatists. Wilson is indelibly marked with the cultural stamp of the 1960s Black Arts Movement.[1] His dramas, anchored in African-centered rituals and cosmology, evoke Ed Bullins's Afrocentric dramatic principles: "The future of Black theater will be in its evolution into a profound instrument of altering the slave mentality of Black Americans. In an evil, white world of ever shifting values and reality, for the Black man there must be a sanctuary for re-creation of the Black spirit and African identity" (Bullins 14). Wilson subscribes to the Black Arts Movement's aesthetic dictate that art be rooted in the cultural exigencies of black people; he proudly claims this as his artistic template. But underlying his dramatic vision is not a doctrinaire conception of race that calls for black drama to "raise" and "raze"—that it simultaneously uplift and bludgeon, as Baraka and Bullins mandated. Instead, he centers the boundless possibilities for his black male subjects, their pressing desire to reconnect and reclaim a sense of self, community, and history. By no means am I suggesting that he depicts culturally indifferent or amputated black men who lack racial animus. But even more so than Baraka's stentorian dramatic call to arms, Baldwin's own call issued in *Notes of a Native Son* for the inscription of a "field of manners and ritual of intercourse" (35–36) is the creative appeal to which Wilson responds. Challenging atavistic figurations of the black male dramatic protagonist, the playwright offers innovative forms through which he presents his reconceptualized subjects. He downplays ideological blandishments and centers the rituals that might reconnect not merely fragmented selves but experientially and historically related black men. Though he does not present unfettered and "whole" black men in plays such as *Ma Rainey's Black Bottom* (1984) and *Seven Guitars* (1996), he assiduously chronicles black men's resolute desire for intimacy and community—an impulse that is sometimes thwarted, sometimes realized, but never abandoned.

While some critics—Wilson's nemesis Robert Brustein being the most zealous—have assailed Wilson for covering familiar dramatic terrain, he is grounded in both American and African-American dramatic traditions.[2] Having garnered Pulitzer Prizes for *Fences* (1985) and *The Piano Lesson* (1991), his works evoke comparisons to the pantheon of "great" white dramatists (O'Neill, Miller, and Williams). Craig Hansen Werner has commented on this coterminous relationship:

> Wilson employs numerous themes and motifs familiar to theater audiences grounded in the O'Neill tradition, which includes Tennessee Williams, Sam

Shepherd, Lillian Hellman, Lanford Wilson, Beth Henley, and numerous others. Among these are the disruption of the surface of family life by repressed or buried secrets, the blurring of the line separating "psychological" and "physical" realities, and the transformation of everyday diction and syntax into a heightened vernacular poetry. (*Playing* 278)

However, if one can argue that there exists an archetypal twentieth-century American dramatic story, it might be the staging of men's internecine conflicts. Vestiges of the psychological torpor of O'Neill's tortured male Tyrone triumvirate in *Long Day's Journey into Night* (1957) or the verbal bloodletting that occurs between the male real estate agents in David Mamet's *Glengarry Glen Ross* (1984) surface in the same-gender conflicts that pervade Wilson's plays. This is not to say that Wilson's dramatic design is strictly mimetic. However, denying these intersections would be tantamount to overlooking Ellison's discursive conversations with Dostoevsky, Twain, Poe, Whitman, and other European and Anglo-American male writers.

Notwithstanding Wilson's place in this American dramatic tradition, his plays ultimately transcend such parochial comparisons. The centering of black music stands as his most striking modal departure from his white dramatic predecessors, as Wilson venerates it in ways that echo Baraka's observations in his seminal study of African-American music, *Blues People*. As Wilson makes clear in his interview with Sandra G. Shannon, "I have always consciously been chasing the musicians. You see their expression has been so highly developed, and it has been one expression of African American life. It's like culture is in the music. And the writers are way behind the musicians I see" (Shannon, *Dramatic* 234). Though Wilson repeatedly claims the blues as his artistic reservoir, his plays have their thematic origins in the blues while simulating the structure of jazz—"blues tales" related in a "jazz mode."[3] While the distinction between blues and jazz modalities can be alternatively contrived and amorphous, Werner observes that, "Seen in relation to the blues impulse, the jazz impulse provides a way of exploring implications, of realizing the relational possibilities of the self, and of expanding consciousness (of self and community) through a process of continual improvisation" (*Playing* 268–69). One might therefore interpret Wilson's blues plays as being comparable to jazz compositions: his protagonists' sagas of personal, artistic, and familial turmoil are thematically hewn from the blues, while the plays' improvisational strategies of revelation through performance approximate jazz structurally. Not coincidentally, Wilson consistently configures his plays around quartets of black men: Levee, Slow Drag, Cutler, and Toledo in *Ma Rainey* and Floyd, Canewell, Red Carter, and Hedley in *Seven Guitars*. Hence, he invokes the organic and polyvoiced qualities of the jazz combo, replete with unfurling statements and counterstatements, restatements and revisions. This distinctly African-American discursive practice distinguishes his plays from the well-trodden paths of realism and naturalism, which often mute the black playwright's "blues voice."[4] Analogous to Baldwin's claim that the English language is anathema to the "spirits and patterns" of his fellow Harlemites and that he had to "find a way to bend it the way a blues singer bends a note" (Gresham 162), Wilson's elastic dramatic language and dramaturgy permit him to record the multiexpressiveness of African-American life and culture.

Simultaneously drawing on and departing from American dramatic conventions, Wilson constructs his plays in ways that are comparable to Gaines's fictive apparatus, which focuses less on emplotment and more on the stories of black people, especially black men. To this end, he abandons the hallmarks of the well-made play. Contrary to the specious claim that "our most highly acclaimed dramatists are still shaping their works to sequential diagrams" (Brustein, *Reimagining* 25), Wilson is less concerned with causality, linearity, or verisimilitude, which explains why his "history cycle" has not been composed chronologically. Comparing his formal design to the collages of the African-American painter Romare Bearden, he posits that "I've got all these images, and the point is how I put them together. The pieces are always there; it's how I put them together, the relationships between them that counts" (Rocha, "Conversation" 32). Because he constructs action associatively rather than chronologically, the dramatist doesn't so much abjure "sequential diagrams" as he de-emphasizes emplotment. He opens dramatic space for his characters' attempts to "sing their songs," a recurrent trope Wilson uses to signify his black male protagonists' wrenching but exigent spiritual journeys—a prerequisite for wholeness.

Wilson does not jettison plot in the vein of the absurdist dramatists of the 1950s (i.e., Eugene Ionesco or Jean-Paul Sartre). Nor does he metadramatically bring attention to the medium itself as a comment on the efficacy of form. Nor is Wilson a proponent of a neo–"theatre of cruelty," which reflects the French playwright and theorist Antonin Artaud's core belief that theater should incite and catapult spectators into revolutionary action.[5] Rather, Wilson's multiple dramatic discourses—simultaneously realist and naturalist, fabulist and mystic, ritual and spiritual—are rooted in black men's retrieval and voicing of personal histories, which inform the plays' thematic and formal configurations. Hence, personal story takes precedence over the erection of a seamlessly crafted dramatic story.

The lexicon critics use to describe Wilson's plays—words such as "ritualistic," "vernacular," and "musical" recur—invites comparisons between his plays and the revolutionary drama of the 1960s. From a dramaturgical stand-point, his works employ many of that genre's conventions, which Bullins particularizes:

> Some of the obvious elements that make up the alphabet of the secret language used in Black theater are, naturally, rhythm—black, blues, African; the racial consciousness and subconsciousness of Third World peoples; Black Cultural Nationalism, Black Revolutionary Nationalism and traditional Black people's familial nationalism; dance, as in Black life style and patterns; Black religion in its numerous forms—gospel, negro spiritualism to African spirit, sun, moon, stars and ancestor worship; Black astrology, numerology and symbolism; Black mysticism, magic and myth-science; also, history, fable and legend, vodun ritual-ceremony, Afro-American nigger street styles, and, of course, Black music. (9)

A cursory glance at the Wilson oeuvre reveals his indebtedness and adherence to 1960s dramatic aesthetics: the quasi nationalism of characters such as Toledo (*Ma Rainey*) and Sterling (*Two Trains Running*); the African-imbued cultural rituals and myths of *Joe Turner's Come and Gone;* and the seven disjointed, blues-inspired characters in *Seven Guitars* whose lives converge with tragic and transformative consequences. His "polyrhythmic"[6] dramas are undeniably the by-products of this watershed artistic moment.

Though Wilson's plays abound with connections to Black Arts drama, there are substantive differences. The poet and critic Larry Neal's 1968 essay "The Black Arts Movement," considered the cultural manifesto for Black Arts drama, lays bare the distinctions between Wilson and his acknowledged dramatic standard-bearers. Neal earnestly proclaims that the Black Arts Movement eschews "protest literature" but paradoxically insists that "The motive behind the Black aesthetic is the destruction of the white thing, the destruction of white ideas, and white ways of looking at the world" (258–59). It would be erroneous and critically irresponsible to extract these comments from their social and cultural contexts, but it would also be myopic to overlook the race-speak that sometimes diluted the movement's aesthetic aims. A percipient observation by the drama scholar Tejumola Olaniyan addresses the problems of such binary thinking. According to him, there is an inherent "problematic feature of counterdiscourses: their deep and intricate relations with the dominant. They share the same ground with the dominant and thus run the risk of a fixation with the restrictive binary logics of the latter and of recycling its epistemological premises" (20). At the heart of Neal's treatise lies a symbiotic relationship with the dominant, an unshakeable need to invert the cultural and artistic hegemony, to replace one orthodoxy with another.

I interpret Wilsonian aesthetics as less counterdiscursive than recursive and reclamative. Refusing to privilege or valorize Anglo-American culture as dominant, Wilson strives to reposition and recapture blackness not as the mirror opposite of whiteness but for its own historical resonance and complexity. By vowing to compose what he calls a "dramatic history of black Americans" (Shannon, *Dramatic* 232), he has committed to interrogating and displaying the rituals and intricate relationships that unify and/or estrange blacks from each other—again, what Baldwin labeled a "field of manners." Much less a dramatist of didacticism than a dramatist of ideas, Wilson distills the blackness of blackness, that unique and contradictory web of individual and collective narratives of blues people, irrespective of the cultural forces committed to their evisceration. Throughout his work, he dissects the codes of conduct that govern blacks' relationships to each other, foregrounding especially black men's excruciating attempts to gather together in the name of individual and collective affirmation.

Talking B(l)ack, Talking Blues: Repositioning the Black Male Dramatic Subject

By placing black vernacular, oral, and performance traditions at the heart of his art, August Wilson foregrounds the intersection of African-American cultural practices and identity formation. Expounding on the dramatist's literary apprenticeship, the novelist Ishmael Reed conveys how Wilson's native Pittsburgh shaped his artistic ethos as definitively as Louisiana informed Gaines's:

> Wilson's official education ended in the ninth grade, but another education took place in the highest academies of the African literary oral tradition: the gambling dens, or the street corners like the one at Fullerton and Wylie in Pittsburgh, which the Harlem Renaissance author Claude McKay called "the crossroads of the world." Then there were the restaurants, also in Pittsburgh: Eddie's restaurant, on Centre Avenue, Sef's Place, Pat's Place—places where the old-timers gather to "play the dozens," "signify," and indulge in all their other volatile, hyperbolic word games. (Reed, "Shy Genius" 95)

A sense of place as sentient and organic pervades Wilson's drama-world. The playwright's omnipresent fascination with various communal enclaves— stages, really—piqued his interest in community, performance, and voicedness. Moreover, that the gambling dens and street corners were probably male-dominated venues elucidates the author's persistent concern with the black subjectivity-masculinity nexus. With disarming candor he admits that "I doubt seriously if I would make a woman the focus of my work simply because of the fact that I am a man, and I guess because of the ground on which I stand and the viewpoint from which I perceive the world" (Shannon, *Dramatic* 222). Though one might take umbrage with this sort of gender essentialism,[7] the playwright's point is crucial to demythologizing his concentration on black men. Ultimately, his plays are neither misogynistic nor phallocentric, but they are male-centered. Wilson dismantles hackneyed definitions of maleness, for clusters of male characters dramatize the arduous internal excavation that must be undertaken in negotiating individual and collective identity.

When one begins to consider Wilson's representations of black men within the context of black drama in the second half of the century, comparisons with archetypal protagonists such as Hansberry's Walter Lee Younger and Baraka's Clay Williams are inevitable.[8] What resurfaces throughout the canon is a concern with black men's valiant though often misguided efforts to situate themselves into a fiction of archetypal masculinity—attempts that are often derailed by a virulently hostile hegemonic culture. Baraka spells out the ideological basis of black male dramatic representation in "The Revolutionary Theatre": "The Revolutionary Theatre must Accuse and Attack anything that can be accused and attacked. It must Accuse and Attack because it is a *theatre of Victims.* It looks at the sky with the victims' eyes, and moves the victims to look at the strength in their minds and their bodies. . . . Our theatre will show victims so that their *brothers* in the audience will be better able to understand that they are the *brothers of victims,* and that they themselves are victims if they are blood *brothers*" (211, 213; emphasis added). One could read these proclamations as cultural and artistic calls to arms that exhort the victims—"blood brothers"—to liberate and empower themselves. The repeated emphasis on "brothers" here is telling as well: all the blacks are Victims; all the victims are men; and women are accorded neither status.

I return briefly to Wilson's most adamant critic, the former dean of the Yale school of drama, Robert Brustein, to illustrate a more contemporary variation on the notion that black drama can be simplistically relegated to "agit-prop" or "guilt" literature. Assailing *Fences* as an ersatz *Death of a Salesman* in blackface, Brustein concludes: "Yet, for all his sense of black uniqueness, his recurrent theme is the familiar American charge of victimization. What is remarkable is the way in which audiences sit still for their portion of guilt" (*Reimagining* 26). The patina of racial and critical chauvinism notwithstanding, the terms "victimization" and "guilt" deserve especial attention, for they exemplify the tendency of some critics to objectify black writing and consign it to the rubric of "victim literature," where it can be summarily dismissed.[9] Thus, Brustein and Baraka become strange bedfellows, for each critic's underlying assumption is that black art has as its primary object a white audience. In Barakan discourse, this cruel theater of victims should flay said audience; in Brustein's, the audience masochistically accepts the lashings.

I concur instead with Wilson's assertion that "I try not to portray any of my characters as victims" (Shannon, *Dramatic Vision* 222). Plays with black protagonists do not necessarily present a bifurcated view, with irredeemable white victimizers and infallible black victims. Wilson does not repudiate protest inasmuch as he depicts characters that may have experienced crushing racism. But while these experiences may spawn the dramatic action, the author is not obsessed with redress. I would take issue with the notion that Wilson's plays "continue and deepen the motif of facing the white man which Baraka developed so fully" (Rocha, "Four B's" 7). Instead, one might conclude that his works contain shreds of protest but are not subsumed by it; "facing" the ubiquitous "Man" is by no means their raison d'être.

To this end, Wilson decenters singular characters by dramatizing communities of black men in order to depict their various phases of identity formation. As Shannon argues, "Often depicted on the verge of an emotional breakdown, Levee [*Ma Rainey*], Herald Loomis [*Joe Turner's Come and Gone*], Troy Maxson [*Fences*], and Boy Willie [*The Piano Lesson*] dominate center stage and become Wilson's primary spokesmen" ("Good Christian's" 127). While some characters do maintain more crucial roles in the hierarchy of dramatic action, Wilson resists the discursive tendency to represent any singular figure as *the* sociocultural incarnation of the long-suffering black man. Seldom does he heap the burden of "spokesvictim" upon any singular protagonist, though inevitably certain characters, such as Troy Maxson in *Fences,* who experiences the insidious racism that pervades professional athletics, reflect the author's social sentiments.

In situating a panoply of black male voices in central roles, Wilson envelopes his plays with multiple perspectives to convey the multifaceted nature of post-1960s black male dramatic subjectivity, a discursive figuration far more complex than a simple replication of Anglo-American patriarchal subjectivity. Robert Vorlicky speaks to this shift in dramatic representations of the masculine in *Act Like a Man: Challenging Masculinities in American Drama:* "several contemporary American playwrights are confronting the assumptions that underlie the representation of male subjectivity. They are embracing the notion that the *asymmetries of gender affect the construction of male subjectivity,* resulting in a varied range of male identities when dramatizing men alone together" (3; emphasis added). Wilson's plays foreground multiple conceptions of gender that are often contradictory and conflicting.

However, the Baldwinian "ritual of intercourse" becomes his strategic blue-print for dramatic writing, and his primarily—though not exclusively—male communities become sites where the terms of subjectivity can be negotiat-ed and redefined. His characters cannot be categorized binarily as whole or psychically fragmented; there exist too many "asymmetries," too broad a range of masculinities. His characters' interactions reflect black men in the process of resituating themselves as individual and as communal subjects, in the process of "trying to find their songs."

Taken cumulatively, Wilson's men embark upon spiritual journeys into unexplored parts of themselves as well as their counterparts. Schematizing the melange of voices that populate his mise-en-scène, I offer the following paradigm of the Wilson subject:

1. The *mimetic* subject: This figure is physically present in his community but has misguidedly inculcated values that preclude emotional and spiritual bonds. This character often valorizes some aspect of a patriarchal masculini-ty: an obsession with economic independence and capitalistic values, an anachronistic, extramasculinized conceptualization of malehood rooted in violence and the objectification of women, or a debilitating belief that his subjectivity depends upon disproving/abrogating whites' depreciative mas-ter-narrative of black masculinity. Characters such as Levee in *Ma Rainey* and Floyd Barton in *Seven Guitars* (as well as Troy Maxson in *Fences*) exem-plify this discursive formation.

2. The *aggregate* subject: This character lays claim to subject status through communal ties—the psychological and emotional connection to people with whom he shares geographic space. This fusing of psychic space and physical place allows these protagonists to achieve a sense of community that traverses temporal or spatial boundaries. Connecting with other blacks across time and space is an essential part of these characters' understanding of their subjectivity. Men such as Cutler and Slow Drag in *Ma Rainey* and Canewell in *Seven Guitars* exemplify many of these traits.

3. The *inchoate* subject: This liminal character is betwixt and between the pre-vious configurations. Characters who fall under this category include Hedley in *Seven Guitars*. Such figures are often on the cusp of regeneration—or de-generation—and undergo some experience that alters their identities in the course of the play.

Of course, some characters may not be confined to the above categories or may embody characteristics of each, and the categories are not mutually exclusive; there is often overlap. But most significant is the scope of Wilson's depictions and his attempts to provide a panoramic representation of black men.

In effect, *Ma Rainey* and *Seven Guitars* (as well as *Joe Turner* and *Fences*, to which I will allude here but not discuss in depth) are structured around an imbrication of stories, intricately woven and related. At the vortex of Wilson's plays lies the performance principle, his deeply ingrained belief in the inspiriting and empowering possibilities of African and African-American vernacular, oral, and musical traditions in the reformation of the black male subject. Olaniyan's delineation of a "performative" identity illustrates why black vernacular culture is the sine qua non in investigations of Wilson's representation of black male subjectivity: "The performative . . . stresses the historicity of culture, that is, its 'made-ness' in space and time. . . . Identity in the performative conception is a *process* marked by endless negotiations. It is never closed or positive but always vulnerable, fragile" (30–31). Wilson depicts how the performative, in addition to being an organic process, requires a psychic and spiritual intermingling of self and others. To this end, musical performance, storytelling, story-listening, witnessing, and testifying represent authentic acts of cultural preservation, empowering acts of self-representation, and vehicles for collapsing emotional barriers black men erect between each other. These complex negotiations represent blues acts, the constant statement and restatement, articulation and signification that governs the characters' interactions and articulations of identity. Thus, the self's ability to "perform identity" in order to access its myriad possibilities becomes the cornerstone of Wilson's dramaturgy. Foremost, this mandatory act is a prerequisite for achieving communitas, which emblematizes male intimacy and connectedness. These performances become Wilson's recurrent formal strategy, one fashioned not around a series of linearly constructed events but around the sentient and multirhythmic blues voices that inhabit his drama-world.

The "Spooked" Bluesmen: The Thwarted Quest for Community in *Ma Rainey's Black Bottom*

Wilson's first Broadway play, *Ma Rainey's Black Bottom*, is emblematic, for he will continually return to the male artistic community to interrogate various facets of male subjectivity. This play presents a range of black men, encompassing all of the stages in my schematization of the Wilsonian subject. *Ma Rainey* chronicles the life of the 1920s blues icon and the recording industry's pandemic economic racism. *Ma Rainey* "dramatizes the production of blues race-records as a critique of commercial and racial exploitation of blacks by whites" (Smith, "*Ma Rainey's*" 177). When Ma Rainey expresses this exploitation as artistic and sexual defilement—"As soon as they [the white men conducting the recording session] get my voice down on them recording machines, then it's just like if I'd be some whore and they roll over and put their pants on" (64)—she speaks not only for Wilson but also for generations of black performers who were similarly bamboozled. But this seeming "protest" situation, which pits the fiercely independent Ma against the rapacious white record producers Sturdyvant and Irvin, is of less dramatic cogency than the play's rigorous examination of the internecine struggles among a cadre of African-American artists irrespective of white avarice. We must look beyond the dramatic scaffolding—the blatant critique of the recording industry—to locate the play's foundation: the male band members' tortured attempts to achieve spiritual and psychological connections among themselves.

The artists who make up Ma's band, Cutler, Levee, Toledo, and Slow Drag, are deformed to varying degrees and for myriad reasons: the inculcation of patriarchal masculinity; a preoccupation with hegemonic, market-based values; and the sanctioning of a hypermasculine ethos that locates violence and competition as part of men's genetic makeup. *Ma Rainey* evolves as a series of vignettes in which the male characters perform episodes from their lives. The play's multiple voicings and responses suggest a free jazz composition, where statements are made, reacted to, revised, reversed, and restated. Wilson departs from his usual dramatic strategy, given that *Ma Rainey* is not divided into scenes. His decision to use only act demarcations—the play consists of two acts—gives the work a jazz ambiance because the characters' voices respond emotively to each other. Wilson organizes the play around the layered telling and hearing of stories. As he points out, "What I tried to do in *Ma Rainey,* and in all my work, is to reveal the richness of the lives of the people, who show that the largest ideas are contained by their lives, and that there is a nobility to their lives" (Powers 52). The revelations of personal histories become the play's locus and central organizing device, more so than the overworked dramatic conceit of black victims versus white perpetrators.

Ma Rainey's quartet consists of Cutler, the group's leader, Toledo, a quasi Black Nationalist, Levee, a mercurial young artist manqué, and Slow Drag, the convivial pianist. The play, as Paul Carter Harrison notes, depicts "itinerant blues musicians in a rehearsal room engaged in the male ritual aggression of 'lyin' and signifyin'" while exchanging survival tales about coming and going in a hostile world, taunting each other with a contrapuntal—call 'n' response—choral configuration which presses them to the edge of physical confrontation" (306–7). Through the ceremonial process of testifying and witnessing, the bluesmen attempt to dismantle the barriers—whether erected by themselves or the larger society—that preclude community and contribute to black men's disaffection. And though the climactic violence would seem to place the play within the rubric of protest, the author's insistence on the curative and regenerative power of voicing history makes racial retribution more ancillary. Though physical violence punctuates the play, it cannot abrogate the insurmountable power of even a single voice in this gathering of male artists.

The title is both rhetorical and metaphorical. "Bottom" could be interpreted as an addendum to Clay's climactic aria in *Dutchman,* where he interprets Bessie Smith's coded admonition to whites to "kiss my black ass." "Bottom" has multiple connotations in the black literary canon. In the context of this play, the bottom is concretized by the "band room," the space the musicians most frequently occupy, "in the basement of the building" below the recording studio. Though this room may symbolize the band members' low rank on the socioeconomic totem pole, space takes on a metaphorical meaning, representing a potentially regenerative realm, a site that inaugurates the storytelling rituals. In terms of the gender-space nexus, Vorlicky raises a salient point about what he labels "male-cast" plays:

> It is precisely when American men are in institutional settings of confinement, and to a lesser extent in workplaces, that the likelihood of their self-expression— or their self-disclosure—increases. By self-disclosure I mean something almost wholly contained within the realm of language: an individualization that overcomes the restrictions of cultural coding, in particular the powerful masculine ethos, but an individualization wholly manifested in the characters' articulation of personal truths. (6–7)

This comment speaks to the tropic function of setting, where speech acts potentially animate healing and communion. Just as the prison in *A Lesson before Dying* stimulated Grant's and Jefferson's self-disclosures and their subsequent emotional-spiritual union, so too does the band room stimulate the interior psychic and historical journeys upon which the characters embark. The black male stories Wilson creates are alternatively comical, scatological, and tragic. Collectively, they bespeak the vastness of black male interiority, and the telling and hearing of them dramatizes the valuable though tenuous nature of community.

Storytelling in the play catalyzes spiritual connections and exposes the gulf that often separates black men who share common physical places but not psychic space. One story-performance that marks the constructive and reformative potential of voice is Cutler's rendition of the way Slow Drag acquired his name. Though Slow Drag refuses the invitation to recite the story himself, Cutler becomes his surrogate and weaves for the other men a ribald anecdote steeped in the blues, replete with music, sex, competition, violence, and survival.

According to Cutler, Slow Drag earned his name at a competition for the "best slow draggers." He "looked over the competition, got down off the bandstand, grabbed hold of one of them gals, and stuck to her like a fly to jelly" (45). When the woman's knife-wielding lover threatened him, "Slow Drag just looked over the gal's shoulder at the man and said, 'Mister, if you'd quit hollering and wait a minute . . . you'll see I'm doing you a favor. I'm helping this gal win ten dollars so she can buy you a gold watch.' The man just stood there and looked at him, all the while stroking that knife. Told Slow Drag, say, 'Alright, then, nigger. You just better make damn sure you win.' That's when folks started calling him Slow Drag" (45; author's ellipsis). This humorous episode is also a microcosm of the play: the dance, like the story-telling ritual, is an authentic cultural practice that potentially fosters communal ties; simultaneously, however, it portends doom when the specters of financial and sexual competition are introduced. Cutler doesn't tell a complete, self-contained story, because the resolution of his blues riff is much less significant than the act of performing it. The retelling of this story marks the blossoming of a speech community, a site where black men's voices are not bound by the strictures imposed by Anglo-American culture. Wilson conjures the image of Zora Neale Hurston's Janie Crawford, who entrusts her story to her "kissin' friend," Phoebe: "'You can tel 'em what Ah say if you wants to. Dat's just de same as me 'cause mah tongue is in mah friend's mouf'" (9). Through the ritual retelling of his story, Slow Drag's tongue, like Janie's, is figuratively in Cutler's "mouf," his story metamorphosing into blues literally and metaphorically. Just as Hurston casts black women's speech acts as a celebratory form of sisterhood and as an act of resistance, Wilson depicts black men as brothers who are experientially, psychically, and historically bound. This ritualistic story-performance, as a tale told, retold, and re-created, embodies the play's overall jazz contours and sensibilities.

Cutler's centrality as a griotic figure is borne out not only in his insouciant recollection of Slow Drag's naming but also during his bracing tale about "Reverend Gates," a figure not present in the play but whose dehumanizing experience Cutler vividly re-creates. At this moment, he becomes a cultural custodian and conduit, for he presides over the stories about black men's lives irrespective of geographic or temporal boundaries. Reminiscent of Reverend Homer Barbee's resonant sermon and the Invisible Man's address on the dispossessed,[10] Cutler's "invocation" recalls the black preacher, who establishes a call-and-response relationship with his audience: "I'm gonna tell you something. Reverend Gates . . . you know Reverend Gates? . . . Slow Drag know who I'm talking about. Reverend Gates . . . now I'm gonna show you how this go where the white man don't care a thing about who you is" (78–79; author's ellipses). This prelude links Cutler to a black sermonic tradition, where the speaker piques the congregation's interest by delaying information and employing certain rhetorical flourishes.[11] In setting the stage for his performance, Cutler satisfies what the story theorist Livia Polanyi deems the "burden of making the relevance of the telling clear" (21). Unlike Toledo, Cutler intuitively gauges his audience because he is culturally and cosmically embedded in its vernacular and customs.

Though he embroiders a disquieting tale of how a group of white men forced Reverend Gates to dance for their sadistic pleasure (a stark reversal of his comic "Slow Drag" anecdote), most crucial is the reception of Cutler's story by men who share his emotional space. Slow Drag offers intermittent affirmative responses, while Toledo "witnesses" by adding, "You don't even have to tell me no more. I know the facts of it. I done heard the same story a hundred times. It happened to me too. Same thing" (80). While Eileen Crawford argues that the men "discuss in their many moving stories their suffering and tribulations, these narratives, in essence, must be seen as rituals of complaint directed primarily *at* the white man" (42), it is significant that the bonds forged here are not based solely on common discriminatory experiences. Instead, they are produced by the amalgam of men telling stories, listening to, inspiring, and affirming each other's voices. When Cutler asserts the tale's veracity—"Reverend Gates sat right in my house and told me that story from his own mouth" (81)—we get a vivid idea of what Wilson himself envisioned when he articulated the organic power of storytelling: "If you're going to tell someone a story, and if you want to keep information alive, you have to make it memorable so that the person hearing it will go tell someone else. This is how it stays alive" (Moyers 168). The stories Wilson's black men impart transmit their mutual histories, as the playwright demonstrates that these narratives are integral to the ritual process of reconstructing black male subjectivity.

Given the layered story-voicings that constitute the play's central action, I take issue with the notion that Toledo represents the play's "singular choral figure, an unofficial griot or chronicler of the collective history" (Harrison 308). He represents the unmediated Black Nationalist voice, evinced by his Clay-esque soliloquy on why blacks are the "leftovers" of an oppressive white history (47). But whereas Toledo's pseudointellectual culinary analogy puts him at odds with the other band members—he derides them for misinterpreting his esoteric racial analyses—Cutler's stories speak definitively to the experiences the men share in a language they comprehend. Hence, he closely resembles what I have delineated as the aggregate subject, a figure who valorizes and immortalizes black men's past and present individual life-stories and re-creates them within a communal, affirming milieu.

However, the relationship between speakers and hearers isn't completely harmonious, for Levee represents a disruptive presence throughout the play. For instance, when Cutler is preparing his audience for his "Reverend Gates" story, Levee constantly challenges him over picayune details such as a train's itinerary: "You can stop telling that right there! That train don't stop in Sigsbee" (79). Unlike the other men, Levee is antagonistic throughout the storytelling event, foreshadowing his murder of Toledo and the psychological implosion that follows. By contesting minute facts of Cutler's tale, Levee fails to grasp the larger truths, not merely the repugnant treatment meted out to Reverend Gates but the importance of hearing and affirming the voices of other black men. He discounts their words, thereby replicating the white record producers' protracted devaluation of the black musicians; Levee and Sturdyvant patronizingly refer to them as "boys" throughout the recording session. Wilson casts Levee as an inveterately discordant voice that undermines the liberating potential of the burgeoning speech community, thereby portending the character's psychic degeneration at the play's conclusion.

As Levee's central role in the storytelling and listening evinces, there exists no hierarchy of voices and stories in the play. On the contrary, Wilson democratically grants each character an opportunity to speak his own reality. Though openly contemptuous of his fellow musicians' stories, Levee also has the opportunity to relate a life-altering experience, one that might explain his volatile and subsequently anticommunal behavior. At the conclusion of the first act, he delivers a Wrightian southern gothic story that not only demonstrates whites' searing hatred of blacks but the scars that such hatred leaves on the black body and psyche. Recalling an experience in Natchez, Mississippi, when he was only eight years old, Levee reveals the sexual and economic violence whites perpetrated in response to his father's business acumen. After his father declares young Levee "man of the house" before departing to buy farming supplies, Levee witnesses the barbarous gang rape of his mother by white men. Despite his futile attempts to defend her, one of the men "reached back and grabbed hold of that knife and whacked me across the chest with it" (57). Afterwards, his father devises a plan in which he resettles his family while feigning acceptance of his wife's violation. Refusing to go quietly, he embarks on a reconnaissance mission: he returns to avenge the rape by hiding in the woods and waiting for the perpetrators. Though his father is lynched in the ensuing battle, Levee divulges that he "got four of him before they got him" (58). While the attempt to defend his mother leaves a scar across his chest, the emotional wounds traumatize Levee as an adult. To make whites pay for his irreparable psychic scars, he vows to sell his songs to white record producers by engaging in obsequious behavior. Levee apparently hopes to parlay the mask that grins and lies into a monetary reward borne from his parents' blood.[12]

However, his means of salving his pain and avenging a racially violent childhood are severely wrongheaded, rendering him a mimetic subject—one determined to define himself within the constricting construct of patriarchal masculinity. Levee's childhood is a potential hotbed of Freudian hermeneutics: his psychological castration, the unresolved Oedipal complex, his lingering distrust of black men. Almost inevitably, his adulthood is burdened by the sins of fathers, both white and black. Thus his blues becomes not the jagged grain that sustains but a weight that encumbers his reconnection to other black people. Peter Middleton's comments on the role of oppression in male subject formation shed further light on Levee's psychosocial trauma: "Oppression confers an identity. For members of an oppressed group to recognize that they are oppressed is crucial, because that is the moment when they perceive that their experience is not the result of their own specific nature or the nature of the world, but the result of an alterable state of things (however difficult change might be in practical terms)" (146). Hence, Levee's life is subsumed by an inviolable narrative of oppression—his perpetual view of himself as a victim of an insurmountable white patriarchy. However, he does not view his situation as "alterable"; instead of challenging the pathological patriarchal masculinity that led to his mother's rape and father's lynching, Levee inculcates that pathology, which contributes to his devaluation of self.

Moreover, his adoption of a hypermasculine mindset leads him to view women as conquests, perhaps a reaction to his childhood psychological emasculation. Though Cutler warns him that she is "Ma's gal," Levee pursues Dussie Mae, claiming that the projected windfall from his songwriting will allow him to provide gifts far more lavish than those she receives from Ma. This becomes the most perverted form of mediated desire, since Levee's pursuit of Dussie Mae is fueled by competition. In addition to seeing Ma as a sexual opponent, Levee views her as an ersatz white male who thwarts his artistic endeavors (e.g., when Ma proclaims that the band will perform her version of "Black Bottom," not Levee's). Incarnating the mimetic subject, Levee harbors a distorted conceptualization of subjectivity, one garnered through material accoutrements and sexual spoils.

Throughout the play, Levee's relationship with Ma Rainey amplifies his conflicted definition of masculinity. Because she maintains a limited degree of power in her dealings with white men, he casts her as an adversary. Whether it be his insistence that the band play his version of "Black Bottom" or his pursuit of Dussie Mae, Levee views Ma as an obstacle on his road to self-elevation. In a modified form of plantation politics, he envisions Ma as a Mammy figure, an operative of the white power structure. For Levee to gain access to culturally sanctioned definitions of masculinity, her authority and voice must be neutralized. A fictive descendent of Bigger Thomas, Levee elevates black women to the position of faux white men, the gatekeepers of masculine privilege. In a bizarre conflation, he simultaneously loathes and emulates black women because they wield power even within the white patriarchy—evinced by Ma's behavior. Simultaneously, however, he devalues women by reducing them to objects of male sexual domination—hence his objectification of Dussie Mae. Deposing and possessing the ersatz white men, black women, enables Levee to revise and correct the childhood tragedy that reduced him to an invisible, powerless spectator and object-victim.

Though I have focused primarily on Wilson's representations of black men and the tenuous nature of community, Levee's interactions with Ma emphasize her essential role in the play. Wilson immerses her within the black male community through her masculine persona: she brazenly loud-talks and curses white men (record producers and policemen alike), she flaunts her lesbianism, and she freely interacts with the men in the band. In a memorable scene with Cutler, she castigates white producers for "raping" her economically and claims the blues as blacks' cultural and epistemological property whose true meaning, she insists, will forever elude whites. Wilson's fictive reincarnation of the blues legend blurs and subsequently shatters gender boundaries and constructions. In fact, the men would have done well to emulate her behavior instead of confining themselves to provincial notions of male subjectivity. The most conspicuous examples of this include Levee's frequent challenges to others' voices, his fight with Cutler over religion (in the latter portion of act two), and, most catastrophically, his murder of Toledo at the play's end.

Only during the instances of storytelling or musical performance do the male musicians begin to break out of their debilitating notions of masculinity. One particularly effusive example occurs early in the play. Waiting for the ever-tardy Ma to arrive at the recording session, the men dispute whether they will record her or Levee's version of "Ma Rainey's Black Bottom." Cutler then decides to have the band practice "Hear Me Talking to You" and instructs Slow Drag to "sing Ma's part," which opens thusly:

Rambling man makes no change in me
I'm gonna ramble back to my used-to-be
Ah, you hear me talking to you
I don't bite my tongue
You wants to be my man
You got to fetch it with you when you come. (27)

The title and lyrics of this blues abound with gendered connotations. The title underscores the play's concern not merely with the importance of speaking one's self but the necessity of having an audience participate in the "talking" by actively listening; Wilson considers this dynamic a fundamental dimension of the blues. This cultural performance is made more valuable and instructive by the performer himself. Wilson's substitution of Slow Drag for Ma blurs the gender boundaries that the men otherwise hold unimpeachable; the name Slow Drag comically corroborates this.[13] Slow Drag's performance of the song alters its meaning substantially. No longer a woman's assertion of verbal and sexual dominance, Slow Drag's rendition of "Hear Me Talking to You" restates the play's central concern: the conditions and difficulties surrounding black male intimacy and community. The performative realm thus represents a potentially transgendering space where black men can flout the dictates of normative masculinity that forbid even nonsexual intimacy among men, race notwithstanding.

Given the paucity of "blues moments" like Slow Drag's performance or Cutler's tragic-comic tales, *Ma Rainey* might leave the impression that black men are perpetually relegated to lives of abuse and oppression; the denouement ostensibly seems to corroborate such a conclusion. Like *Dutchman*, the play ends with an act of paroxysmal violence: Levee stabs Toledo because Toledo "stepped on my shoe with them raggedy-ass clodhoppers!" (92). However, the source of Levee's discontent is not the soiling of his cherished shoes but another crushing defeat: Sturdyvant, the more hostile of the two white record producers, refuses to listen to several songs he has composed and "takes them off [Levee's] hands" for a paltry five dollars. But Wilson moves beyond defining black male subjectivity as being overdetermined by economic exploitation. The predominantly white recording industry irrefutably has a long and shameful history of defrauding black artists; thus, Wilson does not have to dwell on this point. From a sociological standpoint, what has putatively come to be known as "black-on-black violence" would offer one plausible though facile explanation for the murder. Such an interpretation would situate the play securely in the shopworn category of protest drama, the requisite thesis being that whites are incorrigibly evil and that blacks are the powerless objects of their diabolical maneuvers who respond by mutilating each other.

However, in terms of the play's emphasis on black men's communal rituals and interactions, the murder is a part of a wider anthropological context that goes beyond a parochially racial one. Rene Girard has examined the etiology of violence, concluding that "When unappeased, violence seeks and always finds a *surrogate victim.* The creature that excited its fury is abruptly replaced by another, chosen only because it is vulnerable and close at hand" (2; emphasis added). In this context, violence involves a series of displacements and replacements that are not inherently racial. Perhaps Levee murders Toledo not premeditatedly but because he hastily finds in Toledo a substitute for Sturdyvant. Levee's action may therefore be as much the result of transference and convenience as the result of any racial animus. Thus Wilson's conclusion invites alternatives to jejune discussions of black male "pathology," a popular calumny at a moment when warehousing black men has become a lucrative practice and is seen as a necessary remedy to stem the black male "menace."

Because Levee's murder of Toledo engenders his own spiritual and emotional death,[14] it is significant that Cutler and Slow Drag survive and will likely perpetuate the vernacular rituals that promote communal intercourse. Unlike Levee and Toledo, who are haunted by and obsessed with white male hegemony, Slow Drag and Cutler embody the power of storytelling and blues as liberating rituals in black men's attempts to define or negotiate alternative vehicles for subjectivity. The play's violent conclusion does not undermine its central point: black men maintain the ability to deliver each other from a state of deformation, an asphyxiating realm where so many have perished. Though *Ma Rainey's Black Bottom* may appear to be a treatise on the wages of economic and racial violence as well as black men's destructive responses to oppression, it traverses the tradition of black masculinist protest literature. Its tiered[15] structure allows Wilson to subvert the requirements of realistic and protest drama by centering not how whites "pimp" black art but by interlarding the play with black men "performing self" in ways that are potentially regenerative and healing. Though Cutler and Slow Drag do not represent a thriving male artistic or vernacular community, they embody black men's potential to locate within each other their nascent blues voices.

As is his dramatic signature, Wilson presents an array of subjectivities in *Ma Rainey's Black Bottom.* Levee, the mimetic subject who wrongheadedly adopts the same values that led to his parents' deaths, may haunt us as an irremediably tragic figure. Aggregate subjects like Cutler and Slow Drag survive him, however. Their voices, linking black men's experiences through time and space, reverberate as the invaluable "bottom" that moors blues people like Ma Rainey. The often devalued internal lives of black men may appear ancillary, but they are invariably essential—the blackness of blackness. In *Seven Guitars*, Wilson returns to the male artistic community to probe black men's arduous struggle to reposition themselves as subjects.

"You Don't Never Get the Full Story"?: The Perils and Pleasures of Communal Living in *Seven Guitars*

Despite the twelve-year gap between the Broadway premiers of *Ma Rainey's Black Bottom* and *Seven Guitars*, one can easily discern why they might be considered companion pieces. Like its predecessor, *Seven Guitars* foregrounds an assemblage of musicians who work tirelessly to forge spiritual and emotional ties. Another quartet of men engages in myriad performances attempting to voice individual and collective experiences. As is his common dramatic strategy, Wilson locates music as the lens through which he explores black male subjectivity. Moreover, racial oppression and black victimology are not the play's driving forces, underscored by the fact that Wilson uses basically the same agon: a black blues artist is shamelessly commodified, though the perpetrators of this exploitation are not a part of the play's dramatic action. The dramatist underplays protest and instead utilizes his dramatic space to probe the inner lives of his protagonists, who struggle to define their subjectivity. Contrary to one character's declaration that "you don't never get the full story," Wilson attempts to sketch a composite story-portrait of black men in *Seven Guitars*.

Like the spooked bluesmen of *Ma Rainey*, the artistic collective in *Guitars* is marked by its communal impulses and marred by an adherence to paralyzing and anachronistic constructions of subjectivity. Especially noteworthy is the sense of a cosmological male community, as Wilson's characters frequently invoke historical, artistic, and mythic icons, thereby illustrating that black men's attempts to commune transcend time and space. The play poses several trenchant questions: Why are black men's relationships governed by an adherence to hegemonic values and mores? Can confining constructions of gender be vanquished? Or are black men who inhabit common physical ground doomed by a sort of collective entropy, an inexplicable but inexorable predilection for self-destructive behavior? And finally, how do cultural performances become modes of resistance that empower black men to move from a subjectivity that is mimetic (Levee) to one that is more expansive, inclusive, and collective? *Seven Guitars* becomes the dramatic coun-

tersign for *Ma Rainey*, for it reiterates the revivifying effects of male cama-
raderie as well as the self-destructive impulses that hasten the implosion of
scores of black men.

Seven Guitars opens with six friends of the blues singer Floyd Barton returning from his funeral and commemorating his life through stories and
music. While the details surrounding Floyd's death are withheld until the
play's end, its hows and whys are of less importance than the internecine
conflicts between Floyd and those closest to him: his former lover Vera, the
band members Red Carter and Canewell, and his friend Hedley, who is originally from Haiti. The play retrospectively explores Floyd's life in relation to
these three men and three women. Though Wilson deemed *Seven Guitars* a
"murder mystery" (Shannon, *Dramatic* 229), this is somewhat a misnomer.
The author himself hints at this when he states, "you then have to look at
Floyd in whatever relations he is having with anybody in the play" (229). I
interpret *Seven Guitars* less as a prototypical whodunit than as a drama chart-
ing men's attempts to connect and the seemingly insurmountable obstacles
that hinder them. The play unfurls as an examination of competing ideolo-
gies, spawned by Floyd's ill-conceived idea of subjectivity and the conflicting attitudes of those around him. An array of different types of performances, *Seven Guitars* more closely resembles a Bearden collage than a
murder mystery. The mystery genre, with its requisite plot convolutions and
emphasis on action and suspense, is far too prescriptive and confining given
the play's multidiscursive framework.

As one of the play's two strongly ideological figures, Floyd "Schoolboy"
Barton has internalized the mythological narrative of Anglo-American male
selfhood: the ardent belief that any man can parlay hard work and individual talent into success. Like Ben Franklin's black fictive heirs Invisible Man
and Walter Lee Younger, he espouses a Panglossian belief in "opportunity,"
a word he frequently invokes to describe why he must return to Chicago by
any means necessary to record another "hit" for a white recording label. A
distinctly masculinized ethos informs Floyd's ontology and epistemology: he
has served time in prison and the armed services, two institutions historically entrenched in oppressive constructions of black maleness.[16] Think for
instance of the conclusion of Chester Himes's *If He Hollers Let Him Go*, in
which Bob Jones is given two "choices": to serve jail time because of a white
woman's spurious rape charge or to enlist in the army during the Second
World War. Hence, as confining spaces within a fiercely hegemonic culture,
these institutions reify black men's psychic imprisonment and devitalization.

Through these male-dominated venues, Wilson emphasizes Floyd's self-
deluding belief in the American Dream. In fact, this may elucidate Wilson's

choice of name: "Schoolboy" suggests a naive adherence to America's hollow promise that material prosperity is available to all. His insatiable desire for material accoutrements mediates all of his relationships. Floyd expresses these sentiments frequently, first when he recalls meeting Vera, whom he spurned but still desires:

> I had just got out the army. They give me forty-seven dollars. Adjustment allowance or something like that. I come on up Logan Street and I seen you. That's why I always say I had a pocket full of money when I met you. I seen you and said, "there go a woman." . . . My hands got to itching and seem like I didn't know what to do with them. I put them in my pocket and felt them forty-seven dollars . . . that thirty-eight under my coat . . . and I got up my nerve to say something to you. You remember that? Seem like that was a long time ago. (12; author's ellipses)

Floyd's recollections suggest a tainted conception of masculinity, one that objectifies women while fetishizing money and guns. This fetishism and objectification epitomize the supreme patrinarrative, a fiction that black men have willingly inherited from their white counterparts. In a subsequent paean to Chicago, he tells Canewell:

> I'm going there to take advantage of the opportunity. I'm gonna put out some more records. I know what will make a hit record. I leave here on the Greyhound and I bet you in one year's time I be back driving a Buick. Might even have a Cadillac. If you come visit me you be able to use my telephone. I'm gonna have everything. Some nice furniture. The white man ain't the only one can have a car and nice furniture. Nice clothes. It take a fool to sit around and don't want nothing. I ain't no fool. It's out there for somebody it may as well be out there for me. If Vera go up there with me and she don't like it, I'll send her back. But at least she will have the chance to see the opportunities. (80)

In Floyd's value system, the urban North becomes the black Mecca that offers material if not spiritual fulfillment. Using white American men's markers for success as his benchmark, he desires these possessions primarily because they have ascribed them value. In his schematization, Vera becomes another adornment who can be transported or discarded at will. In essence, Floyd adopts a patriarchal black masculinity that is as pernicious as its white counterpart. Like his dramatic predecessor Levee, Schoolboy represents the mimetic subject, for he privileges similar conceptions of masculinity that will induce his psychic and physical demise.

Consistent with his proclivity toward commodification, Floyd's attitudes about art reflect his distorted notions of manhood. The modus operandi of

Floyd's predecessor, Ma Rainey, is worth revisiting. Though one could argue that she allows herself to be compromised and exploited, she nevertheless understands her devaluation. As if she were heeding Dr. Bledsoe's advice to the neophyte Invisible Man, Ma becomes a distaff version of the trickster who knowingly plays the game and manipulates the rules in order to exercise at least nominal agency. By controlling the conditions under which her voice will be recorded, and by also employing sass and invective as modes of resistance, Ma Rainey wields a substantial amount of power in the art-commodity nexus. Floyd, however, gullibly assumes that a sort of laissez-faire capitalism will reward him while also allowing him to maintain economic autonomy. Wilson aptly names him: as "Barton" euphonically suggests, he barters his voice, maniacally attempting to parlay his talents into profits for Savoy Records.[17] Though Wilson's symbolism here is somewhat turgid, the fact that Floyd's guitar remains "in pawn" for the play's duration emblematizes Floyd's role in the compromising and objectifying of his artistic voice. His obsessive attempt to peddle his talents leads ultimately to his psychic implosion, for he will subsequently rob a bank and physically threaten Canewell. He, like many male protagonists, willingly swallows the argot of the American Dream and the attendant mythic Anglo-American male self-creation story.

Wilson foregrounds an array of male characters who serve as countervoices to Floyd's hopelessly credulous one. Throughout *Seven Guitars,* Canewell represents one such voice. As his name suggests, he personifies a Toomerian southern ethos that Wilson insists must remain an abiding part of black life regardless of one's geographic location. The perils of northern exposure are painfully illuminated when Canewell recalls his imprisonment in Chicago's Cook County jail for singing and playing his harmonica on the street: "I said, 'If I'm gonna stand here and play I may as well throw my hat down . . . somebody might put something in it.' The police said I was disturbing the peace. Soliciting without a license. Loitering. Resisting arrest and disrespecting the law. They rolled all that together and charged me with laziness and give me thirty days. I ain't going back up there" (23; author's ellipsis). In Canewell's dissenting opinion, Chicago becomes a black man's no-man's-land, a place that criminalizes not merely the black man's artistic voice but his very being. His subsequent sequestration and silencing lay bare the risks black men undertake when attempting to convert their art into profit without the backing of the puissant white recording industry.

Wilson's depiction of Chicago as inimical to black subjectivity is a discursive pattern in black literature. The city represents the spiritual, emotional, or actual sepulchre for countless protagonists—Bigger Thomas, Lutie Johnson, and Walter Younger Jr. and Sr. come immediately to mind. Throughout the play it is metamorphosed into more than a physical environment. Characters superimpose their most cherished desires upon it until it represents a psychic as much as a geographic space—their psychological Canada. Though his plays are not pastorals in which the city emblematizes social and personal disintegration, Wilson's representation of Chicago as the black man's dystopia dovetails with other black dramatists' portrayals of the urban milieu. As Robert Tener observes, "One of the major views of the fictive city to emerge in the decade of the sixties in African-American drama is that it is no place to be somebody. For those fictional blacks who appear in the plays of Ed Bullins, Amiri Baraka (LeRoi Jones), Charles Gordone, Adrienne Kennedy, and Lorraine Hansberry, the soul has apparently gone out of the city, its structures, and even its streets, producing a demonic world" (236). Canewell's denunciation has its antecedents, as his voice and experiences contradict Floyd's halcyon vision of the city. Thus, Canewell functions as Wilson's spokesman, voicing the playwright's ardent belief that "if we [African Americans] had stayed in the South, we would have been a stronger people" (Rothstein 8).[18]

An even more prominent countervoice, Hedley is simultaneously Floyd's nemesis and doppelganger; their relationship clearly parallels Toledo and Levee's. As a vendor who hawks everything from cigarettes to chicken sandwiches, Hedley ostensibly possesses an economic autonomy that eludes Floyd. Though Wilson does not specify the character's birthplace, his speech patterns and dialect suggest a Haitian origin; this is supported later in the play by his reverential memories of the Haitian revolutionary Touissaint L'Ouverture. Hedley's identity is a veritable callaloo: a Haitian who embodies the mythic, self-made Anglo-American male in economic terms, he castigates the West generally and white men specifically. Fiercely oppositional, he practices a syncretic religion that encompasses Rastafarianism, voodoo, and a distinctly Afrocentric form of Christianity. Hedley melds his polytheism with an impassioned, Diasporan nationalism, fervently exalting the legacies of Marcus Garvey and L'Ouverture. On the surface, at least, his is a corrective voice, one that punctures the shibboleths of Western/American male subjectivity to which Floyd adheres.

Despite these differences, both characters are bound because they imbue white men with the power and authority they so passionately crave. In Toledo's words, they are "spooked up with the white men" (*Ma Rainey* 55). Haunted by memories of dispossession and powerlessness, Hedley seeks redress for whites' colonization of his homeland. For instance, he rhapsodizes about owning a plantation, a place where "the white man not going to tell me what to do" (24). His "white man's disease," perhaps symbolized by the tuberculosis that afflicts him, becomes more chronic as the play progresses; hence, there is a tangible connection between his physical deterioration and his psychic obsession with avenging a multitude of white transgressions. Hedley's ruminations recall other psychically maimed men in Wilson's oeuvre—for instance, Gabriel in *Fences* and Hambone in *Two Trains Running*—whose life-altering encounters with whites prove catastrophic:

> Everybody say Hedley crazy cause he black. Because he know the place of the black man is not at the foot of the white man's boot. Maybe it is not all right in my head sometimes. Because I don't like the world. I don't like what I see from the people. The people is too small. *I always want to be a big man. Like Jesus Christ was a big man. He was the Son of the Father.* I too. I am the son of my father. Maybe Hedley never going to be big like that. But for himself inside . . . that place where you live your own special life . . . I would be happy to be big there. And maybe my child, if it be a boy, *he would be big like Moses.* I think about that. *Somebody have to be the father of the man to lead the black man out of bondage.* Marcus Garvey have a father. Maybe if I could not be like Marcus Garvey then I could be the father of someone who would not bow down to the white man. Maybe I could be the father of the messiah. I am fifty-nine years old and my time is running out. Hedley is looking for a woman to lie down with and make his first baby. Maybe . . . Maybe you [Ruby] be that woman for me. Maybe we both be blessed. (67–68; emphasis added)

This eruption buttresses the notion that Hedley functions as the play's "slightly deranged and misunderstood conscience" (Shannon, "Transplant" 663) and renders Hedley what I delineated as a mimetic and inchoate subject.

However, aside from the mental disorientation suggested by his copious second-person references, Hedley's belief system is deeply flawed. Envisioning whites as the incarnation of evil, he fashions himself as a neo-Garveyite. That he cannot effect change, however, makes him a quasi race man and thereby compounds his frustration and psychic disintegration. As a result, a sort of race neurosis sets in because he ascribes to whites such impenetrable power and authority. Moreover, by invoking Moses and Christ, Hedley emulates venerated icons of Anglo-male religious authority—a glaring contradiction in his conceptualization of whites as evil that recalls Gabriel Grimes's infelicitous preachments in Baldwin's *Go Tell It on the Mountain*. His biblical desire for a line of heirs is the zenith of hegemonic male privilege. Stated another way, Hedley's inculcation of archetypal forms of patriarchal masculinity is exposed by his obsession with fathering a race as a bulwark against white oppression. Wilson foregrounds the shortcomings in Hedley's Sutpenian design, one glaring problem being the ecclesiastical preference for male children and the belief that women exist merely as the vessels through which this royal line is sired. Like Floyd Barton, Hedley envisions black male subjectivity as an inverted form of its white counterpart, a replication of a historically and categorically malignant construct.

Wilson's characterization of Hedley dramatizes the pitfalls of and links between cultural domination and identity formation: the sociopolitical colonization of his Caribbean homeland leaves him mentally colonized, reified in his fixation on white male hegemonic privilege as the foundation of black subjectivity. Not surprisingly, this fixation begets not only a sense of alienation among his compatriots but, more profoundly, a cosmological disconnection. Throughout this study, I have argued that the communal resituation of black men physically and emotionally has a curative effect; "Sonny's Blues" and *A Lesson before Dying* attest to the empowering and liberating potential of community. Conversely, however, Hedley's psychohistorical and multiethnic male triumvirate, consisting of Jesus, Moses, and Marcus Garvey, paralyzes him and impedes his psychological development—his attempt to become an aggregate subject. Despite their veneration and historical import, all of these figures personify a masculine power and privilege that Hedley mistakenly valorizes and emulates.

Though teetering on the precipice of psychic decomposition, Hedley reveres male historical figures who form a personal, cultural, and religious godhead. Recalling a boyhood experience in Haiti in which his teacher berated him for being a "black-as-sin nigger" who will never live up to L'Ouverture's legacy, he ruminates:

I go home and my daddy he sitting there and he big and black and tired taking care of the white man's horses, and I say, "How come you not like Toussaint L'Ouverture, why you do nothing?" *And he kick me with him boot in my mouth. I shut up that day,* you know, and then when Marcus Garvey come *he give me back my voice to speak.* It was on my father's deathbed, with Death standing there, I say to him, "Father, I sorry about Toussaint L'Ouverture, Miss Manning say nobody ever amount to nothing and I never did again try. Then Marcus Garvey come and say that it was not true and that she lied and I forgive you kick me and I hope as God is with us now but a short time more that you forgive me my tongue." It was hard to say these things, but I confess my love for my father and Death standing there say, "I already took him a half hour ago." . . . So I dragged him with me these years across an ocean. Then my father come to me in a dream and he say he was sorry he died without forgiving me my tongue and that he would send Buddy Bolden [a blues singer to whom he refers throughout the course of the play] with some money for me to buy a plantation. *Then I get the letter from the white man* who come to take me away. So I say, "Hedley, be smart, go and see Joe Roberts." We sat and talked man to man. Joe Roberts is a nice man. I told him about Toussaint L'Ouverture and my father and Joe Roberts smile and he say he had something to give me. And he give to me this (*He takes out a machete that is wrapped in his burlap apron, crosses over, and sits on his stool*). (86–87; emphasis added)

Hedley becomes part of a coterie of Wilson tragic heroes for whom community remains a desired but elusive goal. Reminiscent of Troy Maxson (*Fences*) and Herald Loomis (*Joe Turner's Come and Gone*), he is burdened by the sins of biological and historical black fathers and omnipotent, vindictive white ones. And like Schoolboy Barton, he invests white men's words (his reception of the letter marking a repetition of an earlier scene in which Floyd received a patronizing letter from the president of Savoy Records) with the power to transform him into a sovereign, empowered subject. After Hedley happens upon some money that Floyd has stolen, he assumes it is the same money he dreamed that his father would bequeath him. That he slashes Floyd's throat is a sadly logical conclusion: the two men most enamored with the emblems of patriarchal privilege—money, property, women, male heirs—in effect suffer the same fate. While Floyd's death is a physical one, Hedley's is emotional and spiritual. In Wilson's dramatic configuration, Hedley and Floyd are Levee's descendents: they apotheosize distorted forms of male subjectivity, thereby doing irreparable damage to themselves and other black men.

Seven Guitars as Intertextual Blues

Though *Ma Rainey* and *Seven Guitars* end violently, Wilson is not validating the culturally sanctioned image of the feral black male. To counter his depiction of maimed black men, the dramatist often portrays ritualized performance to display alternative forms of black manhood. He often employs music and sports as "performances" that enable black men to move beyond cramping constructions of masculinity. *Seven Guitars* maintains a distinct intertextual dimension as Wilson recasts, reverses, and revises crucial scenes from Baldwin and Ellison. This artistic signifying accentuates the work's self-reflexivity, for the dramatist's aesthetic practices reiterate the play's core concerns about the power of black men's interactions. In other words, the curative potential of the gender-specific male community that these performances demonstrate is evidenced by Wilson's invocation of his literary forefathers' legacies. Their inspiriting voices reverberate throughout his artistic production, though he expands and iterates the centrality of performance in black men's identity formation.

Unlike the linearly configured well-made play, *Seven Guitars* contains multiple types of verbal and musical utterances that go beyond dialogue and the development of plot. At the literal center of the play lie two primarily (but not exclusively) masculinized performances—an impromptu blues/gospel sing-along and a boxing match. In the first, Wilson uses "Sonny's Blues" as an intertext to convey the value of gendered cultural performance and the ancestral wisdom available to black men willing to take the journey back. This performance precedes a re-enactment of a Joe Louis fight that centers not the fight itself but the characters' responses to it. Just as Ishmael Reed formally and thematically "tropes" *Invisible Man* in *Mumbo Jumbo,* Wilson revises the "Battle Royal" by dramatizing the potentially regenerative aspects of a historically dehumanizing ritual. That characters such as Hedley recall Ellison's redoubtable Ras the Exhorter subtly suggests that *Seven Guitars* is a tour de force in signifying.

Wilson's revisiting and revising of these two male literary ancestors' texts, where he repositions himself discursively, recalls the different forms of signifying that Henry Louis Gates Jr. labels a "ritual of close reading":

> Reed's use of parody would seem to be fittingly described as motivated Signifyin(g), in which the text Signifies upon other black texts, in the manner of the vernacular ritual of "close reading." [Alice] Walker's use of pastiche, on the other hand, corresponds to unmotivated Signifyin(g), by which I mean to suggest not the absence of a profound intention but the absence of a negative critique. . . . Whereas Reed seems to be about the clearing of a space of narration, Walker seems to be intent on underscoring the relation of her text to Hurston's, in a joyous proclamation of antecedent and descendant texts. (xxvi–xxvii)

While Gates's rubric posits a distinctly gendered signifying, in which male writers critique and distinguish themselves from literary forefathers while Walker and other women authors venerate their foremothers' voices, it does help to situate Wilson among his male predecessors. Though I would not go as far as to say that Wilson's critique of Ellison amounts to a clearing of literary space, the playwright—consciously or unconsciously—tropes what Gerald Early calls "one of the most famous fictional boxing depictions in all of American literature" (25). Wilson recalls Baldwin's use of musical performance to facilitate male bonding and intimacy. That he literally centers these blues moments—they occur at the play's midpoint—underscores the notion that black subjectivity is grounded in cultural practice and ritual, buttressing the link between individual and collective performance and wholeness.

The extemporaneous musical performance precedes the boxing match as a kind of invocation. After the "official" members of Floyd's band begin to play, Hedley pieces together an instrument made with a "two-by-four, a hammer, a nail, and a piece of chicken wire" (49). What commences is the quintessence of black vernacular/oral performance, replete with call and response, witnessing and testifying, and the cadences and rhythms of gospel and blues—a laying on of sacred and secular voices:

> HEDLEY: Now. When I was a little boy I asked my grandfather where his mother was. He say she was long gone far away. Say when he play this he could hear her pray. I asked him, "How?" He say, "Listen."
> (*He plucks the string*)
> I didn't hear her. But I learned it and I used to sit and play and try to hear her. Once. Maybe. Almost.
> (*Hedley begins to play the instrument. It is a simple tune for a simple instrument: really not much more than a piece of wire vibrating. The men listen hard.*)
> FLOYD: *If I could hear my mother pray again*, I believe I'd pray with her. I'd be happy just to hear her voice again. I wouldn't care if she was cussing me out. They say you don't miss your water till your well run dry. *If I could hear my mother's voice again* I never would say nothing back to her. I wouldn't mind hearing her singing either. She used to do that sometime. *Used to sing "Old Ship of Zion."* I believe that was her favorite. Though sometime she used to sing "The Lord's Prayer." I can still hear her singing . . .
> (*He sings* [the Lord's Prayer]) (49–50; emphasis added)

That Wilson interpolates the two central spirituals from "Sonny's Blues" grounds the play in the polyphonic tradition of Baldwin. Recall that the songs "If I Could Only Hear My Mother Pray Again" and "'Tis the Old Ship of Zion" serve as the musical bridges for Sonny's reconnection to his narrator-brother. These spirituals spark the narrator's memory of his mother's injunction that he watch over the younger Sonny and lay the groundwork for the cathartic rendition of "Am I Blue," which catalyzes the final reconciliation of the prodigal Sonny and his solipsistic narrator-brother.

Similarly, Hedley's call elicits Floyd's response, in which he summons the regenerative and healing power of his dead mother's voice. As a result, Floyd spends most of the play raising money for her headstone; Wilson may as well be engaging in a bit of what Gates calls "joyous" signifying, since Walker's marking of Hurston's grave has been documented in Robert Hemenway's biography of Hurston. Moreover, since gospel music in black literature is often associated with women or homosexual men (think of Rose Maxson singing "Jesus, be a fence all around me every day" in *Fences,* or the professional gospel singer Arthur Montana in *Just Above My Head*), Floyd, at least temporarily, overcomes the limitations of hegemonic masculinity by invok-

ing a *female* ancestral voice as a source of empowerment and spiritual renewal. His singing of his mother's song represents an inversion of the major leitmotif in *Joe Turner's Come and Gone,* where the healer-conjurer Bynum extols the knowledge that his father taught him how to recognize and claim his
own "song," which allows him to assist others in resuscitating their voices.
The improvised gospel-blues performances thus mark self-reflexive or meta-
dramatic moments in the play. Wilson, anchored in African and African-
American traditions, invokes the voice of his literary ancestor Baldwin to
sanctify his artistic expression.

The sacred gives way to the secular in the following scene, in which the
characters listen to the broadcast of the 1939 Joe Louis–Billy Conn bout.
Wilson's insertion of this "social text" echoes a discursive feature of Toni
Morrison's fiction in that historical events are interwoven to highlight not
the events themselves but the role they play in the development of self and
community.[19] Many male authors employ boxing metaphorically, and comparisons between its representation here and in *Invisible Man* are inevitable.
However, like Reed, Wilson signifies on Ellison by using boxing as a unify-
ing and almost sacred ritual that crystallizes the community of black men
and women. Recall in *Invisible Man* how the battle functions as both cultural spectacle and symbol: it exemplifies sexism and racism, black myopia and
self-erasure, and a general barbarism hidden beneath the patina of American puritanism.

More reminiscent of Gaines's portrayal of it in *A Lesson before Dying,* the
fight, like the singing it follows, has a transformative and invigorating effect
on those who hear it. An event that ostensibly ennobles an archaic and destructive conception of maleness, one predicated on pugilism and competition, has an almost holy effect on those who experience it. As is often the case
in African-American literature, the line between sacred and secular performance is not only blurred but obliterated. After Louis knocks Conn out, the
characters engage in another impromptu, cathartic expression: "The men
celebrate. They begin to circle the yard chanting 'The Brown Bomber.' Red
Carter grabs Louise and starts to dance with her. He pulls her into the center of the yard. Red Carter begins to dance. Canewell and Louise imitate him.
Canewell stops and watches Red Carter admiringly. Canewell begins playing his harmonica" (53). The black fighter represents what Early calls a "conundrum" for both blacks and whites, a "symbol, political and social, and
as a kind of running commentary, critical and complimentary, in the whole
matter of what it means to be a black American" (33). Nevertheless, instead
of inciting a race/class riot or so-called black-on-black violence, boxing in
Seven Guitars inaugurates more culturally galvanizing rituals such as dance,

another discursive element Wilson often employs to dramatize the liberating potential of African cultural practices.[20] Wilson transforms and represents a heretofore exclusively masculinized ritual as the basis of renewed communal ties; boxing becomes inclusive, abrogating the rigid gender boundaries that it traditionally reinforces. The musical and boxing spectacles together form a verbal and transverbal call and response, each performance complementing the other.

Wilson's reverence for black fighters dates back to the poetry he composed in the early 1960s. He asserts that his poem "Muhammad Ali" is "modeled after an African praise song in which you give praises of any kind" (Shannon, *Dramatic* 202). It is not surprising, then, that he deconstructs a ritual so commonly equated with male barbarism, imbuing it with restorative and cathartic qualities. However, it is rather ironic and a bit misleading that Joe Louis is such a looming historic presence in *Seven Guitars*. The boxer's life was fraught with the same contradictions, shortcomings, and tragedies that befall the men in this play. Nevertheless, the life of another boxer sheds further light on Wilson's tropological use of the sport.

Earlier, I pondered the euphonic salience of Floyd's last name, Barton, as a derivative of "barter." However, his first name carries equal significance, for it conjures memories of another famous black prizefighter, Floyd Patterson; the character's persistent concern with scoring a musical "hit" ironically bolsters this connection. In his pioneering work on literary and cultural figurations of boxing, Early comments on the enigmatic life of Patterson, a man who claimed John Wayne as his "favorite movie actor" and also declared that "'I am a Negro and I'm proud to be one, but I'm also an American'" (33, 38).[21] In this context Floyd Barton's life becomes a gloss on the boxer with whom he shares a first name. The fictionalized blues singer's naive and misguided inculcation of the discourse of American success and masculinity echoes Patterson's own misplaced hero worship and his dual/dueling identities. That he emulated Wayne, whose films and personal life exalted the excesses of white patriarchal masculinity and xenophobia, is both confounding and pitiable—but not shocking, considering the degree to which black men have modeled their behavior on abhorrent constructions of male subjectivity. Wilson uses the prizefighter's biography as an urtext for his portrayal of Floyd Barton: the latter becomes the mimetic double of the former, both men psychically consumed by their desire to include themselves within a narrative of American masculinity that has historically stymied black male liberation.

If one accepts that Floyd's is a warping and deforming conception of black subjectivity, then his murder might be seen as a constructive act. In this light, the health of the community might depend on expunging the materially crazed Floyd, who physically threatens Canewell after he accidentally finds Floyd's stolen money. However, the denouement, in which the characters are returning from Floyd's funeral, is much more ambiguous on this point. Instead of tying up the action in the tradition of the mystery or realistic play, the conclusion of *Seven Guitars* perhaps poses more questions than it answers, thereby resisting what Olaniyan calls the "hegemonic tradition of the 'well-made play'" (21). By revealing Hedley's murder of Floyd to the audience while withholding this information from the other characters, Wilson jettisons the structures and strictures of Western dramatic idioms, instead privileging black men's relationships and their perpetual search for different forms of community. Like Gaines, the playwright de-emphasizes violence by focusing on the destructive and constructive ways in which black men attempt to define their subjectivity. Wilson charts the devolution and disintegration of a character wedded to what Du Bois derided as America's "gospel of work and money" through Floyd Barton. Conversely, however, by centering homosocial and heterosocial rituals such as boxing, musical performance, dancing, and signifying, Wilson offers alternative vehicles for black male selfhood.

That August Wilson steeps his plays in the performative evokes comparisons to the Nigerian dramatist and Nobel Laureate Wole Soyinka, who similarly interfuses his plays with ritual. Dramas such as *Death and the King's Horseman* demonstrate that "For him, ritual is not only a cultural anchor but also a creative ideal for the representation of experience and phenomena that resist simplistic rationalism or socioeconomic calculation" (Olaniyan 62). When thinking of Wilson's performative aesthetic, rituals, especially masculinized ones, are the matrix of his forays into black men's psyches. *Seven Guitars*, like all of his works, problematizes putative and sacrosanct definitions of American manhood, evidenced by the persistent liberating potential of community that allows the remaining characters to sing Floyd Barton's aptly titled song, "That's All Right," in the wake of his emotional and physical evisceration. Though not all of Wilson's men can survive their encounters with the jagged grain, characters such as Red Carter, Canewell, Slow Drag, and Cutler remain resilient and indestructible black blues people who make a way out of no way. Complementing the centrality of ritual is the artistic legacy of Baldwin, whose griotic voice resonates throughout the playwright's oeuvre. Wilson's communal voice is ultimately part of a larger black male artistic landscape, for he painstakingly razes the figurative fences that separate generations of African-American men, be they writers, singers, blues musicians, or history's leftovers.

Conclusion

> Well, I guess Canada, like freedom, is a state of mind.
> —Ishmael Reed, *Flight to Canada*

IN ONE OF HIS MANY thoughtful reflections on the aesthetics of black writing, August Wilson details his creative credo:

> You can be a black writer and write whatever you want. I would never tell anyone what to write. You can only write what you feel to write anyway. I don't want anyone telling me what to write. And that was part of the thing in the '60s. People were talking about the black writer's responsibility. A black writer's responsibility is whatever he assumes that responsibility to be individually. So you can't say you're not doing right because you're not writing this kind of material even though you're black. You may not want to write it. You can't be forced to write it. If they assume that as a responsibility, then you have the basis to sit down and talk about what that responsibility should be—"Did you ever look at it this way?" But you can't force on anyone a responsibility for writing. (Shannon, *Dramatic* 233)

This jeremiad-like denunciation of rigid artistic parameters for black artists might appear to contradict the black male subjectivity-community nexus his plays dramatize. Wilson's repudiation of an artistically correct mandate for black authors has become the manifesto for scores of writers since the 1970s, most notably novelists such as Ishmael Reed, Clarence Major, and Charles Johnson.[1] However, his insistence that each writer formulate his own aesthetic code—that he, like Raven Quicksill, the narrator of *Flight to Canada*, fashion his own artistic Canada—does not undermine the communal impulse I've traced in recent African-American men's writing. Some contemporary authors have been less concerned with producing socially "responsible" works that restrict their artistic vision to circumscribing black-versus-white scenarios—texts that foreground volatile racial conflict (either in narratives of black-white male battle royals or sexualized black male bodies as despoilers of virtuous white ladies); African-American literature is no longer solely a calculated form of racial and social intervention. Eschewing the burden of exclusively addressing and denouncing racial wrongs, black men's writing has become quilt-like, a patchwork of narratives far more layered than a monochromatic fabric of black and white. The emergence of a sort of communally rooted black male subjectivity is a significant facet of a multitextured masculinist discourse.

Perhaps the most notable trend in black men's writing since the 1960s has been the kaleidoscopic vision of authors who focus on male subjects. No longer bound by the discursive shackles of protest, novelists such as Albert Murray and Ernest Gaines constitute one new wave of African-American men's literature. Undeniably, such writers are influenced by the Wright-Ellison tradition while they simultaneously renounce the limiting configuration of subjectivity proffered in earlier fiction. This anxiety of influence is emblematized in Murray's *Train Whistle Guitar* and Gaines's *A Lesson before Dying*, novels harvested from the soil of black southern men's literary art while blossoming in more expansive directions.

Assailing Wright (and Baldwin) for overlooking "the rich possibilities available to them in the blues tradition" (*Omni-Americans* 166), Murray transposes his extensively theorized blues aesthetic into *Train Whistle Guitar*, the antithesis of the racially charged and dystopic southern landscape of Wright's short story "Big Boy Leaves Home." *Train Whistle Guitar* pulsates as a distinctly black and blues bildungsroman, containing an arabesque of stories and voices—folk idioms and verbal rituals of signifying, toasting, boasting, and storytelling. In Murray's 1920s Alabama, a precocious protagonist's communal and vernacular education supersedes his formal training, as the author showcases oral and aural in his musically inflected writing. Scooter is firmly planted in this community even after he leaves it, for it endures as a sentient, nurturing space that spawns roots and wings through its emphasis on folk epistemology and the hard-won lessons inherent to a blues life. As part of what might be considered a renaissance of black southern men's writing, Gaines also glances backward in *A Lesson before Dying* by recasting Bigger Thomas's metaphorical and literal incarceration as a tale of agency within the context of imprisonment and psychic dislocation—an agency borne out of one's intraracial and intragender relationships.

Gaines's concern with the place-selfhood nexus has resurfaced in the writings of other southern male authors. The late novelist Raymond Andrews, for instance, devoted much of his writing to depicting the black male subject's formation. His first novel, *Appalachee Red*, echoes Murray and Gaines in its commingling of personal, communal, and geographical biographies. Andrews's novel is also a discursive intervention: he re-envisions and revises Faulkner's Yoknapatawpha, where blacks were often abstracted and silenced. And ultimately it is a testament to the indisputable impact the black community has on black men's emotional development. In the tradition of Murray, Gaines, and scores of other southern novelists, Andrews personalizes and fictionalizes his native Georgia, vivifying interlocking racial, social, and historical dramas.

In addition to Gaines, pioneering writers such as Reed, Johnson, and Major have used the 1960s Black Arts Movement not merely as their artistic raison d'être but as an incubation period that helped them to conceive a plethora of black male subjects. These novelists unapologetically emblematize Wilson's "responsibility-less" approach to art. As writers who cut their artistic teeth during the volatile civil rights and Black Power movements, they have reimagined black men's writing through innovative approaches to theme, narrativity, and masculinity. Reed's and Johnson's historiographic novels re-examine slavery, recasting overworked accounts of sinister whites and subjugated, agencyless blacks. Both *Flight to Canada* and *Oxherding Tale* have emerged as classic neo–slave novels, a subgenre of African-American fiction that includes Margaret Walker's *Jubilee*, Gaines's *The Autobiography of Miss Jane Pittman*, and Toni Morrison's *Beloved*. *Flight to Canada* and *Oxherding Tale* deconstruct the standard narrative of black victimization by exposing how it constricts the black male subject's opportunities for growth and renewal. They invert and dismantle the conventions of male slave accounts such as Frederick Douglass's 1845 *Narrative* and Olaudah Equiano's 1789 *Interesting Narrative*. Though Reed's uproarious satiric discourse might ostensibly differ from Johnson's opaque, philosophy-laden texts, both demythologize historical facts such as slavery to elucidate how individual truths are neither culturally bound nor explained by facile, preconceived notions of race and racialized conflict. Just as Baldwin conveys Rufus Scott's complicity in his own demise in *Another Country*, Reed and Johnson free their black male protagonists from the debilitated position of blaming whites for their plights and metamorphose them into shapers of their own destinies and subjectivities. As the most technically experimental, Major epitomizes the black writer as literary outlaw. One finds in his disarming metafictive novels such as *Reflex and Bone Structure* shades of John Barth, for Major emphasizes what he considers the artificiality of the medium itself by consistently resisting story or

plot in the most normative sense. However, his work retains as its underpinnings black musical and vernacular cadences and an ongoing concern with
American and African-American popular culture.

Perhaps more so than any of his contemporaries, John Edgar Wideman
has fashioned a black male subject who emblematizes the communal impulse
evident in much contemporary masculinist literature. Though he spent his
literary apprenticeship as a disciple of the white modernist icons Eliot and
Joyce (reflected prominently in his first novel, *A Glance Away*), Wideman's
work in the 1980s and 1990s synthesizes poststructuralist devices such as
narrative discontinuity with contemporary and historical events in black
men's lives. Novels such as *Reuben* reflect an ardent belief that the black self
and community exist symbiotically and that their devitalization does not
preclude their revitalization. His docunovel, *Philadelphia Fire*, is exemplary:
it takes as its intertext a historical event, the incendiary MOVE bombing in
1985 in Philadelphia, which was ordered by a black mayor and claimed the
lives of eleven blacks (all members of the revolutionary black organization,
including children). This novel—with its spatiotemporal violations and fragmentation, its copious allusions to and revisions of Euro-Anglo and African-
American texts, its violation of the standard novelistic convention that places
the author outside of the text, and its insistence that the black community
represents the locus of black life and holds the potential for the self's renewal and regeneration—marks the apogee of black postmodernism. Moreover,
Wideman's forays into his own personal history have produced the autobiographical *Brothers and Keepers* and *Fatheralong: A Meditation on Fathers and
Sons, Race and Society,* self-explorations that hearken back to Wright's *Black
Boy.* In these extensive biocritical commentaries, Wideman explores his relationships with men in his family (most notably his son and brother, both
imprisoned). Unlike Wright, however, he repositions himself as a subject to
be interrogated, complicating his familial role and actions in ways that are
far less self-aggrandizing than Wright's self-portrait.

Embodying the legacy of his fellow southern authors, Wright and Gaines,
Randall Kenan has woven layered narratives that capture the sentience of the
black vernacular/southern folk community, the arabesque of communal,
national, and personal histories, and the disquieting issue of sexual difference. His two books of fiction, the novel *A Visitation of Spirits* and the short
story collection *Let the Dead Bury Their Dead,* are awash in black southern
history, vernacular and gospel cadences, and an organic sense of place. One
might say that his melding of geographic space and an emerging black gay
male identity makes him the literary progeny of both Gaines and Baldwin—
the product of a figurative marriage of heterosexual and homosexual, rural

South and inner-city North, folk and urban realism. Traveling through much of the same artistic terrain is the late Melvin Dixon, an accomplished literary critic turned novelist whose voice complements Kenan's. Dixon's first novel, *Trouble the Water,* is set in North Carolina (as is *Visitation*) and projects a Toomerian insistence that the South is an inescapable part of the black self's personal geography. Above all, this troubling region must be navigated if self-actualization is to be achieved. His second novel, *Vanishing Rooms,* looks backward to Baldwin's audacious *Giovanni's Room* in its homoerotic content but dramatizes the commingling of race, gender, and sexual orientation in a manner that goes beyond Baldwin's Anglo-Americanized gay tragic-romance.

Writers such as Kenan and Dixon (prior to his premature passing) incontestably represent a profusion of young black male writers who dismantle commonly held notions about black masculinity and subjectivity. Placing heretofore out-of-bounds issues such as sexual otherness at the locus of their artistic imagination, several African-American male authors in the 1990s have unabashedly challenged anachronistic and prescribed constructions of race, malehood, sexuality, and family and have simultaneously engaged *and* transcended the masculinist tradition embodied in the Wright-Ellison dyad. And though one could argue that there exists a paucity of budding new male dramatists (aside from established ones like Wilson and Charles Fuller, author of *A Soldier's Play*), the popularity of writers like E. Lynn Harris (*Invisible Life*) and the detective writer Walter Mosley (*Devil in a Blue Dress*) attests to the diversity of black men's writing and the wider audience to which it appeals. The ghost of Bigger Thomas will always lurk in the African-American masculinist literary imagination, but many of Richard Wright's literary sons and keepers have managed to capture black protagonists' multi- and intersubjectivities. The black male subject has been resituated, his boundless possibilities exceeding the constraining discourse of protest that shrouded the voices of countless native and invisible sons.

Notes

Introduction

1. Anthony P. Cohen theorizes the multiple configurations of community: "'Community' is one of those words—like 'culture,' 'myth,' 'ritual,' 'symbol'—bandied around in ordinary, everyday speech, apparently readily intelligible to speaker and listener, which, when imported into the discourse of social science, however, causes immense difficulty" (11). With this in mind, my project attempts to particularize the notion of community by exploring how it interfaces specifically with black men's literary discourse.

2. Though I do not include Baldwin's autobiographical first novel in this study, I have discussed *Go Tell It on the Mountain* elsewhere. See "Baldwin, Communitas, and the Black Masculinist Tradition."

3. See Gates, *The Signifying Monkey,* esp. section 2 in chapter 3, "Figures of Signification" (103–24).

4. Of course, African-American male novelists prior to the 1950s have narrativized black men's homosocial relationships vis-à-vis the black community and family, though not with nearly the same regularity as their female counterparts. Novels such as Langston Hughes's *Not without Laughter* and George Wylie Henderson's *Jule* are two such works. However, James Baldwin was one of the first major writers of fiction to build an oeuvre around the examination of black men's communal and same-gender—both sexual and nonsexual—relationships. Short stories such as "The Rockpile" and "The Outing" from *Going to Meet the Man* as well as his more widely known novels are part of an important albeit underrecognized discursive trend.

5. See, for instance, Houston A. Baker Jr.'s "Generational Shifts and the Recent Criticism of Afro-American Literature" and Karla F. C. Holloway's *Moorings and Metaphors.*

6. I wish to acknowledge two professors in the English department at Howard University, Lettie Austin and Jennifer Jordan. During a presentation on my research, they encouraged me to consider how cultural events such as the civil rights movement and the authors' own lives could offer valuable insights into the evolution of black men's writing in the 1950s and 1960s.

7. Recent studies such as *Baldwin Now* (edited by Dwight McBride) provide a more comprehensive and balanced assessment of the trajectory of Baldwin's life and art.

Chapter 1: Countering the Counterdiscourse

1. Robert B. Stepto uses the phrase "articulate hero" to describe Douglass's ascent to the public roles of abolitionist, orator, and author (25).

2. Thadious M. Davis provides a useful overview of subjectivity in canonical male writers who preceded Wright.

3. See Houston A. Baker Jr.'s "Generational Shifts and the Recent Criticism of Afro-American Literature," where he asserts that "The dominant critical perspective of Afro-American literature during the late 1950s and early 1960s might be called the poetics of integration" (3). Baker goes on to discuss Wright's comments on the *Brown v. Topeka Board of Education* case as evidence of blacks' optimism about "overcoming" America's cancerous racial past.

4. Critics such as James W. Coleman have done a commendable job of showing how contemporary novelists such as John Edgar Wideman have been influenced by white modernist icons like James Joyce and T. S. Eliot. Coleman points out that Wideman "during his career as a novelist has moved from uncritical acceptance of the forms and themes of mainstream modernism as practiced by white literary masters to a black voicing of modernism and postmodernism that is consistent with Afro-American perspectives and reflects a commitment to the needs of the black community" (6). In Coleman's estimation, early Wideman novels such as *A Glance Away* are his most "postmodernist," that is, most deeply influenced by modern and postmodern "masters."

5. I take this term from Terry Eagleton's *Literary Theory.* He uses it in his chapter "Psychoanalysis," where he explores gender formation in terms of Freudian and Lacanian psychoanalytic theory.

6. The French philosopher Gaston Bachelard discusses the psychosocial influence of setting on the self. For example, he notes that, during snowy winters, houses as enclosures "derive reserves and refinements of intimacy from winter" and that, "As a result of this universal whiteness, we feel a form of cosmic negation in action" (40–41). These observations provide apt metaphors for the protest subject, who often conceives of whites and white spaces as intractable natural phenomena that concretize his sense of powerlessness. Note, for example, how Wright describes Bigger's conception of whites: "To Bigger and his kind white people were not really people; they were a sort of great natural force, like a stormy sky looming overhead, or like a deep swirling river stretching suddenly at one's feet in the dark" (*Native Son* 109).

7. John M. Reilly's "Giving Bigger a Voice" and Laura E. Tanner's "Uncovering the Magical Disguise of Language" address the tension between Bigger's attempts to articulate his tortured story and the text's narratological apparatus, where the author's presence overwhelms and, to some degree, undercuts the protagonist's quest.

8. See James A. Miller's "Bigger Thomas's Quest for Voice and Audience in Richard Wright's *Native Son*," which examines the novel through the critical frame of Russian formalism.

9. Paul Gilroy explores a much-neglected dimension of Wright artistic vita: his post-

American period of "artist as world citizen." Like the white American writer Paul Bowles, Wright's Diasporan sojourn resulted in some of his most intriguing writing. See Gilroy's chapter "'Without the Consolation of Tears': Richard Wright, France, and the Ambivalence of Community" for a thorough assessment of Wright's post–*Native Son* canon.

10. Richard Majors and Janet Mancini Billson use this term to describe the hypermasculine "performance" that adolescent and some adult African-American men enact to compensate for their perceived psychosocial emasculation. Majors and Billson state that "By cool pose we mean the presentation of self many black males use to establish their male identity. Cool pose is a ritualized form of masculinity that entails behaviors, scripts, physical posturing, impression management, and carefully crafted performances that deliver a single, critical message: pride, strength, and control" (4).

11. Another instance of Johnson problematically assessing other African-American writers was his caustic criticism of Morrison after she won the Nobel Prize in 1993. This was particularly baffling, since in *Being and Race* he lauded her talent: "However, the greatest praise for technical prose mastery among black women must go to the much-celebrated Toni Morrison. More than any other contemporary writer, she is a direct descendant in style and sensibility of Ralph Ellison. Perhaps even his rightful heir in her ability to place fictional excellence above political appeal, yet without softening the social importance of her works" (101).

12. I am indebted to the pioneering scholarship of Robert B. Stepto and Houston Baker, specifically their studies *From Behind the Veil* and *Blues, Ideology, and Afro-American Literature,* respectively. Stepto draws from Turner's work in his discussion of the geography-self nexus in Douglass and Du Bois's works; in the chapter entitled "A Dream of American Form: Fictive Discourse, Black (W)holes, and a Blues Book Most Excellent," Baker employs anthropological paradigms originated by van Gennep and Turner to elucidate the cultural dimensions of literary texts such as *Black Boy* and *Invisible Man.* I use these authors' paradigms as models for my own, especially in my discussion of Gaines's *A Lesson before Dying.*

13. See Henry Louis Gates Jr.'s "Zora Neale Hurston and the Speakerly Text" in *The Signifying Monkey,* (170–216), where he explores Hurston's aesthetic attempt to inscribe black speech patterns in *Their Eyes Were Watching God.*

14. I borrow this term from Alessandro Portelli.

15. That Baldwin, Gaines, and Wilson claim their respective black vernacular communities as their artistic crucibles is well documented. Baldwin's Pentecostal upbringing in Harlem, Gaines's bucolic Louisiana terrain, and Wilson's urban Pittsburgh enclaves—all of these rich cultural spaces illuminate the links between these authors and the fictive communities they create. For biocritical discussions of the community-artist nexus, see David Leeming, *James Baldwin;* Marcia Gaudet and Carl Wooton, *Porch Talk with Ernest Gaines;* and Sandra G. Shannon, *The Dramatic Vision of August Wilson.*

Chapter 2: The Perilous Journey to a Brother's Country

1. For perceptive discussions of the identity-environment nexus, see Melvin Dixon's *Ride Out the Wilderness* and Fred L. Standley's "'But the City Was Real.'"

2. Broadening their critique beyond men of color, Delgado and Stefancic observe that

"the social construction of masculinity is problematic. The stereotype of the ideal man is forceful, militaristic, hyper-competitive, risk-taking, not particularly interested in culture and the arts, protective of his woman, heedless of nature, and so on. And in many families, boys are conditioned actually to behave that way" (211). This already troubling construction is exacerbated when race is taken into account.

3. See West's *Race Matters*.

4. Baldwin never stated whether he based Sonny on an actual person (unlike Rufus Scott, whom he modeled after his friend Eugene Worth), but Sonny's biography parallels the actual life of Amiri Baraka: both served in the armed forces, both immersed themselves in the bohemian, largely white Greenwich Village counterculture of the 1950s, and both are passionate about jazz.

5. See section five of Horace A. Porter's *Stealing the Fire*, "'Outside of Disorder, the Order Which Is Art': James Baldwin and the 'Mighty' Henry James," and section six of Bryan R. Washington's *The Politics of Exile*, "Writing the American Scene: James Baldwin, James/Baldwin, and James Baldwin." Baldwin also discusses how James's aesthetics informed his first novel. See his interview with Jordan Elgrably and George Plimpton, "The Art of Fiction LXXVIII: James Baldwin."

6. Keith Byerman's "Words and Music" explores the narrator's excessively "literary," pedantic sensibilities, noting how he "misreads" messages throughout the text: "The story, in part, is about his inability to read properly. The source of this inability is reliance on a language that is at once over rationalistic and metaphoric. His sentences are always complete and balanced, and his figurative language puts on display his literary intelligence" (367). While I agree with most of Byerman's observations, I would argue that the narrator's immersion in language in and of itself does not preclude an understanding of Sonny's tumultuous life, nor does it undermine the story's communal ethos.

7. In *Black Women in the Fiction of James Baldwin,* the only book-length study devoted exclusively to Baldwin's representations of black women, Trudier Harris delineates what she sees as Baldwin's tendency to confine black women to stereotypically gendered roles. She concludes that the nameless mother in "Sonny's Blues" has "become the universal bosom of comfort in this world until her troubled husband could reach the world beyond. No background information on her allows us to see how she has come to be where she is, but she has uncomplainingly fallen into the role of WOMAN: saving her man, keeping his suffering private so that he could remain respectable in the public eye, planning for her children as she sees her own death approach" (79).

8. Victor Turner uses these terms in describing the conclusion of the liminal phase in his schematization of the ritual process he outlines (*Ritual Process* 94).

9. See Isaiah 51:17 and 22: "Awake, awake, stand up. O Jerusalem, which hast drunk at the hand of the Lord the cup of his fury; thou has drunken the dregs of the cup of trembling, and wrung them out"; "Thus saith thy Lord the Lord, and thy God that pleadeth the cause of his people, Behold, I have taken out of thine hand the cup of trembling, even the dregs of the cup of my fury; thou shalt no more drink it again."

10. An example of an established scholar breaking this critical trend is Mae G. Henderson in "James Baldwin." Henderson uses Baldwin's positions on gender, sexuality, and queer critical discourse as the basis for her nuanced reading of *Giovanni's Room.*

11. See Washington's *The Politics of Exile* and Kendall Thomas's "'Ain't Nothing Like the Real Thing.'"

12. Thomas questions the Black Nationalist critic Ekwueme Michael Thelwell's attempts to efface Baldwin's sexual orientation. He links this erasure to a broader campaign in which contemporary rap artists similarly proffer a masculinity rooted in a vituperative rejection of homosexuality. Thelwell and such artists impose a "heteronormative logic that conditions the ascription of 'authentic' black identity on the repudiation of gay or lesbian identity. The jargon of racial authenticity insists, as the gangsta-rapper Ice Cube has put it, that 'true niggers ain't gay'" (59).

13. See Sarotte's *Like a Brother, Like a Lover* (98) and David Bergman's *Gaiety Transfigured* (168).

14. Regrettably, Bawer fails to connect the shortsightedness of some queer critics to many white gay critics' dismissal of Baldwin as insufficiently gay. Witness his own whitewashing of Baldwin's insistence on foregrounding race in his counterhegemonic narrative discourse: "Baldwin became *fixated* on racial issues, writing books and articles that often seemed resolutely *antiliterary*" (*Aspect of Eternity* 27; emphasis added).

15. Phillip Brian Harper expounds on some black homosexuals' distaste for the term "gay" in his examination of African-American constructions of masculinity: "The invocation of 'homosexuality' . . . is deliberate. My point is not to register what many have protested are the clinical connotations of *homosexual* in contrast to the putatively more expansive resonances of *gay* or *queer*, but to indicate the limited degree to which many men of color feel identified with these latter terms. Indeed, *gay*, especially, conjures up in the minds of many who hear it images of a population that is characteristically white, male, and financially well-off; thus it can actually efface, rather than affirm, the experiences of women and men of color" (205).

16. Kobena Mercer takes a similar position regarding contemporary gay movements' proclivity for eliding racial issues: "While some feminists have begun to take on issues of race and racism in the women's movement, white gay men retain a deafening silence on race. Maybe this is not surprising, given the relatively depoliticized nature of the mainstream gay 'scene'" (131).

17. I would be remiss in suggesting that Baldwin has not portrayed same-sex relationships between black men. He does so, albeit briefly, in *Tell Me How Long the Train's Been Gone*. In fact, the novel's protagonist, Leo Proudhammer, bears a striking resemblance to Arthur Montana. A performer in a different medium, the actor Leo, like Arthur, is stricken by a severe illness at the age of thirty-nine. Unlike Arthur, however, he survives his heart attack. Similarly, Leo has sexual encounters with both men and women, though he is involved in a relationship with a black man by the novel's end.

18. Baldwin's portrayal of Leo Proudhammer's relationship with "Black Christopher" establishes a precedent for the novelist's cursory treatment of relationships between black men. Though entitled "Black Christopher," the last book of *Tell Me How Long* concentrates primarily on Leo's affair with Barbara King, a white actress, and his incestuous encounter with his brother, Caleb. Christopher enters abruptly and then disappears altogether, appearing briefly at its conclusion.

19. In "The Politics of Intimacy," the black feminist theorist Hortense Spillers critiques the alternatively phallocentric and saccharine representations of manhood and heterosexual love in *If Beale Street Could Talk*.

20. In *My Ántonia*, Cather invests the character Jim Burden with the narrative burden of speaking for and about the eponymous heroine and a host of women characters who

flout conventions regarding women's sexuality and the cult of domesticity. Perhaps such fictive cross-dressing was necessary for gay writers in the first part of the twentieth century given social prohibitions against homosexuality. One can also detect similar sexual self-veiling in works such as Tennessee Williams's *A Streetcar Named Desire*. The sexually transgressive actions of Blanche DuBois approximate stereotypical constructions of gay men and could therefore be interpreted as the playwright's attempt to dramatize his own plight as a southern homosexual male.

21. One need only consider the closeted lives of many black male luminaries as an indicator of the black community's history of heterosexism. Recent studies on the lives of Langston Hughes, the civil rights activist Bayard Rustin, and the songwriter Billy Strayhorn have shed light on these men's private lives and the lengths to which they went to separate the racial-public and sexual-private.

22. Lash's "Baldwin Beside Himself" represents an early foray into the politics of Baldwin's gender-racial delineations. He identifies and fleshes out what he sees as Baldwin's stratifying of men based on their hetero-, bi-, or homosexuality; Lash explores what he calls "the sissy," "virile and earthy male," and "freaks" (50) who populate *Giovanni's Room* and *Another Country*.

23. For a slightly different interpretation of the novel's geosexual dynamics, see Harris's "The South as Woman."

24. Nero provides an insightful look at the scant scholarly and fictive attention devoted to black gays and lesbians, regardless of the gender of the critic or writer. Particularly illuminating is his interpretation of Toni Morrison's neo–slave novel *Beloved* and what he interprets as her refusal to offer homosexuality as a viable alternative for the male slaves on the "Sweet Home" plantation, who nobly refuse to use Sethe to satiate their sexual desires. Instead of engaging in sex with each other, they resort to bestiality: "Morrison's description is homophobic because it reveals her inability to imagine homosexual relationships among heroic characters. By implication, sex with farm animals is preferable to homoerotic sex" ("Toward" 232).

25. "B-boy" signifies in 1990s black vernacular culture "banjee-boy," a term with several connotations. James Earl Hardy's novel *B-Boy Blues,* described as a gay "black-on-black love story," defines b-boys as young black men "who stand on street corners, doin' their own vogue—striking that 'cool pose' against a pole, a storefront, up against or on a car, leanin', loungin', and loiterin' with their boyz . . . tryin' to rap to the females, and daring anyone to stake their territory, to invade their domain" (25). See also Majors and Billson.

26. I borrow this descriptor from chapter four of C. W. E. Bigsby's *The Second Black Renaissance,* "The Divided Mind of James Baldwin."

Chapter 3: Reimagining Richard

1. The black feminist scholar Mary Helen Washington admonishes Douglass because women in his autobiography are "simply rendered invisible" (8), while Valerie Smith accuses him of "mythologizing rugged individuality, physical strength, and geographical mobility," thereby "enshrin[ing] cultural definitions of masculinity" (34).

2. Callahan uses this term to describe Gaines's schematization of black men in *Bloodline.*

3. I'm influenced here by Daphne Spain's socioarchitectural study *Gendered Spaces,* where she establishes a connection between gender, knowledge, and power in terms of men's and women's spheres.

4. I explore the polyphonic dimensions of this novel in "Re-(W)righting Black Male Subjectivity."

5. Criticism exploring Gaines's configuration of community in novels such as *A Gathering of Old Men* and *A Lesson before Dying* includes Bonnie TuSmith's *All My Relatives* and Philip Page's *Reclaiming Community in Contemporary African American Fiction.*

6. In "Tell Old Pharaoh," Craig Hansen Werner extrapolates the explicit and implicit revisionist praxes of African-American novelists such as Ellison, Gaines, Gayl Jones, and David Bradley with respect to Faulkner's excessively flawed characterizations of black characters.

7. In "Black Manhood in Ernest J. Gaines's *A Lesson before Dying,*" Charles E. Wilson Jr. accurately observes, "That Gaines uses two men to serve as protagonists indicates his appreciation for the shared commitment of black folk as he adapts the typical protagonist/antagonist model to suit his purpose of redefining the African American experience" (100).

8. I first employed this concept to describe Faulkner's double marginalizing of this character in his 1948 novel *Intruder in the Dust* (Clark, "Man on the Margin"). Lucas Beauchamp is rendered invisible within the narrative's action through his estrangement from other blacks and in terms of narrative space, since his voice all but disappears by the latter stages of the text.

9. For a discussion of Gaines's use of modernist literary devices, see Valerie Melissa Babb, "Old-Fashioned Modernism."

10. Philip Auger explores the voice-manhood-power nexus and the "complete imprisoning function of white discourse" that Grant's act of narration as well as Jefferson's eventual assertion of his voice help to destabilize (74).

11. I borrow this phrase, with a slight alteration, from Baker, who uses the term "expressive black community" in schematizing Wright's personal evolution in *Black Boy* (*Blues* 154).

12. In a chapter entitled "School Feminization, Black Males, Initiation Rites, and Historical Change," Joseph H. Pleck explores how the predominantly female environment of the classroom impacts black male identity and gender formation. In what he labels the "school feminization hypothesis," he conjectures: "Boys experience academic and psychological difficulties at school because it exacerbates their sex role identity problems, due to the predominance of female teachers, teachers' encouragement of femininity, and the image of school as feminine" (117). His analysis might explain Grant's anxiety of masculinity, since his occupation is a traditionally "feminine" one.

13. Chapter four of Greene's *Blacks in Eden,* "New Slaves and Lynching Bees," examines the psychosexual dimensions of lynching in the South, which evolved from the perceived threat that black male bodies posed to white women—the exemplars of purity, chastity, and white masculine privilege.

14. Abdul JanMohamed uses this term to describe the hegemonic culture's social tools for subjugating African Americans. According to JanMohamed's schematization, the Jim Crow South views even minor transgressions by blacks as a threat to its restrictive, apartheid-like codes. This potentially oppositional impulse, where blacks are seen as challenging their assigned "place," must be curbed, usually through violent means: "in order for complete subordination to be maintained in an absolute manner, the slightest resistance is immediately interpreted as a major rebellion, which in turn makes the communication of death instantly and whimsically revocable" (209).

Chapter 4: Race, Ritual, Reconnection, Reclamation

1. Wilson reiterated how the Black Power movement of the 1960s nurtured his personal and artistic flowering at the eleventh biennial national conference of the Theatre Communications Group at Princeton in June 1996: "I find it curious but no small accident that I seldom hear those words 'Black Power' spoken, and when mention is made of that part of black history in America, whether in the press or in conversation, reference is made to the Civil Rights Movement as though the Black Power movement—an important social movement by America's ex-slaves—had in fact never happened. But the Black Power movement of the '60s was a reality; it was the kiln in which I was fired, and has much to do with the person I am today and the ideas and attitudes that I carry as part of my consciousness" ("Ground" 14–15).

2. The verbal jousting between Brustein and Wilson has surfaced in public and print. Wilson named names in his Princeton address (printed in the September 1996 edition of *American Theatre*), calling Brustein's criticism of grant-awarding procedures that benefit some minority artists "sophomoric" ("Ground" 71). Brustein offered an acerbic rebuttal: "For me, Wilson's speech, not to mention his letter [in *American Theatre*, October 1996], resounds with separatist and exclusive demands. As a 'race man,' dedicated to 'Black Power,' he would force us into extreme color consciousness. Yet, he continues to refer to 'white' culture as if it were a monolithic entity without its own shades of color and varieties of difference" ("Forum" 63, 81).

3. I am riffing here on Eleanor W. Traylor's eloquent description of Baldwin's *Just Above My Head,* which she calls "a gospel tale told in the blues mode" (95).

4. Paul Carter Harrison makes this point when he articulates the shortcomings of Hansberry's dramatic poetics of the late 1950s: "The missing ingredient was style, some form of particularized presentation—more textual in its orientation than the highly esoteric kinetic rituals of Barbara Ann Teer's National Black Theatre—resourceful enough to reveal mythic layers of folk culture without becoming burdened with the familiar sociological formulations on the black experience that had constrained the *blues voice* of Lorraine Hansberry's *Raisin in the Sun,* subordinating her dramaturgy to the structural limitations of social realism popularized in the traditional American theater" (Harrison 298–99).

5. See Artaud's classic 1958 drama manifesto *The Theater and Its Double,* where he provides a theory and context for what he delineates as the theatre of cruelty.

6. The term "polyrhythmic" appears in Werner's essay on Wilson, "The Burden and the Binding Son: August Wilson's Neo-Classical Jazz," in *Playing the Changes.* Werner

notes that Antonio Benitez-Rojo uses the phrase "polyrhythmic literature" in discussing the "interaction of European binary systems with Native American, Asian, and African traditions" (278).

7. One particularly problematic reading of Wilson is Kim Marra's "Ma Rainey and the Boyz": "Like most of his canonized predecessors, Wilson writes in a predominately realistic mode whose narrative structure posits a male protagonist and constructs female characters as Other" (123).

8. Darwin T. Turner's "Visions of Love and Manliness in a Blackening World" remains an informative exploration of how male representation in African-American drama has evolved. More recent studies include Carla J. McDonough's *Staging Masculinity.* In her chapter "August Wilson: Performing Black Masculinity," she provides an overview of social constructions of gender and uses Hansberry's Walter Lee Younger as a prototype for black male dramatic protagonists. She asserts that "Wilson's work is affected by and responds to a broad theatrical tradition: it encompasses the white fathers of American drama and the dramatic predecessors who helped to establish a theatrical tradition for African American dramatists" (140).

9. Along the same lines of Brustein's generally dismissive attitude toward black artistic production, David Littlejohn's *Black on White* remains one of the most execrable "studies" on black writing. This book is, with few exceptions, a protracted homily on black literature's failure to be "universal" and "positive." It opens thusly: "It may one day be different, but a white American today will find it an exhausting and depressing enterprise to immerse himself for long in the recent literature of the American Negro—for a number of reasons. Much of the writing, like much of the writing of any race, is simply poor, the product of small minds that happen to be Negro" (3).

10. For an insightful critical investigation of the sermonic tradition in black literature, see Dolan Hubbard's *The Sermon and the African American Literary Imagination.*

11. See Sandra G. Shannon's "The Long Wait" and Sandra Adell's "Speaking of Ma Rainey/Talking about the Blues" for discussions of the rhetorical and strategic function of "waiting" in the play.

12. Levee's violence-riddled past evokes comparisons with Wright's autobiography *Black Boy* and short story "Long Black Song." In the former, Wright's Uncle Silas Hoskins is killed by whites who are jealous of his thriving business; in the latter, another entrepreneur, also named Silas, is murdered by a gang of white men after he kills a white salesman with whom his wife has slept. Finally, Levee's birthplace, Natchez, is about twenty miles from Wright's birthplace in Mississippi.

13. Harry Elam makes a similar point about the significance of Slow Drag's "female impersonation": he contends that it "suggests a critique of restrictive gender roles and potentially symbolizes the artificiality of gender." However, I disagree with his assertion that Slow Drag's rendition "emphasizes principally the song's humor and cynically mocks the theme of female empowerment" (172). Slow Drag's version seems not to mock female empowerment but to expose the limitations of masculinity that are challenged only because of Ma's tardiness and not in the men's daily lives.

14. Harrison insightfully concludes that in murdering Toledo, "Levee has not only desecrated a natural life, but also cut himself off from ontological continuity, a sort of cosmic suicide" (311).

15. Victor Turner's work on ritual drama and performance is instructive in thinking about the myriad ways of interpreting the play's conclusion: "The many-leveled or tiered structure of a major ritual or drama, each level having many sectors, makes of these genres flexible and nuanced instruments capable of carrying and communicating many messages at once, even of subverting on one level what it appears to be 'saying' on another" (*Anthropology* 24).

16. For a sustained discussion of the intersections between race, masculinity, and war, see Greene's chapter "The Wars of Eden" in *Blacks in Eden*.

17. One cannot help but note a similar aural connection from *A Raisin in the Sun:* the character Murchison—"merchant's son"—who upheld his father's mercantilistic and classist values during his courtship of Beneatha Younger.

18. Shannon's "A Transplant That Did Not Take" elaborates on Chicago's thematic salience in the play specifically and in black history generally.

19. For a comprehensive discussion of the fight itself, see Jeffrey T. Sammons's *Beyond the Ring*, especially the section "Lull before the Storm" (120–22).

20. Mary L. Bogumil and Kim Periera discuss the role of the West African Juba as well as other African cultural practices alluded to in *Joe Turner's Come and Gone.*

21. Quoted from Floyd Patterson's 1962 autobiography *Victory over Myself.*

Conclusion

1. Major's position is representative. Anticipating Wilson's decrying of a strict blueprint for writers that dictates the scope and form of black literature, he considers "repulsive" the notion that "black writers do anything other than what they each choose to do. . . . No style or subject should be alien to them. We have to get away from this rigid notion that there are certain topics and methods reserved for black writers. I'm against all that. I'm against coercion from blacks and from whites" (O'Brien 127).

Works Cited

Adell, Sandra. "Speaking of Ma Rainey/Talking about the Blues." In *May All Your Fences Have Gates: Essays on the Drama of August Wilson.* Ed. Alan Nadel. 51–66. Iowa City: University of Iowa Press, 1994.

Andrews, Raymond. *Appalachee Red.* 1978. Athens: University of Georgia Press, 1987.

Andrews, William L. "The Black Male in American Literature." In *The American Black Male: His Present Status and His Future.* Ed. Richard G. Majors and Jacob U. Gordon. 59–68. Chicago: Nelson-Hall, 1994.

Artaud, Antonin. *The Theater and Its Double.* Trans. Mary Caroline Richards. New York: Grove Press, 1958.

Auger, Philip. "A Lesson about Manhood: Appropriating 'The Word' in Ernest Gaines's *A Lesson before Dying.*" *Southern Literary Journal* 27.2 (1995): 74–85.

Babb, Valerie Melissa. "Old-Fashioned Modernism: 'The Changing Same' in *A Lesson before Dying.*" In *Critical Reflections on the Fiction of Ernest J. Gaines.* Ed. David C. Estes. 250–64. Athens: University of Georgia Press, 1994.

Bachelard, Gaston. *The Poetics of Space.* Trans. Maria Jolas. New York: Orion Press, 1964.

Baker, Houston A., Jr. *Blues, Ideology, and Afro-American Literature: A Vernacular Theory.* Chicago: University of Chicago Press, 1984.

———. "Generational Shifts and the Recent Criticism of Afro-American Literature." *Black American Literature Forum* 15.1 (1981): 3–21.

———. *The Journey Back: Issues in Black Literature and Criticism.* Chicago: University of Chicago Press, 1980.

Bakhtin, M. M. *The Dialogic Imagination.* Ed. Michael Holquist. Trans. Caryl Emerson and Michael Holquist. Austin: University of Texas Press, 1981.

Baldwin, James. "Alas, Poor Richard." In *Nobody Knows My Name.* 146–70. New York: Dell, 1961.

———. *Another Country.* New York: Dial, 1962.

———. *Giovanni's Room.* New York: Dell, 1956.

———. *Going to Meet the Man.* New York: Dell, 1965.

————. *If Beale Street Could Talk.* New York: Signet, 1974.

————. *Just Above My Head.* New York: Dial, 1978.

————. "Many Thousands Gone." In *Notes of a Native Son.* 1955. 24–45. New York: Beacon, 1983.

————. *Nobody Knows My Name.* New York: Dell, 1961.

————. *Notes of a Native Son.* 1955. New York: Beacon, 1983.

————. "Sonny's Blues." In *Going to Meet the Man.* 86–112. New York: Dell, 1965.

————. *Tell Me How Long the Train's Been Gone.* New York: Dell, 1968.

Baraka, Amiri. *Raise, Race, Rays, Raze.* 1969. New York: Vintage, 1972.

————. "The Revolutionary Theatre" In *Home: Social Essays.* 210–15. New York: Morrow, 1966.

Barnard, Ian. "Fuck Community; or, Why I Support Gay-Bashing." In *States of Rage: Emotional Eruption, Violence, and Social Change.* Ed. Renee Curry and Terry L. Allison. 74–88. New York: New York University Press, 1996.

Bawer, Bruce. *The Aspect of Eternity.* St. Paul, Minn.: Graywolf Press, 1993.

————. "The Poet Out and About." *Washington Post Book World,* 31 August 1997, 3+.

Baym, Nina. "Melodramas of Beset Manhood: How Theories of American Fiction Exclude Women Authors." In *The New Feminist Criticism: Essays on Women, Literature, and Theory.* Ed. Elaine Showalter. 63–80. New York: Pantheon, 1985.

Benveniste, Emile. "Subjectivity in Language." In *Critical Theory since 1965.* Ed. Hazard Adams and Leroy Searle. 728–32. Tallahassee: Florida State University Press, 1986.

Bergman, David. *Gaiety Transfigured: Gay Self-Representation in American Literature.* Madison: University of Wisconsin Press, 1991.

Bieganowski, Ronald. "James Baldwin's Vision of Otherness in 'Sonny's Blues' and *Giovanni's Room.*" *College Language Association Journal* 32.1 (1988): 69–80.

Bigsby, C. W. E. *The Second Black Renaissance: Essays in Black Literature.* Westport, Conn.: Greenwood Press, 1980.

Blount, Marcellus, and George P. Cunningham. Introduction to *Representing Black Men,* ed. Marcellus Blount and George P. Cunningham. ix-xv. New York: Routledge, 1996.

Bogumil, Mary L. "'Tomorrow Never Comes': Songs of Cultural Identity in August Wilson's *Joe Turner's Come and Gone.*" *Theatre Journal* 46.4 (1994): 463–76.

Brooks, Peter. *Psychoanalysis and Storytelling.* Oxford: Blackwell, 1994.

Brown, Tony. "Blacks Need to Love One Another." In Alice Walker, *The Same River Twice: Honoring the Difficult.* 223–25. New York: Scribner, 1996.

Brustein, Robert. "Forum: Race, Art, and Inclusion." *American Theatre* 13.9 (November 1996): 62–63, 81–82.

————. *Reimagining American Theater.* New York: Wang, 1991.

Bryant, Jerry H. *Victims and Heroes: Racial Violence in the African American Novel.* Amherst: University of Massachusetts Press, 1997.

Bullins, Ed. *The Theme Is Blackness: "The Corner" and Other Plays.* New York: Morrow, 1973.

Byerman, Keith E. *Fingering the Jagged Grain: Tradition and Form in Recent Black Fiction.* Athens: University of Georgia Press, 1985.

————. "Words and Music: Narrative Ambiguity in 'Sonny's Blues.'" *Studies in Short Fiction* 19.4 (1982): 367–72.

Callahan, John F. *In the African-American Grain: The Pursuit of Voice in Twentieth-Century Black Fiction.* Urbana: University of Illinois Press, 1988.

Cather, Willa. *My Ántonia.* 1918. Boston: Houghton Mifflin, 1988.

Chesnutt, Charles W. *The Conjure Woman.* 1899. Ann Arbor: University of Michigan Press, 1969.

Clark, Keith. "Baldwin, Communitas, and the Black Masculinist Tradition." In *New Essays on "Go Tell It on the Mountain."* Ed. Trudier Harris. 127–56. Cambridge: Cambridge University Press, 1996.

———. "Man on the Margin: Lucas Beauchamp and the Limitations of Space." *Faulkner Journal* 6.1 (1990): 67–79.

———. "Re-(W)righting Black Male Subjectivity: The Communal Poetics of Ernest Gaines's *A Gathering of Old Men.*" *Callaloo* 22.1 (1999): 195–207.

Cleaver, Eldridge. *Soul on Ice.* New York: Dell, 1968.

Cohan, Steven, and Linda M. Shires. *Telling Stories: A Theoretical Analysis of Narrative Fiction.* New York: Routledge, 1988.

Cohen, Anthony P. *The Symbolic Construction of Community.* London: Routledge, 1995.

Coleman, James W. *Blackness and Modernism: The Literary Career of John Edgar Wideman.* Jackson: University Press of Mississippi, 1989.

Cooke, Michael G. *Afro-American Literature in the Twentieth Century: The Achievement of Intimacy.* New Haven, Conn.: Yale University Press, 1984.

Crawford, Eileen. "The B-flat Burden: The Invisibility of *Ma Rainey's Black Bottom.*" In *August Wilson: A Casebook.* Ed. Marilyn Elkins. 31–48. New York: Garland, 1994.

Davis, Thadious M. "A Female Face; or, Masking the Masculine in African American Fiction before Richard Wright." In *Teaching African American Literature: Theory and Practice.* Ed. Maryemma Graham, Sharon Pineault-Burke, and Marianna White Davis. 98–131. New York: Routledge, 1998.

Delgado, Richard, and Jean Stefancic. "Minority Men, Misery, and the Marketplace of Ideas." In *Constructing Masculinity.* Ed. Maurice Berger et al. 211–20. New York: Routledge, 1995.

Dixon, Melvin. *Ride Out the Wilderness: Geography and Identity in Afro-American Literature.* Urbana: University of Illinois Press, 1987.

———. *Trouble the Water.* New York: Washington Square Press, 1989.

———. *Vanishing Rooms.* 1991. New York: Plume, 1992.

Douglass, Frederick. *Narrative of the Life of Frederick Douglass, an American Slave, Written by Himself.* 1845. New York: Penguin, 1986.

duCille, Ann. *Skin Trade.* Cambridge, Mass.: Harvard University Press, 1996.

Eagleton, Terry. *Literary Theory: An Introduction.* Minneapolis: University of Minnesota Press, 1983.

Early, Gerald. *The Culture of Bruising: Essays on Prizefighting, Literature, and Modern American Culture.* Hopewell, N.J.: Echo Press, 1994.

Elam, Harry J., Jr. "August Wilson's Women." In *May All Your Fences Have Gates: Essays on the Drama of August Wilson.* Ed. Alan Nadel. 165–82. Iowa City: University of Iowa Press, 1994.

Elgrably, Jordan, and George Plimpton. "The Art of Fiction LXXXVIII: James Baldwin."

In *Conversations with James Baldwin.* Ed. Fred L. Standley and Louis H. Pratt. 232–54. Jackson: University Press of Mississippi, 1989.

Ellis, Trey. "The New Black Aesthetic." *Callaloo* 12.1 (1989): 233–43.

Ellison, Ralph. *Invisible Man.* New York: Random House, 1952.

———. *Shadow and Act.* New York: Random House, 1964.

Estes, David C. Introduction to *Critical Reflections on the Fiction of Ernest J. Gaines.* Ed. David C. Estes. 1–11. Athens: University of Georgia Press, 1994.

Equiano, Olaudah. *The Interesting Narrative of the Life of Olaudah Equiano or Gustavus Vassa the African.* 1789. 2 vols. Ed. Paul Edwards. London: Dawsons of Pall Mall, 1969.

Foucault, Michel. "What Is an Author?" In *Critical Theory since 1965.* Ed. Hazard Adams and Leroy Searle. 138–48. Tallahassee: Florida State University Press, 1986.

Franklin, Clyde W., II. "'Ain't I a Man?' The Efficacy of Black Masculinities for Men's Studies in the 1990s." In *The American Black Male: His Present Status and His Future.* Ed. Richard G. Majors and Jacob U. Gordon. 271–83. Chicago: Nelson-Hall, 1994.

———. "Men's Studies, the Men's Movement, and the Study of Black Masculinities: Further Demystifications of Masculinities in America." In *The American Black Male: His Present Status and His Future.* Ed. Richard G. Majors and Jacob U. Gordon. 3–20. Chicago: Nelson-Hall, 1994.

Gaines, Ernest J. *The Autobiography of Miss Jane Pittman.* New York: Dial, 1971.

———. *Bloodline.* 1968. New York: Norton, 1976.

———. *A Gathering of Old Men.* 1983. New York: Vintage, 1984.

———. *A Lesson before Dying.* New York: Vintage, 1993.

———. *Of Love and Dust.* New York: Dial, 1967.

———. "Three Men." In *Bloodline.* 1968. 122–55. New York: Norton, 1976.

Gates, Henry Louis, Jr. *The Signifying Monkey: A Theory of African-American Literary Criticism.* New York: Oxford University Press, 1989.

Gaudet, Marcia, and Carl Wooton. *Porch Talk with Ernest Gaines: Conversations on the Writer's Craft.* Baton Rouge: Louisiana State University Press, 1990.

Gibbs, Jewelle Taylor. "Anger in Young Black Males: Victims or Victimizers?" In *The American Black Male: His Present Status and His Future.* Ed. Richard G. Majors and Jacob U. Gordon. 127–43. Chicago: Nelson-Hall, 1994.

Gibson, Donald B. *The Politics of Literary Expression: A Study of Major Black Writers.* Westport, Conn.: Greenwood Press, 1981.

Gilroy, Paul. *The Black Atlantic: Modernity and Double Consciousness.* Cambridge, Mass.: Harvard University Press, 1993.

Girard, Rene. *Violence and the Sacred.* Trans. Patrick Gregory. Baltimore: Johns Hopkins University Press, 1977.

Goldstein, Richard. "'Go the Way Your Blood Beats': An Interview with James Baldwin." In *James Baldwin: The Legacy.* Ed. Quincy Troupe. 173–85. New York: Simon and Schuster, 1989.

Greene, J. Lee. *Blacks in Eden: The African American Novel's First Century.* Charlottesville: University Press of Virginia, 1996.

Gresham, Jewell Handy. "James Baldwin Comes Home." In *Conversations with James Baldwin.* Ed. Fred L. Standley and Louis H. Pratt. 159–67. Jackson: University Press of Mississippi, 1989.

Griffin, Farah Jasmine. *"Who Set You Flowin'?": The African-American Migration Narrative.* New York: Oxford University Press, 1995.

Hall, Leland K. "Support Systems and Coping Patterns." In *Black Men.* Ed. Lawrence E. Gary. 159–67. Beverly Hills, Calif.: Sage, 1981.

Hansberry, Lorraine. *A Raisin in the Sun.* New York: Signet, 1966.

Hardy, James Earl. *B-Boy Blues.* Los Angeles: Alyson, 1994.

Harmon, William, and C. Hugh Holman. *A Handbook to Literature.* 7th ed. Upper Saddle River, N.J.: Prentice Hall, 1996.

Harper, Michael. "Gayl Jones: An Interview." In *Chants of Saints: A Gathering of Afro-American Literature, Art, and Scholarship.* Ed. Michael Harper and Robert Stepto. 352–75. Urbana: University of Illinois Press, 1979.

Harper, Phillip Brian. *Are We Not Men? Masculine Anxiety and the Problem of African-American Identity.* New York: Oxford University Press, 1996.

Harris, Trudier. *Black Women in the Fiction of James Baldwin.* Knoxville: University of Tennessee Press, 1985.

———. "The South as Woman: Chimeric Images of Emasculation in *Just Above My Head.*" In *Black American Prose Theory.* Vol. 1 of *Studies in Black American Literature.* Ed. Joe Weixlmann and Chester J. Fontenot. 89–109. Greenwood, Fla.: Penkevill, 1984.

Harrison, Paul Carter. "August Wilson's Blues Poetics." In *Three Plays,* by August Wilson. 291–318. Pittsburgh: University of Pittsburgh Press, 1991.

Hemenway, Robert. *Zora Neale Hurston.* Urbana: University of Illinois Press, 1977.

Henderson, George Wylie. *Jule.* New York: Creative Age Press, 1946.

Henderson, Mae G. "James Baldwin: Expatriation, Homosexual Panic, and Man's Estate." *Callaloo* 23.1 (2000): 313–27.

Henriques, Julian, et al. *Changing the Subject: Psychology, Social Regulation, and Subjectivity.* London: Methuen, 1984.

Himes, Chester. *If He Hollers Let Him Go.* 1945. New York: Thunder's Mouth Press, 1986.

Holloway, Karla F. C. *Moorings and Metaphors: Figures of Culture and Gender in Black Women's Literature.* New Brunswick, N.J.: Rutgers University Press, 1992.

hooks, bell. *Black Looks: Race and Representation.* Boston: South End Press, 1992.

Hubbard, Dolan. *The Sermon and the African American Literary Imagination.* Columbia: University of Missouri Press, 1994.

Hughes, Langston. *Not without Laughter.* 1930. London: Collier-Macmillan, 1969.

Hurston, Zora Neale. *Their Eyes Were Watching God.* 1937. New York: Fawcett, 1969.

Hutcheon, Linda. *A Poetics of Postmodernism: History, Theory, Fiction.* New York: Routledge, 1988.

JanMohamed, Abdul. "Rehistoricizing Wright: The Psychopolitical Function of Death in *Uncle Tom's Children.*" In *Richard Wright.* Ed. Harold Bloom. 191–228. New York: Chelsea, 1987.

Johnson, Charles. *Being and Race: Black Writing since 1970.* Bloomington: Indiana University Press, 1982.

———. *Oxherding Tale.* New York: Grove Wiedenfeld, 1982.

Johnson, James Weldon. *The Autobiography of an Ex-Coloured Man.* 1912. New York: Hill and Wang, 1960.

Jones, Gayl. *Liberating Voices: Oral Tradition in African American Literature.* Cambridge, Mass.: Harvard University Press, 1991.

Jones, LeRoi. *Blues People: The Negro Experience in White America and the Music That Developed from It.* New York: William Morrow, 1963.

———. *Dutchman and the Slave.* New York: William Morrow, 1964.

Kenan, Randall. *Let the Dead Bury Their Dead.* New York: Harcourt Brace and Co., 1992.

———. *A Visitation of Spirits.* New York: Grove Press, 1989.

Killens, John Oliver. *And Then We Heard the Thunder.* 1963. New York: Pocket Books, 1964.

Kinnamon, Keneth, and Michel Fabre, eds. *Conversations with Richard Wright.* Jackson: University Press of Mississippi, 1993.

Lash, John S. "Baldwin Beside Himself: A Study in Modern Phallicism." In *James Baldwin: A Critical Evaluation.* Ed. Therman B. O'Daniel. 47–55. Washington, D.C.: Howard University Press, 1981.

Leeming, David. *James Baldwin: A Biography.* New York: Knopf, 1994.

Lilly, Mark. *Gay Men's Literature in the Twentieth Century.* New York: New York University Press, 1995.

Littlejohn, David. *Black on White: A Critical Survey of Writing by American Negroes.* New York: Viking, 1969.

Lorde, Audre. "The Master's Tools Will Not Dismantle the Master's House." In *Sister Outsider: Essays and Speeches.* 110–13. Freedom, Calif.: Crossing Press, 1984.

Lukács, Georg. "The Ideology of Modernism." In *The Meaning of Contemporary Realism.* Trans. John Mander and Necke Mander. 17–46. London: Merlin, 1963.

Major, Clarence. *Reflex and Bone Structure.* New York: Fiction Collective, 1975.

Majors, Richard, and Janet Mancini Billson. *Cool Pose: The Dilemmas of Black Manhood in America.* New York: Touchstone, 1992.

Marable, Manning. *Race, Reform, and Rebellion: The Second Reconstruction in Black America, 1945–1982.* Jackson: University Press of Mississippi, 1984.

Marra, Kim. "Ma Rainey and the Boyz: Gender Ideology in August Wilson's Broadway Canon." In *August Wilson: A Casebook.* Ed. Marilyn Elkins. 123–60. New York: Garland, 1994.

McBride, Dwight, ed. *Baldwin Now.* New York: New York University Press, 2000.

McDonough, Carla J. *Staging Masculinity: Male Identity in Contemporary American Drama.* Jefferson, N.C.: McFarland and Co., 1997.

McDowell, Deborah E. *"The Changing Same": Black Women's Literature, Criticism, and Theory.* Bloomington: Indiana University Press, 1995.

Mercer, Kobena. *Welcome to the Jungle: New Positions in Black Cultural Studies.* New York: Routledge, 1994.

Middleton, Peter. *The Inward Gaze: Masculinity and Subjectivity in Modern Culture.* London: Routledge, 1992.

Miller, James A. "Bigger Thomas's Quest for Voice and Audience in Richard Wright's *Native Son.*" *Callaloo* 9.3 (1986): 501–6.

Morrison, Toni. *Beloved.* New York: Knopf, 1987.

———. *Song of Solomon.* New York: Knopf, 1977.

Moyers, Bill. "August Wilson, Playwright." In *A World of Ideas: Conversations with*

Thoughtful Men and Women about American Life Today and the Ideas Shaping Our Future. Ed. Bill Moyers. 167–80. New York: Doubleday, 1989.

Murray, Albert. *The Omni-Americans: Black Experience and American Culture*. New York: De Capo, 1970.

———. *Train Whistle Guitar*. 1974. New York: Vintage, 1998.

Myrdal, Gunnar. *An American Dilemma: The Negro Problem and Modern Democracy*. New York: Harper and Brothers, 1944.

Neal, Larry. "The Black Arts Movement." In *The Black Aesthetic*. Ed. Addison Gayle Jr. 257–74. Garden City, N.Y.: Doubleday, 1972.

Nero, Charles I. "Gay Men." In *The Oxford Companion to African American Literature*. Ed. William L. Andrews, Frances Smith Foster, and Trudier Harris. 312. Oxford: Oxford University Press, 1997.

———. "Toward a Black Gay Aesthetic: Signifying in Contemporary Black Gay Literature." In *Brother to Brother: New Writings by Black Gay Men*. Ed. Essex Hemphill. 229–52. Boston: Alyson, 1991.

O'Brien, John T. *Interviews with Black Writers*. New York: Liveright, 1973.

Olaniyan, Tejumola. *Scars of Conquest/Masks of Resistance: The Invention of Cultural Identities in African, African-American, and Caribbean Drama*. New York: Oxford University Press, 1995.

Ostendorf, Berndt. "Black Poetry, Blues, and Folklore." *Amerikastudien–American Studies* 20 (1975): 209–59.

Page, Philip. *Reclaiming Community in Contemporary African American Fiction*. Jackson: University Press of Mississippi, 1999.

Pereira, Kim. *August Wilson and the African-American Odyssey*. Urbana: University of Illinois Press, 1995.

Pleck, Joseph H. *The Myth of Masculinity*. Cambridge, Mass.: MIT Press, 1984.

Polanyi, Livia. *Telling the American Story: A Structural and Cultural Analysis of Conversational Storytelling*. Cambridge, Mass.: MIT Press, 1989.

Portelli, Alessandro. *The Text and the Voice: Writing, Speaking, and Democracy in American Literature*. New York: Columbia University Press, 1994.

Porter, Horace A. *Stealing the Fire: The Art and Protest of James Baldwin*. Middletown, Conn.: Wesleyan University Press, 1989.

Powers, Kim. "An Interview with August Wilson." *Theatre* 16.1 (1984): 50–55.

Reed, Ishmael. *Flight to Canada*. New York: Random House, 1976.

———. "A Shy Genius Transforms the American Theater." *Connoisseur* 217 (1987): 92–97.

Reilly, John M. "Giving Bigger a Voice: The Politics of Narrative in *Native Son*." In *New Essays on "Native Son."* Ed. Keneth Kinnamon. 35–62. Cambridge: Cambridge University Press, 1990.

———. "'Sonny's Blues': James Baldwin's Image of the Black Community." In *James Baldwin: A Critical Evaluation*. Ed. Therman B. O'Daniel. 163–69. Washington, D.C.: Howard University Press, 1981.

Rocha, Mark. "August Wilson and the Four B's: Influences." In *August Wilson: A Casebook*. Ed. Marilyn Elkins. 3–16. New York: Garland, 1994.

———. "A Conversation with August Wilson." *Diversity: A Journal of Multicultural Issues* 1 (1993): 24–42.

Rothstein, Mervyn. "Round Five for the Theatrical Heavyweight." *New York Times,* 15 April 1990, 1+.

Rotundo, E. Anthony. *American Manhood: Transformations in Masculinity from the Revolution to the Modern Era.* New York: Basic Books, 1993.

Sammons, Jeffrey T. *Beyond the Ring: The Role of Boxing in American Society.* Urbana: University of Illinois Press, 1988.

Sarotte, Georges-Michel. *Like a Brother, Like a Lover: Male Homosexuality in the American Novel and Theatre from Herman Melville to James Baldwin.* Trans. Richard Miller. New York: Doubleday, 1978.

Scarry, Elaine. *The Body in Pain: The Making and Unmaking of the World.* New York: Oxford University Press, 1985.

Sedgwick, Eve Kosofsky. *Between Men: English Literature and Male Homosocial Desire.* New York: Columbia University Press, 1985.

Seidler, Victor J. *Rediscovering Masculinity: Reason, Language, and Sexuality.* New York: Routledge, 1989.

Shange, Ntozake. *for colored girls who have considered suicide/when the rainbow is enuf.* New York: Macmillan, 1977.

Shannon, Sandra G. *The Dramatic Vision of August Wilson.* Washington, D.C.: Howard University Press, 1995.

———. "The Good Christian's Come and Gone: The Shifting Role of Christianity in August Wilson's Plays." *MELUS* 16.3 (1989–90): 127–42.

———. "The Long Wait: August Wilson's *Ma Rainey's Black Bottom.*" *Black American Literature Forum* 25 (1991): 151–62.

———. "A Transplant That Did Not Take: August Wilson's Views on the Great Migration." *African American Review* 31.4 (1997): 659–66.

Shire, Chenjerai. "'Men Don't Go to the Moon': Language, Space, and Masculinities in Zimbabwe." In *Dislocating Masculinity: Comparative Ethnographies.* Ed. Andrea Cornwall and Nancy Lindisfarne. 147–58. London: Routledge, 1994.

Smith, Philip E., II. "*Ma Rainey's Black Bottom:* Playing the Blues as Equipment for Living." In *Within the Dramatic Spectrum.* Ed. Karelisa V. Hartigan. 177–86. Lanham, Md.: University Presses of America, 1986.

Smith, Valerie. *Self-Discovery and Authority in Afro-American Narrative.* Cambridge, Mass.: Harvard University Press, 1987.

Smitherman, Geneva. *Talkin and Testifyin: The Language of Black America.* Boston: Houghton Mifflin, 1977.

Some, Malidoma Patrice. *Ritual: Power, Healing, and Community.* Portland, Ore.: Swan/ Raven and Co., 1993.

Spain, Daphne. *Gendered Spaces.* Chapel Hill: University of North Carolina Press, 1992.

Spillers, Hortense. "The Politics of Intimacy: A Discussion." In *Sturdy Black Bridges: Visions of Black Women in Literature.* Ed. Roseann P. Bell, Bettye J. Parker, and Beverly Guy-Sheftall. 87–106. Garden City, N.Y.: Anchor, 1979.

Standley, Fred L. "'But the City Was Real': James Baldwin's Literary Milieu." In *The City in African-American Literature*. Ed. Yoshinobu Hakutani and Robert Butler. 138–49. London: Associated University Presses, 1995.

Standley, Fred L., and Louis H. Pratt, eds. *Conversations with James Baldwin*. Jackson: University Press of Mississippi, 1989.

Stepto, Robert B. *From Behind the Veil: A Study of Afro-American Narrative*. 2d ed. Urbana: University of Illinois Press, 1979.

Tanner, Laura E. "Uncovering the Magical Disguise of Language: The Narrative Presence in Richard Wright's *Native Son*." *Texas Studies in Literature and Language* 29.4 (1982): 412–31.

Tener, Robert L. "The Inner and Outer City: A Study of the Landscape of the Imagination in Black Drama." In *The City in African-American Literature*. Ed. Yoshinobu Hakutani and Robert Butler. 236–53. London: Associated University Presses, 1995.

Thomas, Kendall. "'Ain't Nothin' Like the Real Thing': Black Masculinity, Gay Sexuality, and the Jargon of Authenticity." In *Representing Black Men*. Ed. Marcellus Blount and George P. Cunningham. 55–72. New York: Routledge, 1996.

Thorsen, Karen, dir. *James Baldwin: The Price of the Ticket*. California Newsreel, 1990.

Traylor, Eleanor W. "I Hear Music in the Air: James Baldwin's *Just Above My Head*." In *James Baldwin: The Legacy*. Ed. Quincy Troupe. 95–106. New York: Simon and Schuster, 1989.

Troupe, Quincy. "James Baldwin, 1924–1987: A Tribute—The Last Interview." In *Conversations with James Baldwin*. Ed. Fred L. Standley and Louis H. Pratt. 287–92. Jackson: University Press of Mississippi, 1989.

Turner, Darwin T. "Visions of Love and Manliness in a Blackening World: Dramas of Black Life from 1953–1970." *Iowa Review* 6.2 (1975): 82–98.

Turner, Victor. *The Anthropology of Performance*. New York: PAJ Publications, 1988.

———. *The Ritual Process: Structure and Anti-Structure*. Chicago: Aldine, 1969.

TuSmith, Bonnie. *All My Relatives: Community in Contemporary Ethnic American Literatures*. Ann Arbor: University of Michigan Press, 1993.

Vorlicky, Robert. *Act Like a Man: Challenging Masculinities in American Drama*. Ann Arbor: University of Michigan Press, 1995.

Walker, Alice. *Meridian*. New York: Washington Square Press, 1976.

Walker, Margaret. *Jubilee*. New York: Bantam, 1966.

Wallace, Michele. *Black Macho and the Myth of the Superwoman*. New York: Dial, 1978.

Warren, Robert Penn. *Who Speaks for the Negro?* New York: Vintage, 1966.

Washington, Bryan R. *The Politics of Exile: Ideology in Henry James, F. Scott Fitzgerald, and James Baldwin*. Boston: Northeastern University Press, 1995.

Washington, Mary Helen. "Meditations on History: The Slave Woman's Voice." In *Invented Lives: Narratives of Black Women, 1860–1960*. 3–15. New York: Anchor, 1987.

Werner, Craig Hansen. *Playing the Changes: From Afro-Modernism to the Jazz Impulse*. Urbana: University of Illinois Press, 1994.

———. "Tell Old Pharaoh: The Afro-American Response to Faulkner." *Southern Review* 19.4 (1983): 711–35.

West, Cornell. *Race Matters*. Boston: Beacon Press, 1993.

Wideman, John Edgar. *Brothers and Keepers*. New York: Holt Rinehart, 1984.

———. *Fatheralong: A Meditation on Fathers and Sons, Race and Society.* New York: Random House, 1994.

———. *A Glance Away.* 1967. Chatham, N.J.: Chatham Booksellers, 1975.

———. *Philadelphia Fire.* New York: Henry Holt, 1990.

———. *Reuben.* New York: Henry Holt, 1987.

Williams, Shirley Anne. *Dessa Rose.* New York: William Morrow, 1986.

Williams, Tennessee. *A Streetcar Named Desire.* New York: Signet, 1974.

Wilson, August. *Fences.* New York: New American Library, 1986.

———. "The Ground on Which I Stand." *American Theatre* 13.7 (September 1996): 50–52, 71–74.

———. "How to Write a Play Like August Wilson." *New York Times,* 10 March 1991, sec. 2, 5+.

———. *Joe Turner's Come and Gone.* New York: New American Library, 1988.

———. *Ma Rainey's Black Bottom.* In *Three Plays.* 1–93. Pittsburgh: University of Pittsburgh Press, 1991.

———. *Seven Guitars.* 1996. New York: Plume, 1997.

———. *Two Trains Running.* New York: New American Library, 1993.

Wilson, Charles E., Jr. "Black Manhood in Ernest J. Gaines's *A Lesson before Dying.*" *Journal of African American Men* 1.1 (Summer 1995): 99–112.

Wright, Richard. "Big Boy Leaves Home." In *Uncle Tom's Children.* 1938. 17–53. New York: Perennial, 1965.

———. *Black Boy.* New York: Harper, 1945.

———. "Long Black Song." In *Uncle Tom's Children.* 1938. 103–28. New York: Perennial, 1965.

———. *Native Son.* 1940. New York: HarperPerennial, 1992.

———. *Uncle Tom's Children.* 1938. New York: Perennial, 1965.

———. *White Man, Listen!* 1957. Garden City, N.Y.: Anchor, 1964.

Index

fiction, 67–72; figurations of the black male literary subject, 12–15; in Gaines's *A Lesson before Dying,* 73–93; hooks on scholarship on, 13; hypermasculinity, 5, 24, 62, 63, 104, 109; interiority of black men seen as alien, 70; internalizing demonization of black men, 5; the military in, 36; multiple components of, 2; Negro problem in literary construction of, 16–17; in the new wave of African-American literature, 127–31; oppression in the formation of, 109; in protest discourse, 17, 18–21; resituating the black male subject, 13, 24–29; ritual in the regeneration of, 26–27; triply confined, 70; victimization as a component of, 69–70, 100–101; white patriarchal masculinity in conceiving, 67, 81; and white women, 56; Wilson repositioning, 99–103; in Wilson's *Ma Rainey's Black Bottom,* 103–13; in Wilson's *Seven Guitars,* 113–25
black music: rap, 4, 5, 28, 137n.12; spirituals, 29; subjectivity refashioned through, 28; Wilson centering, 96–97, 113. *See also* blues; gospel; jazz
Black Nationalism: and Baldwin's sexuality, 52, 137n.12; Black Power, 25, 129, 140n.1; community affirmed by, 8; rigid configuration of masculinity in, 6–7. *See also* Black Arts Movement
Black on White (Littlejohn), 141n.9
Black Power, 25, 129, 140n.1
black speech. *See* vernacular
black women: in Baldwin's "Sonny's Blues," 42, 136n.7; dissociative black subject denigrating, 82–83; gospel associated with, 122; Hedley of Wilson's *Seven Guitars* on, 119; Levee of Wilson's *Ma Rainey* on, 110; in protest literature, 42; as teachers, 83, 139n.12; Wright on, 23
Black Women in the Fiction of James Baldwin (Harris), 136n.7
Bloodline (Gaines), 68, 70–71, 72, 76
Bloom, Harold, 65
Blount, Marcellus, 2
blues: audience participation in, 111; in Baldwin's *Just Above My Head,* 50, 140n.3; in Baldwin's "Sonny's Blues," 47; in Baldwin's work, 29, 34; black men achieving voice in, 70; and Gaines's *A Lesson before Dying,* 88, 92; liberating nature of, 112; in Murray's *Train Whistle Guitar,* 128; Wil-

son as employing, 94, 96; in Wilson's *Ma Rainey's Black Bottom,* 103, 110; in Wilson's *Seven Guitars,* 122
Blues, Ideology, and Afro-American Literature (Baker), 135n.12
Blues People (Baraka), 96
Bone, Robert, 51
Borges, Jorge Luis, 94
Bowles, Paul, 134n.9
boxing, 123–24
Bradley, David, 25
Brooks, Peter, 14–15
Brothers and Keepers (Wideman), 130
Brown, Tony, 1
Brown vs. Topeka Board of Education (1954), 17
Brustein, Robert, 95, 97, 100–101, 140n.2, 141n.9
Bryant, Jerry H., 5
Bullins, Ed, 95, 98, 117
Byerman, Keith, 46, 66–67, 76, 136n.6

Callahan, John F., 70, 139n.2
call and response, 50, 104, 122
Cather, Willa, 58, 137n.20
Cherry, Don, 47
Chesnutt, Charles W., 15, 16, 20, 65
Chicago, Ill., 23, 116–17
classroom, 83, 139n.12
"Clean, Well-Lighted Place, A" (Hemingway), 86
Cleaver, Eldridge, 6, 8, 58
Cohan, Steven, 12, 25, 73, 86–87
Cohen, Anthony P., 133n.1
Coleman, James W., 134n.4
Coleman, Ornette, 47, 48
colonialism, 23
communitas, 26–27
community: in Baldwin's "Sonny's Blues," 31, 42, 44, 47, 119; in Baldwin's work, 4, 5, 15, 25, 30, 34, 38; in Black Arts aesthetic, 7; in black male literary subjectivity, 4–5; Black Nationalism affirming, 8; collective identity as a function of African-American literature, 11–12; communitas, 26–27; in Douglass's *Narrative,* 5; exclusive as well as inclusive, 8; in Gaines's work, 5, 15, 72, 74, 79–80, 119; gendered nature of, 3; homosocial relationships, 34, 51, 55, 76, 133n.4; multiple configurations of, 133n.1; as a vehicle for the reconceptualization of black male subjectivity, 15; white Ameri-

can male writers on, 19; in Wilson's *Ma Rainey's Black Bottom,* 103–13; in Wilson's *Seven Guitars,* 113–20; in Wilson's work, 4, 15, 95, 99. *See also* black community
Conjure Woman, The (Chesnutt), 15
Conrad, Joseph, 15, 87
Constitution, U.S., 11, 16, 18
Cooke, Michael G., 20
cool pose, 24, 135n.10, 138n.25
Cooper, James Fenimore, 19
Cosby, Bill, 70
Crane, Hart, 53
Crawford, Eileen, 107
Cunningham, George P., 2

Davis, Angela, 4
Davis, Thadious M., 24, 134n.2
Death and the King's Horseman (Soyinka), 125
Delgado, Richard, 35, 36, 135n.2
Dessa Rose (Williams), 93
Devil in a Blue Dress (Mosley), 131
dialect, 90
dissociation, narratives of, 77
Dixon, Melvin, 4, 51, 58, 131
Douglass, Frederick: as an articulate hero, 134n.1; Baldwin, Gaines, and Wilson linked to, 25; on community, 5; and configuring the authentic African-American self, 12; finding his voice, 14; patriarchal masculinity valorized by, 81; struggle for the masculine status of, 1. See also *Narrative of the Life of Frederick Douglass*
Du Bois, W. E. B., 12, 125
duCille, Ann, 3
Dunbar, Paul Laurence, 65
Dutchman (Baraka), 69, 100, 105, 111

Eagleton, Terry, 134n.5
Early, Gerald, 121, 123, 124
Elam, Harry, 141n.13
Eliot, T. S., 66, 130
Ellis, Trey, 29
Ellison, Ralph: Baldwin, Gaines, and Wilson linked to, 25; characters abstracted in, 6; on jazz, 44, 45; Johnson on Morrison and, 135n.11; literary models of, 66; setting as employed by, 21; *Shadow and Act,* 11, 44; on white configurations of the black subject, 33; white literary aesthetic influencing, 72, 96; Wilson's *Seven Guitars* recast-

ing scenes from, 120; Wright as an influence on, 14, 65; on Wright on the novel, 75–76; Wright repudiated by, 66. See also *Invisible Man*
Equiano, Olaudah, 129
Estes, David C., 67–68

Fatheralong (Wideman), 130
Faulkner, William: *Absalom, Absalom!,* 84; Andrews's re-envisioning, 129; black writers submitting to the aesthetic of, 72, 139n.6; dysfunctional notion of maleness in, 19; Ellison influenced by, 66; Gaines influenced by, 68, 90; *Intruder in the Dust,* 139n.8; *The Sound and the Fury,* 90
Fences (Wilson): Brustein on, 100; emotional breakdown in, 101; Gabriel as psychically maimed, 118; Gaines's *A Lesson before Dying* compared with, 80; Hedley of Wilson's *Seven Guitars* compared with Troy Maxson, 120; imbrication of the stories in, 103; mimetic subject in, 102; Pulitzer Prize for, 95; Rose Maxson singing gospel, 122; Troy Maxson as reflecting the author's social sentiments, 101
first-person narration, 28, 38
Flight to Canada (Reed), 127, 129
for colored girls who have considered suicide/ when the rainbow is enuf (Shange), 20
Forster, E. M., 73
Foucault, Michel, 16
Franklin, Clyde W., II, 18, 67
free jazz, 47–48, 104
From Behind the Veil (Stepto), 11, 135n.12
Fuller, Charles, 36, 131

Gaines, Ernest J., 65–93; authorial presence de-emphasized by, 28–29, 72; *The Autobiography of Miss Jane Pittman,* 129; Baldwin as an influence on, 64; black masculinity as a driving force of the fiction of, 67–72; *Bloodline,* 68, 70–71, 72, 76; commitment to storytelling of, 91; community in the work of, 5, 15, 72, 74, 79–80; dominant conception of masculinity countered by, 70; on Ellison's *Invisible Man,* 72; *A Gathering of Old Men,* 67, 72; Kenan influenced by, 130; literary models of, 66; masculinism in the works of, 3; in the new wave of African-American literature, 29, 128; *Of Love and Dust,* 68; orality

77; Grant and Vivian, 83–84; Grant as the narrator of, 77–85; Grant's meeting with Guidry, 81–83; interlocking stories in, 75; Jefferson's diary, 88–92; Joe Louis in, 80–81, 123; plurivocality of, 28, 76, 139n.7; ritual in, 76, 91; trial of Jefferson, 75, 89; tropological function of space in, 27, 70–71, 105; and Wright's *Native Son*, 73–74, 75, 89, 92, 128
Let the Dead Bury Their Dead (Kenan), 130
Lilly, Mark, 51, 55
liminal stage of ritual, 26, 41
Littlejohn, David, 141n.9
Living Colour (rock band), 29
"Long Black Song" (Wright), 141n.12
Long Day's Journey into Night (O'Neill), 96
Lorde, Audre, 51, 55
Louima, Abner, 89
Louis, Joe, 80–81, 121, 123, 124
Lukács, Georg, 17
lynching, 18, 84, 139n.13

Mailer, Norman, 53
Major, Clarence, 25, 127, 129–30, 142n.1
Majors, Richard, 135n.10
Mamet, David, 96
"Many Thousands Gone" (Baldwin), 32
Marable, Manning, 16
Ma Rainey's Black Bottom (Wilson), 103–13; aggregate subjects in, 102, 112–13; artists of Ma's band, 96, 104; Baldwin's "Sonny's Blues" prefiguring, 41; band room in, 105; blues in, 103, 110; "bottom's" meaning in, 105; central concern of, 104, 111; community in, 105, 110, 111; Cutler as a storyteller in, 105–7; emotional breakdown in, 101; free jazz structure of, 104; imbrication of stories in, 103; Levee as a disruptive presence in, 108; Levee's murder of Toledo, 108, 110, 111–12, 141n.14; Levee's pursuit of Dussie Mae, 109, 110; Levee's relationship with Ma, 109–10; Levee's traumatic past, 108–9; Ma compared with Floyd Barton of *Seven Guitars*, 116; Ma's essential role in, 110; mimetic subject in, 102, 109, 112; quartet of black men in, 96, 104; quasi nationalism of Toledo, 98, 107; range of black men in, 103, 112; Rev. Gates story in, 106–8; *Seven Guitars* as a companion piece to, 113–14; Slow Drag singing "Hear Me Talking to You," 110–11, 141n.13; Slow Drag's name, 105–6; storytelling in, 104;

105–8, 110; Toledo on being "spooked up with the white men," 117; violence in, 104, 105; voice in, 108
March on Washington (1963), 8
Marra, Kim, 141n.7
masculinism: Baldwin in the masculinist tradition, 31, 33; Gaines and the neo-masculinist literary imagination, 65–93; Gaines critiquing, 68; in *Native Son* and *Invisible Man*, 6; pejorative nature of, 3; quest for wholeness in the tradition of, 31; space in masculinist literature, 46–47; as used in this study, 3; white masculinist literary aesthetic and black poetics, 72
masculinity: Anglo-American definitions of, 18–19, 67, 70; men's propensity to forget themselves, 84; patriarchal, as valued by protest discourse, 81; socially conceptualized, 2; violence in the construction of, 35, 36, 135n.2; white patriarchal, John Wayne as a model of, 124; white patriarchal, xenophobia in, 85, 124
McBride, Dwight, 134n.7
McDonough, Carla J., 141n.8
McDowell, Deborah E., 68, 76
McKay, Claude, 99
Mercer, Kobena, 137n.16
Meridian (Walker), 93
Middleton, Peter, 21, 84, 109
military, 36
Miller, James A., 134n.8
Million Man March (1995), 4, 11
misogyny: in Anglo-American definitions of masculinity, 18; in the Black Arts Movement, 7; colonialism and the Shona, 23; and Wright's *Native Son*, 3
modernism: Baldwin's "Sonny's Blues" critiquing, 45; black male writers influenced by, 134n.4; Gaines's use of, 90; subject of, 17–18; Wideman and, 130
Morrison, Toni: *Beloved*, 49, 83, 85, 92, 129, 138n.24; communities of black women in the works of, 76; on her novels' opening lines, 56; historical events in the works of, 123; Johnson on, 135n.11; literary foremothers acknowledged by, 67; and the New Black Aesthetic, 29; *Song of Solomon*, 85; *Sula*, 76
Mosley, Walter, 131
MOVE bombing, 130
"Muhammad Ali" (Wilson), 124
Mumbo Jumbo (Reed), 121, 123

KEITH CLARK teaches in the Department of English at George Mason University. He is the editor of *Contemporary Black Men's Fiction and Drama* and the author of articles on James Baldwin, William Faulkner, Ernest J. Gaines, Lorraine Hansberry, and Ann Petry, which have appeared in journals such as *African American Review, Callaloo,* and *Faulkner Journal.*

The University of Illinois Press
is a founding member of the
Association of American University Presses.

Composed in 10.5/13 Adobe Minion
at the University of Illinois Press
Manufactured by Maple-Vail Book Manufacturing Group

University of Illinois Press
1325 South Oak Street
Champaign, IL 61820-6903
www.press.uillinois.edu